The Progressive City

The Progressive City:

Planning and Participation, 1969–1984

Pierre Clavel

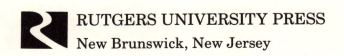

RUTGERS UNIVERSITY PRESS
New Brunswick, New Jersey

Library of Congress Cataloging in Publication
Data

Clavel, Pierre.
  The Progressive City.

  Bibliography: p.
  Includes index.
    1. Municipal government—United States—
Case studies. 2. Political participation—United
States—Case studies. I. Title. II. Title: The
Progressive City.

  JS341.C59 1986   302.8′0973   85–1987
  ISBN 0–8135–1119–4
  ISBN 0–8135–1020–8 (pbk.)

To Cora Ward Clavel

Contents

Tables and Figure

Preface

If there was a main motive for writing this book, it was the discovery that people somewhere were inventing a new form of social organization, while academic and journalist colleagues continued to report on the old ones as if nothing had changed. It was as if some orthodox model comfortable to, say, the readers of the *New York Times* had to limit the way we see things, to protect us from the unexpected.

I had seen something like this before. I was doing research in West Virginia, during the coal strike in the spring of 1978. Driving from place to place, I saw that a majority of the people on the street had sallow complexions, were badly dressed, and were driving cars usually five to ten years old; little evidence showed of new private or public capital investment. Back home, the news and conversations were full of accounts of the high salaries the coal miners were making and reports that largely misrepresented the issues. Clearly national perceptions were one thing, events on the ground were another. On the same trip I had interviewed a community organizer in the Tug Valley who had organized the area's relief effort in the wake of disastrous floods. After months of delay, the federal Department of Housing and Urban Development had agreed to establish an office to expedite the delivery of temporary housing to flood victims, but in a city two hours away from the site of the problem. She had called to protest. The H U D official had said (she reported) "but there is no Holiday Inn in your town." That conversation typified for me the way our nation handles the efforts at social organization and innovation that tend to spring up in our communities. If there was a reason to write, I thought, it was to try to correct this drift toward uniformity, this avoidance of the unexpected, and to encourage concepts tolerant of diversity.

In the case of the book that follows, the social invention at issue is a form of progressive local government that began in a few cities like Hartford, Cleveland, Berkeley, and Madison in the 1970s and has been carried on in places like Santa Monica, Santa Cruz, Burlington and Berkeley in the mid-1980s; it has bridgeheads elsewhere—Chicago and Boston, to name two recent prominent cases. These governments have tended to encourage participation and were willing to experiment with property rights in the interest of the majority of the population; they sometimes engaged in dramatic confrontations with long established powers. As perhaps a natural response, they came under fire as "socialist" and were attacked, sometimes viciously, by local opponents. In the heat of controversy, press reports tended to sensationalize or trivialize them and to omit the real essence of what was being created. It seemed as if observers wanted to throw up journalistic defenses to keep us from seeing what was really going on.

My aim here is mainly to report what went on in a sample of these cities: Hartford, Cleveland, Berkeley during the 1970s, Santa Monica and Burlington at the beginning of the 1980s. I have not theorized extensively about these cases. They provide some rich opportunities for theoretical reflection: Why did these governments take the form they did; what light do they shed on the question, Why is there no socialism in the United States? More generally, How do innovations occur in government? What are the processes of class formation? What are the conditions of territorial politics or localism?

But I avoided a theoretical effort for two reasons. First, there was an obvious story in the cases themselves, that took most of my attention. I decided to jump in with both feet. I had friends in Cleveland and Santa Monica, and used my position and contacts to make friends in other cities. Having identified "progressive" groups in situations where there was clear polarization, it was my strategy to ally myself somewhat with them. I did adopt some scholarly conventions (I never did "off the record" interviews, and always warned people that I was trying for an "objective" study), but I did not worry too much about getting close to my subjects. The consequence was that I got much more information, but spent less time than I might have thinking through some of the more abstract implications of what I learned. A second reason for my decision not to theorize too much was that my main analysis came out of the situation. On the one hand, I was part of the situation. My background and predisposition led me to look at planning (this included my recent work in West Virginia, where I had elaborated a concept of opposition planning and had devised a role for planning in opposition politics). I wanted to see if planning played a similar role in these U.S. cities. On the other hand, there were theoretical propositions that informed my progressive subjects. As in my earlier work, much of the logic of the analysis came from the cases.

This book takes a reporting approach. I came to see that reporting could be profoundly supportive of the diversity in social organization I saw these governments helping to create. I found that progressive governments were handicapped not only by inaccurate and incomplete reporting, but by their own inability to record and circulate sufficient information about their own work. I was most struck by this inability in Hartford, where there existed few or no published records of the experience of government under Nicholas R. Carbone, the progressive city council leader who held office there from 1969 to 1979. I asked one of Carbone's associates about this and he explained it by saying "we were too action-oriented to spend much time blowing our own horn." This proved true in each city: people engaged in government and politics were typically exhausted by their work, and the last thing anyone had time for was to write about it or even to keep clipping files and scrapbooks. Nor were there enough occasions to communicate with their counterparts in other cities. Derek Shearer of Santa Monica once told me: "We desperately need to talk to people in Berkeley, but even when we see each other at a meeting or conference, it is always on somebody else's program. We are lucky to get five minutes to talk about the issues we care about."[1]

There is a network of people engaged in progressive local government. In the mid-seventies, Shearer and others formed the Conference on Alternative State and Local Policies, which, under the leadership of its director, Lee Webb, held a series of annual conferences in which local administrators and elected officials could meet each other and share their ideas. But the progressives suffered from the informality of these arrangements, from a constant lack of funding, and from presentations that were vital but ephemeral in nature. What these practices needed more than anything, I came to think, was students: people who could take the time to carefully record what went on and to stay in touch with other people similarly engaged in other places. This might build up a base of recorded knowledge, which later could be reflected on, so that more profound evaluations could be made and fed back to those involved. Such persons did exist, but they tended to be isolated, and their efforts were sporadic and underfunded.

The main possibility for reinforcing the constructive reporting and the interpretation of progressive governments is in our universities. The one support that could be most useful in the long run would simply be to generate attentive attitudes on the part of the universities' scholars: attitudes of open-minded attention to record actual happenings. This is not as easy as it sounds. The most fundamental barrier to this kind of attention is the way applied social science has been practiced generally: researchers work in the university while the community (or some other social entity) is the object to be observed. This leaves the organization of attention too much in the researcher's hands, too little attentive to new developments on the ground.[2] It gradually became clear to me that my approach in this study has been at odds with that research tradition. I do not give up my responsibility for making the ultimate judgments about what to write, but my underlying assumption is that the primary discoveries occur in the community. The role of the researcher is to observe and perhaps to codify what went on, in the first instance, out in the real world. The community is the subject as well as the object, and there are occasions when the observer becomes the object of the community. The relationship of the researcher to the community is two-way.

This book was aided by more than the usual number of people. I interviewed between thirty and fifty persons in each of five cities, some of them repeatedly. I engaged some of them in collaborative ventures—one or two joint articles, panel discussions, workshops. Several of them gave lectures and seminars at Cornell. On research trips, some of the subjects for this book graciously provided me with living accommodations. For various of these kindnesses, I want to thank Eve Bach, Nicholas R. Carbone, Peter Clavelle, Ruth Goldway, Edward Kirshner, Norman Krumholz, Michael Monte, Bernard Sanders, Derek Shearer, and Robert Wiles. Other people were crucial to my logistics in various ways: Sue Burton, Fred Collignon, Andrew Gold, Michael Heiman, Carol Maurer, Paula Rosenthal, and Jan Schultz. Anne S. Clavel, Susan Fainstein, John Forester, Ken Fox, and William Goldsmith commented in detailed ways on the manuscript, as did John Alschuler, T.J. Kent, Jr., and Marc Weiss on specific chapters. Caroline Clavel typed transcripts and made a substantial contribution to the text. Drianne Benner did bibliographical work, and Carol Chock, Robert Giloth, Renee Jakobs, and Francie Viggiani spent the summer of 1982 producing "An Annotated Bibliography on Progressive Administration," which I later drew upon. Jane Dieckman edited the manuscript and composed the index, and Cynthia Halpern provided copy editing and substantial advice. None of these people bear any responsibility for my failure to use their comments to best advantage. Lynn Coffey-Edelman and Helena Wood typed parts of the manuscript.

I have a particular debt to my colleagues at Cornell University's Department of City and Regional Planning. They supported this work in both material and other ways. Three in particular were generous with their help, even when my work put a burden on them: William Goldsmith allowed me to cut back on teaching and administrative responsibilities on two occasions; Ken Reardon, my teaching assistant, shouldered major responsibilities for a year; and Field Secretary Donna Wiernicki coped with my administrative non-feasance through several extended periods.

I also want to note the extent to which I was able to build on the scholarship of others in regard to the cities I studied. I could not have done what I did in Cleveland without the work of Todd Swanstrom, in Berkeley without the articles organized and collected by Harriet Nathan and Stanley Scott, or in Burlington without the master's thesis done by Renee Jakobs. These sources are cited frequently in the text.

Abbreviations

BART	Bay Area Rapid Transit
BCA	Berkeley Citizens Action
BTU	Berkeley Tenants Union
CASH	Cleveland Action to Support Housing
CCCA	Commission on Catholic Community Action
CD	Community Development
CDBG	Community Development Block Grant
CED	Campaign for Economic Democracy
CEDO	Community and Economic Development Office
CEI	Cleveland Electric Illuminating Co.
CETA	Comprehensive Employment and Training Act
CNP	Community for New Politics
CRT	Community Renewal Team
GBIC	Greater Burlington Industrial Corporation
HART	Hartford Areas Rally Together
HUD	Housing and Urban Development
IPS	Institute for Policy Studies
NAACP	National Association for the Advancement of Colored People
NOACA	Northeast Ohio Area Coordinating Agency
OEO	Office of Economic Opportunity

OPCO	Ocean Park Community Organization
OPIC	Ohio Public Interest Campaign
PACT	People Acting for Change Together
RTA	Regional Transit Authority
SAND	South Arsenal Neighborhood Development
SMFHA	Santa Monica Fair Housing Alliance
SMRR	Santa Monicans for Renters Rights
SMSA	Standard Metropolitan Statistical Area
UDAG	Urban Development Action Grant
VPIRG	Vermont Public Interest Research Group

CHAPTER 1

The Roots of Progressive Urban Politics

This book describes progressive politics in five American cities in the 1970s and 1980s: Hartford, Cleveland, Berkeley, Santa Monica, and Burlington. In a period when urban coalitions built upon the problems of urban renewal, highways, and downtown development became passé and unstable, these cities experimented with radically new forms of participation, public enterprise, property regulation, service structure, and neighborhood involvement. Many of their programs had a populist tone reminiscent of the great democratizing movements of the period around the turn of the century. At the same time, they made attempts to alter more fundamental economic relationships in these cities: alterations in property rights in the form of rent-control proposals, limited-equity cooperative housing, and city real estate ventures are all examples.

The main features of progressive politics as practiced in these cities included attacks on the legitimacy of absentee-owned and concentrated private power on the one hand, and on nonrepresentative city councils and city bureaucracies on the other. These attacks led to programs emphasizing public planning as an alternative to private power, and to grass-roots citizen participation as an alternative to council-dominated representation. In most respects, these new programs produced a flood of institutional inventions.

The experience of these cities needs to be documented. It represents a notable exception to the normal patterns of local government. At a time when urban government in general retreated before and came to accommodation with private interests and factions, these cities established substantive governments. Rather than claim to satisfy all factions, they made explicit choices in favor of broad classes of people. Most important, at a time when national politics had moved to the right, leaders in these cities favored poor and working people, and represented the interests of their cities' residents against suburban, absentee, and property-owning factions. Even though their efforts led to dilemmas, and often to political defeat, at least they moved forward into new sorts of dilemmas, different from those of the coalitions devoted to urban growth that were rooted in the New Deal and had persisted into the 1960s.

Their problems and their promise, in fact, stem from a central discovery. At a time when planning had become associated with stultifying central administration, these cities found ways to recast planning as a link between a vital grassroots citizens movement and the desires of progressive political leaders to formulate redistributive policies. In most places, planning had been carried out in a way that was centralized, secret, regulatory, and inhibitive of nongovernment action. Progressives found ways to share planning with grass-roots organizations and to stimulate innovations both in the private sector and in the top councils of government. These new directions in planning also need to be documented. In the following work, I use the experience of planning in these five cities as a central analytical vantage point from which to comment on administration and politics more generally. In this commentary, the contrast between the programs of these progressive cities and the still-dominant earlier version of urban politics appears repeatedly.

The structure of this book reflects this analytical primacy of planning. Chapters two, three, and four are case studies of the cities of Hartford, Cleveland, and Berkeley. Chapter five presents the related, but later, experiences of Santa Monica and Burlington. Chapter six describes the emergence of planning into urban politics and its significance. Chapter seven attempts to summarize the way the cities studied have attempted to solve their political dilemmas, especially in light of the context and environment that planning and their participatory commitments had given them.

Background: The Decline of Growth Politics

Progressive municipal politics emerged from the decline of urban political coalitions that were rooted in the economics and demography of an earlier period, roughly 1945–1965. Those years marked a period of economic growth, and there was a national consensus to create growth while also paying attention to social issues. Unemployment and welfare dependence were problems in those years, but they did not seem to be insurmountable ones. Public schools, welfare agencies, labor unions and political parties, having accommodated waves of European immigration, seemed ready to accommodate the next wave of blacks and Hispanics. In the 1950s, federal programs for housing, urban redevelopment, and highways were offered to the cities, and growth-oriented political coalitions under strong mayors took control: those led by Dilworth in Philadelphia and Lee in New Haven were the most cited early examples.

Construction unions, professionals, and real estate interests supported these new growth-oriented programs, which promised to create jobs and continued vitality for the cities. Political liberals often advocated these programs because they believed they would help keep middle-class whites in the central cities and thus avoid the creation of black and Hispanic enclaves and make racial integration possible.[1]

By the 1960s, however, these urban growth coalitions were proving to be unstable. Several underlying economic changes were taking place, which shifted the ways liberal politicians and their supporting coalitions related to one another, and the whole system of urban rule was transformed. The following transitions were the most important:

(1) Basic industrial employment stopped growing and even declined precipitously in many central cities. Signs of economic stagnation had been growing since World War II. Growth was taking place in the suburbs, not in the cities. In the older cities, even where manufacturing employment was steady, the labor force had become older and less skilled, and capital inputs had declined. New business starts with high technology and high wages were happening elsewhere. In the 1960s, these trends had resulted in the recruitment of low-wage, minority workers, and by the 1970s, much industrial employment had vanished entirely from many cities, particularly from the Northeast.[2]

(2) The demographic makeup of central city populations changed drastically. Black and Hispanic northward migration had increased from the 1940s onward. By 1970, several major central cities had 40 percent and even 50 percent minority populations. Minority in-migration was complemented by white middle-class

out-migration, and the total central city populations declined. The economic effects of these changes were severe. Median incomes for cities declined relative to metropolitan area averages, poverty and welfare dependency increased, and the disparities between the central city and the suburbs increased, as measured by a number of indicators. A look at the census is revealing of these disparities and partly explains the phenomena described in this book (see the Appendix).

(3) The federal government's outlays to city governments continued to grow throughout the 1970s.[3] What had begun as physical construction programs in the 1950s had become a multifaceted set of services oriented toward urban welfare populations by the 1970s. Such specifically targeted programs as public housing and urban renewal were cut in the seventies, but programs like social security and Aid to Families with Dependent Children increased as a result of the dependency represented in the demographic makeup of the cities. The coalitions of middle-class residents, developers, construction unions, and others interested in employment growth, including the bankers who had profited from financing physical development, dissolved, to be replaced by professionals, dependent on the welfare constituencies, and getting major external support from the federal bureaucratic empires.[4]

(4) The material support needed to stabilize these new service-oriented political coalitions was lacking, however. Central city tax bases had deteriorated, while demands for services had greatly increased. Because business leaders and the state and federal governments were not interested in making up the difference, the cities were forced into varying degrees of fiscal crisis.

(5) Investment surged in the center cities in the 1970s and took the form especially of speculation in housing and office properties; but these activities generated no redistributive effects for the poor. The resultant in-migration of middle- and upper-class people into previously poor and working-class neighborhoods displaced the previous residents and raised housing costs. Such displacement and gentrification became a particular political issue in such sunbelt states as California, but rising housing costs were prominent in the inflationary squeeze everywhere.[5]

(6) A strong counterforce in local politics—the neighborhood movement—developed rapidly in response to the impact of growth-oriented policies during the late 1970s. Political organizers, state and regional activist networks, supportive policy research organizations, and organizer training centers all grew up around this

movement. These organizations received a good deal of philanthropic support. Neighborhood groups formed around grass-roots concerns, fought city halls, and took positions on housing, environmental, and many other issues. The neighborhood movement seemed basic to, but not necessarily sufficient for, the development of an alternative to the growth politics that had prevailed throughout the postwar period. In many respects the neighborhood organizations were fragile, and therefore they were often reluctant to engage in electoral politics to form governing coalitions. Yet the new movement seemed to be crucial to local politics. It remained to be seen in what ways and in combination with what other forces they would develop as a political force.[6]

In most cities, the official political programs maintained the rhetoric of the earlier growth coalitions, while the leadership employed a number of mechanisms to manage dissent. A major example was the redefinition of urban economic problems in racial terms. In the 1960s a prevalent assumption had been that minorities were disadvantaged because of their place in the class structure: if you could improve job opportunities and housing and services, you would remove these disadvantages. Such policies were only conceivable if overall employment was growing. In the 1970s—with their generally diminished hopes for job growth—the public rhetoric was largely reversed: Urban problems were then deemed to be caused by an intractable (minority) "underclass." Meanwhile hiring policies ("affirmative action") that were meant to open up jobs to minorities in fact mainly benefited educated, middle-class minorities, because the general decline restricted the jobs available. Hiring minority professionals and businesses gave the appearance of racial justice, while it may in fact have defused grass-roots minority organization and helped to fuel conflicts between minority and white working-class people.[7]

A complementary management strategy involved the manipulation of fiscal crises so that they were focused disproportionately on the inner cities. Many studies have shown that urban austerity budgets in such places as New York City and Cleveland effectively shifted to these central cities the burden of problems that are rooted much more generally in the economy. With the private capital investment, the better factory jobs, and the more affluent working- and middle-class populations moving to the suburbs and to metropolitan areas in the South and West, older cities tended to lose their financial bases. The obvious effect of these changes was to undermine urban political organizations and to reinforce race politics as against class-oriented social and economic programs.[8]

In this climate, political leaders were hard pressed to find a vote-getting formula that could match the expectations of an earlier politics of growth to the increasingly fragmented and impoverished electorate. Edward Koch of New York may be the archetypical figure: as a symbol, feisty and sharp-tongued, but in substance, conservative and elusive. Mario Cuomo, an old-style liberal, who ran against Koch for governor in the Democratic party primary in 1982, characterized him this way in a campaign debate:

> I find it impossible—at the very least, excruciatingly difficult—to find a single position he's ever taken that was politically unpopular. . . . His philosophy is first to find out what the majority of the people wanted . . . and then go there, on the theory that if they want something, you'll be with them [and] they'll be happy with you, for the time being.[9]

Adopting a slippery, if winning, style, Koch completed an evolution from having a liberal record while he was in Congress from 1968 to 1977 to taking a conservative position on the substance of urban issues: a pro-business position, by some accounts verging on racism toward minorities, and including regressive fiscal policies.

Cuomo's criticism was paralleled by academic commentaries on growth politics. Theodore Lowi described the "end of liberalism" as a regression to a situation in which political leaders, unable to set rules for allocating resources, simply delegated governmental authority to private interest groups. Their rationale was that these groups would balance each other and somehow the general interest would be served. Thus, the concern with substantive rationality—the choice among ends—was replaced by a governmental preoccupation with the balancing of interests.[10] Facilitating these private desires, it was felt, would encourage economic growth, and so benefit everybody.

Lowi's criticism was that government, by avoiding substantive choices, had abdicated its authority as the one legitimate source of coercive force. Among other things, this abdication implied that special interests were free to exploit weaker constituencies. If, as the critics argued, growth-oriented policies benefited the few—land developers, property speculators, and a small number of businessmen and perhaps labor unions—disproportionately, then governments that simply acted as conduits for these factions failed their responsibility to act for the whole population. The *fact* of economic growth, through a combination of real and symbolic economic benefits, was beside the point. It simply masked the failure of government.

The alternative, which became relevant when growth stopped (as in many northeastern and midwestern cities) or when the costs of growth impacted sharply on particular groups (as in many sunbelt cities), was substantive government. But no one had laid out in detail how to achieve it.[11]

Planning in the Context of Growth

My own view of this history comes from my experience in the city planning profession, which was a marked feature of growth-oriented city programs during the 1950s and 1960s. In the 1950s, the planning profession was small, largely committed to physical design, and marginal to politics, with a professional membership never exceeding 2,500.[12] During the 1960s, the profession expanded in numbers and scope: In fact, the demand for planners grew faster than the number of professionals did. Planners struck a popular chord in the politics of central city reform governments. They helped organize the flow of funds into physical development projects. They took credit for spectacular downtown office and commercial revitalizations, while making the politicians look good. They also took part in an increasing number of activities not associated with physical development. They did planning for social service and community action projects and for economic development programs, where their skills were useful, not only to plan the programs locally, but also to monitor them for federal agencies. As federal spending in the cities increased, these monitoring and accounting functions became more important, and much of planning became the embodiment of a required set of roles imposed from above.[13]

These new demands were paralleled by changes within the profession itself. In the 1950s, planning had been mainly "master planning"—designs for the future layout of cities. In its most comprehensive form, this purpose implied foresight about the social and economic ramifications of alternative physical designs, and some planning professionals were quite programmatic, coming out of a tradition that emphasized the public provision of housing and even jobs and extensive regulation of the private economy. But starting in the early 1960s, numerous professional journal articles began advocating a more "rationalistic" view: Planners would provide aid to decision makers, wherever they were, and this meant an emphasis on their methodological and tactical skills, without regard for ideological or goal-setting commitments.[14] Rather than remain committed to a search for a global set of priorities or "master plan," they should simply try to be useful by analyzing the medium-term consequences of specific actions being contemplated by political leaders. This perspective, which spread rapidly among planners and was easily adopted by people with other training who took planning jobs, eased the transition of planning into the broader set of roles demanded by the expansion of federal urban programs.

These rationalist perspectives never completely dominated the profession. For one thing, the design-related planners maintained a stubborn resistance to rationalism, sometimes out of simple ignorance, but also because they thought it important to be setting political goals. In addition, important segments retained links to somewhat more idealistic causes, particularly the civil rights and antiwar movements of the 1960s. These members of the profession organized in many cities as "advocacy planners." They donated their services to community groups, usually minorities, and never adopted rationalist ideas. By the end of the 1960s, planners sympathetic to advocacy activities made up a noticeable part of the profession.[15] Advocacy planning operations had become part of the official programs of some city planning agencies as part of a general effort to give minority and disadvantaged populations access to complex bureaucratic procedures.[16] Professional planning meetings were wracked with controversy, but a good deal of innovation and learning occurred for those who could stand the conflict.

Increasingly, throughout the 1970s, mainstream city planning, like urban politics, changed. Most important, the economic underpinnings of the enterprise were gone. The money for planning had come from physical construction projects, from the need to organize and coordinate them, to anticipate their side effects, to create new institutions to further the social development of the new populations that would use or work in the new facilities. From the time at least of the 1940s, a coalition of business leaders and professionals had sought to distribute the cities' economic surplus to create a better urban environment. The surplus was there, as was a commitment to use it and an expectation that planning would produce a better environment. These precepts had been weakened or totally lost by the 1970s. What remained, in most cases, was the need for planners to engage in a scramble for reduced federal grant dollars and to cooperate with or work for private investors with vastly narrowed objectives.

Progressive Governments in the 1970s and 1980s

By 1970, such cities as Hartford and Cleveland had become enclaves of the poor and of racial minorities, while other cities such as Berkeley, Santa Monica, and Burlington had felt the impact of a combination of increased land and housing costs with substantial populations on modest or fixed incomes.

In this context, it should not be surprising that "radical" or "populist," or more generally "progressive" programs—defined by some progressives as "in the interest of the present populations" of these cities—should emerge, in contrast to the programs of, say, developers, merchants, or investors, who might more accurately be described as promoting the interests of property owners or hoped-for future (and more affluent) populations, or of past populations or suburban populations. Given the demographic and economic shifts that had taken place, some policy innovation could have been expected. Progressive opposition to growth-oriented politics had placed some representatives in city councils or in other important offices: Ruth Messenger in New York and Ken Cockrel in Detroit are examples.[17] Such people kept alternative programs alive and were able to cultivate supporters inside and outside of official agencies. They and their counterparts in state government offices organized in the mid-seventies the Conference on Alternative State and Local Policies, which held conferences over a six-year period and served as a focal point for other meetings and for the dissemination of policy ideas through newsletters and publications.

More dramatic than playing minority roles in government, however, were the outright takeovers of mayoral offices and city councils by people who took a progressive stance. These experiences are the subject of this book. Hartford, Cleveland and Berkeley were among the very few medium-to-large cities that in the 1970s tried new departures from the standard structure of city government, departures reminiscent of the socialist and progressive experiments of the first decades of this century.[18] In Hartford, the main innovator was Nicholas Carbone, who took control of the City Council after getting appointed to a seat in 1969. Other significant victories were those of Dennis Kucinich in Cleveland in 1977, and Gus Newport in Berkeley in 1979, both of whom had been preceded by a decade of administrative and political groundwork. They were pathbreakers and set the stage for later developments in other cities. There were several other cases, but Ruth Goldway in Santa Monica, California, and Bernard Sanders in Burlington, Vermont, both elected in 1981, transformed the political and administrative atmospheres of their cities.[19]

It is tempting to compare these modern governments with the progressive and socialist municipal governments that appeared just before and after the turn of the century in this country.[20] Tom L. Johnson in Cleveland and Hazen Pingree in Detroit had initiated such reforms as the municipalization of streetcar lines and of electric power companies and had articulated local programs in opposition to the concentrations of corporate power that had accrued in the earlier decades of the century. Other places such as Bridgeport, Reading, Schenectady, and Milwaukee had overtly "socialist" governments. Reports suggest that, to stay in office, these governments focused on "good government" innovations that appealed to a middle-class and professional constituency, while for a time at least they maintained broad representation. But working-class mobilization of support in these cities was either too weak or too easily influenced by more powerful factions to exert pressure for more far-reaching changes. By the 1920's, these progressive and socialist governments had largely been replaced by a business-backed managerialism.[21]

The governments described in the following chapters certainly encountered some of these same constraints. As in the earlier political experiments, they were able to make political capital out of reformist innovations: introducing better budgeting procedures and opening up public access to government that had been closed under a ruling clique. But these contemporary governments were also different from their predecessors. Their electoral bases were different, and they addressed the economic and social problems of a different age. Their program can be summarized in terms specific to the 1970s and 1980s:

(1) Most fundamentally and controversially, progressives in government took a more experimental view of property rights than did their preceding administrations. This view took the form of proposals—occasionally successful—for direct or shared control of enterprises through municipal ownership. Carbone's successful move toward city partnership arrangements in Hartford land-development schemes may have been the most extended such incursion. Realizing the city could get control of real estate more easily than it could of capital, Carbone got part ownership for the city in a

number of downtown developments, and used this ownership to force local and minority hiring in construction as well as in the operation of the projects. In Cleveland, Kucinich successfully fought the banks and the private power utility to maintain MUNY Light, the city's public power system. In Berkeley and Santa Monica, rent control and other measures extended the possibilities of the cities' regulatory powers, at the same time constraining large property holders.

(2) Berkeley and Hartford successfully tapped local enthusiasm for collectives. In Berkeley, the city built the Savo Island and University Avenue limited-equity housing cooperatives, enterprises that were planned outside of the government and with the high participation of diverse neighborhood people. Berkeley also gave revenue-sharing funds to social services that were collectively organized. Hartford initiated a community food system that involved collectively run enterprises at many different levels, from production to distribution.

(3) Berkeley and Hartford initiated progressively redistributive fee and taxing schemes, splitting the tax roles between residential and business properties, with higher rates for the latter. Berkeley shifted fee structures in a redistributive way: higher parking meter rates, higher building permit fees, new marina use fees—to start charging for privileges that had been subsidies from all residents to a few users.

(4) In a period when budgets were being cut, Hartford and Berkeley found ways to make the cuts less regressive by restructuring services. In Berkeley, budget revisions restored a series of direct services that had been cut—two fire stations, school crossing guards, foot patrols, a Rape Detail—and, in total, traded the elimination of nineteen higher-paid administrative positions for retention of 46.5 street or point-of-service positions. Hartford imposed city residency requirements for education and recreation positions and substituted paraprofessional positions for professionals. Hartford also initiated new services to reduce costs for neighborhood residents, particularly in food supplies and energy.

(5) Santa Monica, Berkeley, and Hartford found new ways to regulate the private sector. The most dramatic device used was rent control, which passed in Santa Monica in 1979 and in Berkeley in 1980, with support from large renter constituencies who had been squeezed by rent increases after Proposition 13 had promised rent relief. In Hartford, a city with a very large minority population, affirmative action enforcement was the most prominent innovation

made in regulatory activity, applied not only to city jobs but to contractors and vendors doing business with the city. Berkeley and Santa Monica enacted stiff land-development control regulations to protect neighborhoods, to counteract speculation and to help lower-income families.

(6) Particularly in Hartford and Cleveland, progressive city governments took a combative, advocacy stance on the side of city residents (who tended to be poor) against suburban and business interests.

(7) While citizen participation was tolerated in many places, these progressive city governments actually encouraged and organized such participation. In Cleveland, the planning department had nurtured a strong neighborhood movement. Although Kucinich ultimately alienated much of this constituency, his administration continued to serve them. In Berkeley, the Fair Representation Ordinance of 1975 made each board and commission representative of all factions represented on the City Council. The result was to unleash a large amount of enthusiastic political participation: each council person had an appointee on each board who was in effect a staff advisor, and each appointee had an advocate for board or committee positions in council. In Hartford, participation was less organic, more centrally stimulated. The political leadership there nevertheless managed some impressive accomplishments. The Hartford Citizens Lobby organized around property tax issues, and the city established neighborhood service districts.

(8) In 1981, Santa Monica, California elected a progressive City Council and mayor, and Burlington, Vermont, elected a socialist mayor. These administrations built on the experiences of progressive governments in other cities. In Santa Monica, a coalition that had formed around rent control won five out of seven city council seats in 1981. The coalition's most remarkable achievements were the effective administration of rent control, the aggressive recasting of commercial and housing development regulations to recapture and redirect private investment in the interest of the largely moderate-income population of the city, and the initiation of an array of participatory and social programs serving its middle-income constituency. In Burlington, progressive government developed out of the leadership of Bernard Sanders, who captured the mayoralty from the Democratic party organization. With a coalition in the minority position on the Board of Aldermen, Sanders slowly built up his electoral support, eventually becoming able to institute a new set of participatory channels, including six neighborhood planning assem-

blies. He set up a highly developed administration, able to negotiate public participation in real estate and economic development projects.

Dilemmas of Progressive Government

This broad array of new initiatives from municipal governments raises questions that more fundamentally define the content
of progressive urban politics.

First, there is the question of establishing a substantively progressive administrative program. This problem crystalized for progressive politicians when, upon taking majority control, they had to
move from an opposition program to a detailed, substantive one.
This was the problem the Berkeley radicals faced in the form of the
budget-cutting exercise described above: the outgoing government
presented them with proposals to cut some of the programs they had
painstakingly championed while in a minority role. They solved the
problem by adopting an explicitly redistributive set of rules, cutting
programs that had benefited a middle-class constituency and maintaining items that served a wider constituency. They were involved
in substantive government, making choices among ends, instead of
leaving such choices to the most articulate interest groups. Similar
stands were taken by Kucinich in Cleveland (on tax abatements for
corporate offices and on municipal power), Carbone in Hartford (on
affirmative action hiring in major downtown construction projects),
and on various issues by the progressives elected in Santa Monica
and Burlington in 1981.

Second, the question of how to encourage mass participation
while still developing the city's administrative capacity emerged
clearly. Progressives had been elected during surges of mass reaction against city bureaucracies, and in part they based their electoral programs on such reactions. In effect, they based their hopes
for substantive government on the expectation that a mobilized
electorate would support them against special interests. Once in
office, they were energetic in their attempts to create new participatory channels. But this emphasis posed several dilemmas:

(1) For the political leadership—mayors and city council
members—how far could they balance general public participation
against other gains that could be made by entering into private negotiations with such specific interests as minorities, business, orga-

nized labor, neighborhood associations, and liberal professionals around substantively progressive programs?

(2) How quickly, and with what emphases, should the leadership build up administrative capacity? Substantive government meant better administration. Did it also mean a new kind of administration? Progressive city governments developed their administrative capacities by hiring administrators willing to serve their specific political objectives and to respond to greatly increased citizen input. But administration came into conflict, at times, with the participatory thrust of progressive constituencies. The pressures on administrators were immense: they had to elaborate programs for local constituencies as well as meet requirements imposed by federal and state governments for funding; business and land developer factions wanted orderly administration and creative financing of development packages as a condition for capital investment; and there was the additional demand that administration be able to bargain effectively with the private sector in order to serve the interests of less affluent constituents. Despite great technical and interpersonal abilities, these administrators could not always perform all these functions in a sufficiently public way or with sufficient open consultation to satisfy those who wanted a say in government.

(3) How far should the leadership go in getting administrative protection against attacks brought on by the dramatic public confrontations their positions occasioned? They found that crucial appointments could ease these problems. In Santa Monica, outstanding appointments in the city attorney's and city manager's offices gained credibility for the administration with the police and the business community. In Cleveland, the failure to make such appointments cost Kucinich heavily.

(4) To what extent should a progressive government bring its own supporters into government—in either paid or volunteer commission roles? The effect of this kind of participatory strategy was to improve the functioning of government at the expense of siphoning off energy from the government's political base. In Santa Monica, the creation of municipal commissions had begun to debilitate the community organizations that had gotten the progressive majority elected.

Another dilemma was how to set up the planning role, which emerged in a different and more substantial way in these progressive administrations than it had in earlier governments. Planning was central in these cities. Each progressive government had a doctrine with many of the characteristics of a plan long before the administrative and regulatory innovations cited above were instituted. But this doctrinal coherence caused problems in relation to the planning structures already in place. The political planners tended to overshadow the functions of the official planning bodies, creating tensions and conflicts with professional planning staffs and boards. These tensions were resolved in some cases, but not in all.

A Theoretical Structure for Progressive Politics

Although growth politics had lost its economic base, and its co-alition had been severely weakened, it persisted as an agenda, as a structure of thought. This theoretical structure was not only a resource for those who practiced politics or worked in government, it also framed the questions of scholarship and informed the research on which any innovation in practice or theory would have to depend.

A part of this structure of thought was tied to an earlier liberalism that included many tenets that most progressives wanted to preserve—a tolerance of diversity, a maximization of individual liberties, the establishment of stable rules—as well as other attributes that progressives wanted to challenge—liberal discomfort with mass-based participation, distrust of substantive government willing to make judgments on redistributive questions, unquestioning commitment to the rights of private property.[22]

But much of the liberal structure was an accommodation to a set of interests no longer relevant to central city populations. Thus, liberal concern for property rights also meant government support for investors in local property, but many of these investors no longer lived in the city by the 1970s, and it was reasonable to ask what city residents got in return for this governmental support. A commitment to markets or to the council-manager form of government likewise implied markets that city residents could compete in and city agencies that represented city residents' interests. It was reasonable to ask whether, with the movement of the middle class out of the city, the market or the council or the city administration had adequately shifted its attention to its new constituents.

The most fundamental usefulness of these recent experiences with progressive politics is the light they shed on these questions about the agenda and structure of urban political thought and institutions and on the possibility of adapting that structure to new conditions. The first proposition that emerges is that some movement away from trust in markets and toward trust in substantive government, and some movement away from reliance on council and city administration and toward reliance on mass participation, are appropriate adjustments to the changed population compositions of these cities.

But any such shift to substantive politics by progressive governments immediately runs into one of the thorniest problems of Western political experience. Robert Michels stated it seventy years ago: The greatest hope for the mass of people is strong administrative leadership responsive to an organized constituency, yet administration carries with it inherent tendencies toward centralization, recruitment from within, and stultification of any government enterprise.[23] Faced with this dilemma, and, at a more naïve level, simply distrustful of all government, Americans tend to choose the market over any elaboration of substantive government and to choose to participate, not primarily in collective pursuits, but in their own private enterprises. The hope for progressive government seems to fly in the face of this tradition. The desire to achieve substantive policies is put at risk because of the predicted bureaucratization of its movement. The outcome to be anticipated, given these traditions, is a retreat to minimal government.

Thus the more profound question at stake here is whether the experience of the cities studied here offers a better way out of Michels' problem than does this retreat. The experience of these progressive governments does begin to refute Michels. It shows that administration and participation can both evolve together and reinforce one another for a time, under some conditions. But what hope is there that these kinds of changes could be made more permanent or could be replicated in other places? The case histories presented in the following chapters provide an alternative model for city government that may give some guidelines. This alternative model suggests that there are exceptions to Michels' conundrum: Under certain conditions, a significant move toward substantive government and mass participation seems possible. The factors at work in making them possible include the following:

(1) An underlying economic rationale. There was an economic rationale, on the face of it, for residents of many cities to take control of their own governments. The claims of growth enthusiasts that they could provide basic sustenance for the majority of city residents were increasingly difficult to maintain. The plausibility of

such claims was upheld only by tradition. Alternative economic programs were beginning to appear. The main problems began to seem political in nature, not economic or technical.

(2) A developing opposition movement. There was also a cultural rationale: Significant numbers of persons wanted more participation in government than they were getting. A history of educational and organizational experiences in the civil rights, antiwar, and neighborhood movements created these demands, and gross governmental inadequacies opened a way to electoral victory in many of these cities. Out of this opening came organizations, in many cases nurtured by progressives during the years out of power. The neighborhood movement is an obvious, though often limited, example; but various other kinds of grass-roots organizations also developed and pressed their demands for participation in local governments. They went beyond negative programs, keyed to building their own organizations by fighting city hall, moreover, to participate in overarching city policy formation, in many cases. This latter step seems to be a condition for the development of a fully progressive local government.

(3) A separate planning function. A planning function, generally including the creation of a redistributive economic program, developed both inside and outside of the formal governmental structure. In its most vital form, planning developed within or in contact with the grass-roots organizations, and cases of conflict arose between official and unofficial planners. But most important, planning was often developed independently of the administrative leadership, which landed planners in a position to mediate between administration officials and the participatory energies coming from the neighborhood organizations and elsewhere. Three main themes emerged: the elaboration of planning within city hall, the development of new forms of professionalism, and the development of new forms for an independent planning function.

On reflecting on the work of this study, I think the role of planning in these progressive local governments was central because it helped progressives get beyond the conflicts that naturally occur between the requirements of administration and of the public's participation in government. Much thinking on these topics— including that of Michels—and most current practices are impoverished because they contrast administration and participation too starkly. Most people see administration as hierarchical, a bureaucratic function, inherently inimical to political participation. They see political participation as an occasionally useful, but somewhat negative check on administration, a back-up when city councils are ineffective. Neighborhood advocates believed that the way to keep city government under control was to fight it from the outside, to make it more responsive, not to take it over. Generally, the opponents of City Hall sought to leave administrative functions in place and to influence city councils to set policies that would control government through hierarchical responsibilities. Planning is commonly seen as simply another aspect of the hierarchy of administration, one which is done from the top down, and which very likely involves a *post hoc* rationalization of the goals set by the top bureaucratics and their political cronies.[24]

My own view as a city planner led me never to accept these popular perceptions; I resisted the thought of planning as an elite, bureaucratized activity even when all the evidence seemed to confirm it as that. I saw planning as a profession that had long harbored a loosely structured ideal of moving directly among the people (unlike the main currents in other professions) and one that, in principle, was dedicated to visions and models that could be validated by catching the popular imagination. Thus I tested my hypothesis in these cities: how the real role of planning, as it developed from the grass roots and among some city administrators and political leaders, was to nurture a movement culture that could sustain both administration and popular participation, while the city government kept operating.

CHAPTER 2

Hartford: From Projects to Programs, 1969–1979

For ten years, from 1969 to 1979, the city of Hartford, Connecticut, operated with a progressive city council majority led by councilman Nicholas R. Carbone. The following pages describe the background to Carbone's assuming leadership, the factors that figured in his decision to adopt progressive innovations, and the increasing internal and external pressures that led to his defeat and the breakup of the progressive coalition in 1979.

Background

The changes that took place in the Hartford economy form the most important context for understanding the city's shift to progressive politics in the 1970s. Although broad social and political changes, enormous personal energy, and general creativeness were all important factors, it was economics that made Hartford's council majority in the 1970s, and that ultimately defeated it.

By the 1960s, Hartford had become polarized in its economics and demography. On the one hand, not only was Hartford the state capital, but it also contained the central offices of six of the nation's largest insurance companies, with perhaps 30,000 people within the city limits employed in that industry. Its resident population, however, was fast becoming an enclave of minority and poverty-stricken residents. Local manufacturers had begun importing black and

TABLE 2.1. **Population Composition, Hartford and sMSA, 1960–1980**

	1960		1970		1980	
	Hartford	*SMSA*	*Hartford*	*SMSA*	*Hartford*	*SMSA*
Population	162,178	525,207	158,017	663,891	136,392	726,114
White	137,027	495,879	111,862	610,041	68,603	634,985
Black	24,855	28,689	44,091	50,518	46,186	61,892
Hispanic	2,307	2,995			27,898	34,207
Median family income	$7,211	$7,187	$9,108	$12,282	$14,032	$23,853

SOURCE: These figures are drawn from the U.S. Census of Population and Census of Housing, cited in full in ch. 1 note 3.

Puerto Rican labor in the 1940s, and the decline of the Connecticut Valley tobacco industry had released additional minorities who settled in the city, while white middle-class residents moved out to nearby suburbs. The result was that the composition of Hartford's population in relation to its surrounding towns was transformed from 1950 to 1980, as shown in table 2.1.

These changes necessitated reforms within the old power structure.[1] Hartford's business leadership had always been relatively liberal and involved in city politics, a concern attributed by many to the roots of the insurance industry in church-related altruism. After World War II, these business leaders wanted to end old-style machine politics, and they backed a successful charter revision that established a weak-mayor and council-manager form of government. Later, businessmen sought further changes. They made the Chamber of Commerce the main vehicle for their participation in public affairs, and in 1955 hired a talented executive director, Arthur Lumsden, who solidified business involvement in city government through several initiatives, including urban renewal programs, the community action program in the downtown area, and a set of large-scale regional ventures: regional planning, a council of governments, and an ambitious development and planning organization, Greater Hartford Process.

Lumsden's arrival coincided with changes taking place in the structure of Hartford corporations and business leadership, and he was able to adapt to and take advantage of these changes. The insurance corporations had long been family firms with a tradition of community consciousness. But the family-dominated firm was changing to professional management, its executives were living in the suburbs, and a new form of interaction with city government was needed. Lumsden helped fill the need for an intermediary. Jack Dollard, an activist architect involved in many civic projects, remembered Lumsden's role in the 1960s:

> It seemed to me like there was the city over here, and over there, across a moat, there was a castle where the companies were. Every once in a while we in the city would need something, and it would be like shouting across the moat. The drawbridge would then come down, and Lumsden would come out. We would talk, and he would go back, and then after a while he would come back out with something.[2]

As director of the Chamber of Commerce, Lumsden played an intermediary role between the corporations, community organizations, and the city government. Many corporations encouraged community projects, and activists and public officials sought their support. Lumsden was important because he insulated the chief executives from a constant concern with activists and public officials, while he helped them put together a general strategy for dealing with local issues. He met frequently with the corporate leadership. His job, as he saw it, was to talk to the politicians, and also to talk to the corporate leadership about politics. He may have overstated his role at times, but, as he said, "I used to get the head of Travellers, the head of Aetna, the publishers of two newspapers, and sometimes the head of the Chamber in here and we'd decide who ought to be mayor."[3] Out of this kind of interaction there developed an approach to public-private cooperation, beginning in the 1950s, whereby the business leadership would take initiatives to preserve those aspects of the city that it valued.

At least three main forms of this business-community cooperation developed through the 1950s and 1960s. The first strategy was the use of urban renewal, which developed out of the Travellers Insurance Company's decision in the 1950s to keep its headquarters in downtown Hartford. Connecticut General Insurance Company had recently moved to suburban Bloomfield. The corporate leadership of Travellers wanted to find a suburban location, according to Lumsden, while its work force preferred to stay downtown. After much debate, the company decided to stay. They became the key investor in the city's first major urban renewal project, Constitution Plaza. Here was the classic downtown urban renewal project of the late 1950s and early 1960s. It displaced hundreds of families and small businesses, decimating "Little Italy," an area that by that time had become half black. As constructed, Constitution Plaza was an expanse of concrete and office towers, later to be criticized as "sterile." But it was a major investment. It signified a commitment to the city and helped to set the stage for later events. When Aetna Life and Casualty Insurance Company faced the decision to move a decade later, it also decided to stay and became a major financial backer of the Hartford Civic Center.

Urban renewal was followed by community action. Minority groups in Hartford were not large, autonomous, or well organized in the 1950s and 1960s, but their numbers were increasing. Community action emerged as a comprehensive response to the concentration of minorities, and moved beyond physical planning and housing to include coordinated attention to education, community organizing, and social programs. This approach had had one of its first experimental beginnings in nearby New Haven. In 1962, at Lumsden's instigation, the city established the Community Renewal Team (CRT) with representation in the black community of North Hartford.[4] This soon became the city's community action agency under the federal Office of Economic Opportunity (OEO). CRT gradually became a focus for local organizing among blacks. Social programs became more prominent, and the organization of minority neighborhoods became more of a priority.

This essentially remedial approach to community issues, performed by new organizations set up by means of a combination of city and corporate support, and, increasingly, federal subsidies, might have continued and expanded within the existing local organization of economics and politics. However, a series of riots, incidents of arson, and violent confrontations with the police took place in North Hartford, which profoundly shook the city and led to another response: a basic shift in Hartford's politics. The outbreaks that occurred in the summers of 1967 through 1970 raised the profile of CRT, but the whole structure of the economy, of local democracy, and of civil order also became issues; what was at stake was no longer a matter of social programs in a few limited neighborhoods. Excerpts from the *New York Times Index* suggest the shock effects of the 1967–1970 violence in Hartford:

> *July 1967.* Police seal off Negro North End section after dispersing 200 unruly Negroes shouting "black power" in a night of violence in which rocks and firebombs damaged several stores. The car carrying Mayor Kinsella damaged while

Mayor toured area. Negro Councilman C. B. Bennett toured area urging calmness. Negro youths split from adults in demanding immediate action to correct problems. NAACP representative urges long-range programs.

August 1967. Fire bombs thrown into supermarket in North End; Four, including NAACP chapter ex-presidents J. Barber and L. Moton, held on charge of arson.

September 1967. 150 demonstrators, mainly Negro and Puerto Rican, attempt to march from Negro North End to white South End to demand strict enforcement of state's open housing law; 36 youths, arrested after group becomes disorderly, are dispersed by some 300 police using tear gas. Members of militant Negro Black Caucus meet with city's antipoverty agency, Community Renewal Team (CRT) to form separate antipoverty organization to be controlled and operated by poor.

April 1968. Looting, vandalism reported following murder of Martin Luther King.

July 1968. Police use tear gas to disperse unruly crowd, mainly youths, in Negro North End section, who protested police closing of fire hydrants Negroes opened to get relief from heat. Project Concern, program in which 800 Negro and Puerto Rican pupils from Hartford, New Haven, and Waterbury schools are voluntarily bused to schools in white suburbs, has 53 suburban schools also participating on a voluntary basis.

June 1969. Negro youths continue disorders by breaking store windows and looting in Negro North End section; tear gas used to disperse youths. Mayor Uccello and police officials call disorders conspiracy to foment trouble in area. Curfew imposed, minor disorders continue; 2 persons wounded by police in previous disorders, 9 others slightly injured. Curfew halts new disorders. Public officials, community leaders offer reasons for disorders; list of contributing factors are noted. Band of young men roam streets of Negro North End and are seen throwing rocks at store windows and passing cars; 22 Negroes arrested in disorders stemming from police attempt to break up domestic argument.

September 1969. Police use tear gas to disperse looters in North End section and downtown area; several buildings are set afire; police car hit by sniper fire; newspaper reporters abandon cars to flee from attackers; over 35 persons arrested, 5 injured. Curfew imposed in attempt to halt firebombing and sniping; 155 persons arrested, mostly for curfew violation, bringing total arrests to over 300. Policeman and alleged looter shot; state police patrol streets with shotguns; 2 National Guard units placed on standby alert. Mayor Uccello scores disorders; Deputy Mayor Kinsella calls violence 'worst in city's history.'

April 1970. City Council sets up 3-man subcommittee to probe all aspects of shooting by police of 4 persons, in mainly Puerto Rican and Negro northern section; also plans to study Police Department's guidelines on use of deadly force; 2 of shooting victims have died. Ghetto residents see subcommittees offering series of concessions to police, who have threatened to resign en masse, by agreeing not to determine whether police acted properly in shootings and granting police right to testify in private; minority-group leaders describe situation as explosive.

June 1970. Mayor Uccello cautiously optimistic . . . blames agitators, not bad housing or lack of jobs, for disorders; NAACP official W. Smith disagrees.

August 1970. Uccello declares state of emergency, City Manager orders curfew following incidents of scattered rock throwing and looting in black North End section. Police also report sniper fire directed against firemen combatting blaze in area. 143 state troopers arrive on outskirts of city to aid local police; 125 persons have been arrested since disorders began 3 days ago. Puerto Rican E. Gonsales shot and killed by sniper or policeman. Police arrest 7 men at Black Panther party headquarters charging that much of sniper fire in North End section has been traced to Panthers; National Committee to Combat Fascism state official R. Mealey calls police action terrorism. Curfew appears to be effective except for isolated instances; main problem is now large number of fires attributed to racial disorders. Curfew is lifted, state of emergency continues after 6 days of street disorders; city officials link most disorders to bands of young children recruited and trained by older militants.[5]

The confrontations between minorities and the police and the property destruction that accompanied them transformed Hartford's approach to urban policy. The remedial programs, in the face of such new local urgencies, became more prominent, and a further push was made toward minority organization both within and outside of their structure. The leading neighborhood organization of the 1960s was the South Arsenal Neighborhood Development Corporation (SAND). The Community Renewal Team, which had been dominated initially by foundations and the OEO, also began to hold neighborhood elections, thus giving more control to the neighborhoods and stimulating neighborhood organization.

During the late 1960s, an insurgent black leadership had developed through these local organizations, independent of the foundation and OEO funding base, and capable—because they held the key to legitimacy in the black neighborhood—of bargaining with the organizations that controlled resources. They had developed an ideology and program that they tried to sell. John Wilson, who started as an organizer with SAND in 1968, said

> we thought the approach was through education. We thought if our kids could get a good education, they could get a good job and good housing. That would break the cycle. We thought of education, also, as never-ending, and as a thing that suburban people and inner city people could share. We did a bunch of retreats and role-playing sessions with suburban people. We wanted to bus our children out to the suburbs for a day, and suburban children in to the inner city so they would get to understand each other.[6]

SAND and other groups got support from local businesses and participation from suburban people. Connecticut General, which had moved its headquarters out of the city, was nevertheless responsive to requests for funds, and it also gave expertise. In general, the insurance companies hired minority people on more than a token basis. Wilson said, "They understand our argument: if the city goes, it won't be long before the suburbs do too."

Lumsden, who was given to wide-scale social engineering, simply pushed harder for expanded social planning. He had a vision of regional action, and he had been able to push through the creation of a regional planning board and council of governments. But the major effort was the establishment of the Greater Hartford Process. In 1969, James Rouse, who had earlier built the new town of Columbia, Maryland, with Connecticut General, signed a $350,000 contract with a private sector Hartford group to design a "total approach" to dealing with the city's problems. The result was a program to build new towns in Hartford's North End *and* in the suburbs; thus it was a truly regional approach. It was large as well, with a projected population of twenty thousand for the new suburban community. The profits were to be used to subsidize the North End revitalization.

The approach was comprehensive. Much attention was paid to social issues, and Greater Hartford Process tried to work with the neighborhood groups in the North End. The operation required a large staff, which spent the next several years planning for land acquisitions, for development, and for community support. The hope was that, with sufficiently imaginative vision, key decision makers would give the necessary support.

Ultimately, Greater Hartford Process built neither the suburban New Town nor the North Hartford project. It fell victim to shifts in the political climate that made social engineering more difficult and it succumbed to increasing interest rates. But Lumsden, by pushing remedial and social-engineering approaches to urban reform to their limits, helped to create a change in the local political structure. That change, in turn, put Hartford on a new track for both physical and social development.

The Transformation in Hartford Politics

All of these early initiatives implied a certain enlightenment in local politics in which a civilized liberalism in city affairs would be backed up by a business power base; this power base, while fast retreating to the suburbs, would continue to care for the city out of altruism as well as self-interest. Under the conditions that prevailed up until 1967, this arrangement might have worked. A city administrator of the 1970s described the way city business got done.

> There were four powers. There was the city manager, the council, the Chamber of Commerce, and Travellers. The city manager was very strong. He carried out policy but he also set it, by means of his budget functions. The City Council was a bluestocking, Democratic group. They were satisfed to let the administration run the show. If you worked for the city, you did not meet with council without the city manager knowing about it. The separation between business and the city government was clear. Working for the city, you would find out about major land development in the papers. Basically what they asked for, the city would provide. Roger Wilkins, the chairman of Travel-

lers, was very powerful. Art Lumsden was in his heyday. The whole social and economic picture was different then. The minority population was small. There was awareness of problems, but the main 'projects' were physical: park improvements, schools, the zoning revision. Urban renewal was very strong. . . . [7]

The riots changed this picture of Hartford politics. The council-manager form of government, well suited to urban management in cities where there was a basic consensus concerning goals, was inadequate to address the kinds of underlying conflicts that were now coming out into the open. As this form of government was practiced in Hartford, with a weak mayor, a part-time council, and strong administrative manager, it could not generate the authority to govern the city's increasingly diverse and divided constituencies. The council-manager system required a talented city manager to be able to make policy proposals based on his understanding of the issues in the city and to boil them down to a form on which a city council could then decide one way or another. This worked as long as the issues reflected an underlying consensus in the community. But when feelings about the issues became too intense, or when racial divisions confounded the understanding of administrators, then the city administration stood revealed as fatally flawed. People, when faced with seemingly irreconcilable conflicts, would accept only an ultimate authority: the problem with the city manager was that he was not elected. Only the mayor and city council were in that position.

What existed in 1969 was an authority vacuum in Hartford's political leadership caused by those leaders' inability to deal with the riots. Somewhat fortuitously, a new group of council members moved into that vacuum and took control of economic development and social programs. There were three resignations, and the Hartford Town Commitee of the Democratic Party and the council nominated temporary replacements, who would then be in position to win the seats for a regular term in the fall. Balancing the ticket, they appointed Allyn Martin, a black dentist from the North End, George Levine, a Jewish lawyer, and Nicholas R. Carbone. The catalyst was Carbone. He had been active as president of the South Hartford Business Association and represented an Italian ethnic constituency. He was not powerful when he started. He was 32 years old, an Air Force veteran, the youngest of three sons of Carl Carbone, who had founded a well-known restaurant in South Hartford. His older brothers had gone into the family business. He had spent some time at the University of Hartford, then worked in various positions in Hartford businesses and corporations. He had sold insurance and had been a sales representative for a typewriter company.

Later, people said that Carbone grew dramatically after getting on the City Council. His own recollection was that this was partly true. Nothing in life had involved him like being on the City Council. He plunged into committee work, which gave him access to information about the workings of city government, and he read everything he could get his hands on. There were two sides to his growth. One was his development as a public entrepreneur, a skill he put to work most effectively in a series of innovative public land development projects. He had been made chairman of the Capital Improvements Committee and used that committee as a vehicle for his own learning. The committee had been set up, he said, to deal with Greater Hartford Process and with Lumsden. He used the position to absorb their thinking about the land development and social programs that Process was undertaking. It was a crucial position. Greater Hartford Process was developing very large plans with a big, highly paid staff. The city administration was nervous about this. Carbone needed to develop a city response that was even-handed. To do that, he educated himself:

> My job was to coordinate that and be the clearinghouse, to keep the cooperation going, have the frank discussions without insulting anybody. . . . In order to do that, I had to study everything. . . . What made sense, what could work, what didn't work, and it forced me to take a very hard look at the city concept. . . . [8]

Because he was able to grasp the details of projects the city had to accomplish if it wanted to maintain the trust of the business community, and because he was more willing than anyone else on the council to put in the time required, Carbone soon became the central figure on the council. He established a sense of teamwork among the Democratic majority and was able to mobilize majority votes on key issues. Because Hartford had a weak-mayor system, the majority group had essential control over the city government. Under Carbone, the council examined the details of city administration and extended its control. The city manager, Eli Friedman, a well-regarded professional, who previously had had more latitude, resigned in

1970. This made it possible for the council to assert its authority even more directly over city administration.

Another side of Carbone was his sense of social justice. During his first years in office, certain events enormously stimulated him to develop his conception of appropriate city policy. First, the riots in the North End erupted, soon after he was appointed. People who knew Carbone looked back on those riots as an experience that affected him profoundly. His own recollections bear this out:

> In June of 1969, I was at the state capital when the word came about the first of the riots. I went down there. I was shocked and aghast at what I saw, because this was outside the realm of my experience. I never understood anger which was so great as to be totally violent. I suspect I spent most of the rest of that year debating in my mind what the answers were . . . trying to understand the behavior of the blacks and Hispanics in North Hartford and why does the anger take this form, and the denial that was coming from . . . the police and the city manager.[9]

Earlier, Carbone had been sympathetic to the approach taken by the police in reaction to the North Hartford violence, but his attitude changed.

> First I came down on the side of the officials. This had to be looters, thugs, etc. . . . The more I examined and talked to people, the more I learned about the extent of poverty. I had never known real poverty before, even though we had lived in times when we had been short of money in my household and we had suffered denial, but it was denial of a vacation, not a denial of food. So the extent of poverty that I had known or had known through my family was denial of the luxuries of life, but not the basics of life. I was beginning to examine for the first time and [be] . . . forced to see denials of basics. . . . It took like a year of going through this.[10]

As a council member, he got involved in several incidents of police shootings and violence that year. There was one case where a South Hartford youth had been subjected to a fusillade of police gunfire because he was mistaken for a suspect: ". . . they just opened fire on him. There were bullets all around the car into the house. His mother called me and his mother was a relation to a good friend of mine."[11] These incidents made him increasingly critical of the police approach. When there were police shootings in North Hartford in the following year he put on pressure for an investigation. His South Hartford constituency still saw the police as their main protection and reacted angrily, and it nearly cost him his position at the next election.

City Policy under the New Council

Carbone was able to influence or dominate the council with his policies. George Levine and Richard Suisman (elected to the council later) played essential roles in this process, and for several years a majority consensus developed around a series of major positions and initiatives.

THE CIVIC CENTER AND THE REAL ESTATE STRATEGY

Carbone inherited two physical development programs when he came on the council. One involved the schools. The other was the Civic Center. The Civic Center had been conceived in the 1950s as a complement to Constitution Plaza. Its conception is attributed to Lumsden, from the Chamber of Commerce. It was to include a hotel and arena, and later, shops, and its purpose was to make Hartford an appropriate place to hold sporting events, shows, and conventions. A 1960 master plan located it to the west of downtown. By 1969 it was in the planning stages, but the city lacked the capital to get it built.

Carbone's involvement in the Civic Center project increased during 1970. Before he was on the City Council, he had opposed the bond issue for the project. Now he plunged into the project of building the Civic Center, as well as building new schools, and began to see some of the possible ramifications of these projects. He thought the Civic Center project should be a publicly controlled operation. In December of 1970, the council formally adopted a policy stating the city's desire to retain title to the land and to control Civic Center operations through leases. But Carbone thought the private sector should pay for the investment, since they would benefit from it most. In 1971, Harold Geneen of ITT was trying to acquire a Hartford insurance firm, a move that was being blocked by a state regulatory agency. Carbone pursuaded the state agency to change its position, on the condition that ITT would construct a Sheraton Hotel as part of the Civic Center.[12] He then asked local and suburban businessmen to match the ITT investment.

I made a public request for $10 million from the private sector in the suburbs because they were going to benefit from it. Of course, as I expected, we got zero. They got Harold Geneen to make an offer of $5 million, if the other businesses would match it. Of course, all the other businesses reacted and said this was a bad principle. That's when I knew there was a limit to public-private cooperation.[13]

He then went after public refinancing of the project by proposing a bond issue, which would double the city's investment from $15 million to $30 million. The city retained ownership of the complex and made separate agreements for the operation of the hotel and for the stores to be built on the air rights over part of the complex. ITT and its subsidiary, Sheraton, constructed the hotel and agreed to pay a fee each year in lieu of taxes, with ownership reverting to the city at the end of the long-term lease. The air rights agreement was explained later by Carbone in this way:

When we built the Civic Center, Aetna Life and Casualty wanted to buy the air rights. We refused to sell the air rights because we were creating valuable real estate. So, we decided that the ownership remained in the public [realm]. What we did was instead of selling the air rights . . . we negotiated the value [at] a million four [hundred thousand dollars]. We capitalized it out for eight percent a year on the value of the air rights, plus one percent of the gross rentals that they collected on the stores. We took a kicker, like they would. So, the more business the stores did, the more that flowed into the city treasury.[14]

Carbone used ownership and the lease agreements to secure additional benefits for city residents. He secured an agreement that all part-time jobs in the Civic Center would go to Hartford residents, to be distributed through the work-study administrators in the city's four high schools. He secured quotas for Hartford residents and minorities on the construction jobs and in the hotel union. He also influenced the assignment of contracts for construction on behalf of minority businesses, and helped establish Hartford residents in Civic Center shops.

The business community had not planned for the city to take such an aggressive role in its physical development. But as one observer said, "Carbone emerged out of real estate development issues. That was never an intent of [Greater Hartford] Process. He got stronger and more confident, and began to make more and more requests. He became more and more a champion of the inner-city poor."[15] Carbone looked back on this period as one of personal growth, but he also saw it as a time of the revelation to the community of a character he had developed previously.

> The public thought of me probably as a machine politician—which I was—they thought I'd be a conservative Italian ethnic. In fact, I wasn't. I thought a lot different than that. So when the public thought I changed, part of it was just a matter of my not meeting their original perceptions. I changed too. But part of it was that they saw me as different than I was originally.[16]

His original thinking about physical development had been formed partly during the Constitution Plaza project, when dozens of Italian families and small businesses had been forced out of the project area. At that time he saw a trend toward all city property going into the hands of the big corporations. Later, he saw his own policy preferences as "pragmatic." "No one could figure what the hell I was doing, because I didn't get up and say I was a progressive or a socialist. I wouldn't put any labels on me. I was just trying to do pragmatics."[17]

Later, he tried to describe more systematically his approach to real estate. In a lecture called "The City as a Real Estate Investor," he described a rationale for his policies.[18] Hartford had lost the bulk of its middle-class population and many jobs. What it had left was a poor population that needed jobs, and a good deal of vacant and underused land. If the city were going to operate in the interests of its own people, it should convert that land into jobs for these people. There would then be a resource base to provide needed services. Furthermore, if the city could get hold of real estate, it would have made a good investment, because real estate would appreciate. The city administration could then be designed to capture the effects generated by the creation of new jobs and by property appreciation for city residents. Carbone saw four basic levers he could use to influence and command development, as ways to pursue these purposes. First, the city should try to own property and buildings. Such ownership would give the city control over land use and allow the city to realize the increasing value as land prices increased. Second, the city should exert policy controls over construction; it could require such projects to employ local contractors and subcontractors and local and minority labor. Third, the city should have a policy directed toward local employment on such properties after construction. Fourth, the city should develop a policy to capture the benefits from the neighborhood effects of such development: the positive impact of such projects on the values of land, employment, and construction on surrounding properties.

Carbone had begun to develop these policies with the Civic Center project, through the air rights lease agreement with Aetna. Later, in collaboration with the city's Development Commission and its director, Paul Strecker, this strategy was refined. They used, in combination, city leasing policies (which allowed them to maintain control over many aspects of subsequent development), and a series of tax policies.[19] Strecker later described the tax policies as based on the realization that the city's property-taxing authority was a first lien on property and conferred control, just as a mortgage would.[20] A mortgage holder held a certain amount of authority over any development: he could stipulate a set of conditions before releasing the funds so that the project could go ahead. Ordinarily, these conditions would refer to the marketability of the project, conditions designed to insure viability so that the mortgage payments were protected, so that the mortgage holder could be assured of a steady repayment. Strecker and Carbone saw the city as being in an analogous position. Like the mortgage holder, it had a claim on revenue flows from any property in the form of property taxes. Second, it needed a way to transform its latent investment into a catalyst that could determine whether and in what form a project would proceed. This could be accomplished if the city could discount the future tax returns and transform them into a form of presently available capital that it could use as an inducement.

A crude form of such discounting was the tax abatement, used in many places as an inducement for development by the private sector. But in Strecker's view, such an approach was too crude. Using the rationale of the real estate developer, he wanted an approach that could be calibrated to the needs of each project. A more exact procedure would begin from estimates of the income and expense streams of any project. A typical project, as Strecker explained it, might have these characteristics, as shown in table 2.2. Using this example, Strecker explained how the project would have only a tenuous feasibility, chiefly because the margin was not high enough for a mortgage holder to risk lending the funds. That is, debt service took up too great a portion of net income before taxes. In this

TABLE 2.2. **Hypothetical Project Cost Analysis, with City Equity Participation**

Project cost at $45 per square foot, 100,000 square feet	$4,500,000
Gross rentals:	1,000,000
Less 5 percent vacancy	50,000
Net rentals	950,000
Annual expenses before local taxes and debt services	400,000
Net income before taxes and debt services	450,000
Debt service on $4,500,000 at 8 percent	360,000
Net income after debt services	90,000
Taxes at 80c per sq. ft.	80,000
Net annual return	10,000

example, net income was only one-and-one-quarter times debt service. Typically, a lender would want perhaps one-and-one-half times debt service, to have a margin against uncertainty.

In this situation, the city could make the difference, if it could fix the tax rate at lower than the nominal $80,000 annual fringe. This is the logic behind tax abatements. But Carbone and Strecker rejected abatements as too crude and inadequately calibrated to serve the interests of both parties. An abatement did not take into account explicitly the factors that would make an arrangement rational for both city and developer. (The same would be true for the anti-abatement position, leaving the whole financing problem in the hands of private interests—also guaranteeing that there would be no project, in this example.) Instead of a blanket abatement, Strecker described a real estate accounting rationale that could be used for any specific project, giving returns to both city and developer. If, using the present example, the city fixed taxes very low—say at $5,000 annually for ten years—it would in effect be guaranteeing the developer an additional $75,000 per year in income. The effect would be to increase the pretax margin from $90,000 to $165,000 annually, enough to make the project viable.

In return, the city could take a proportional share in the equity of the project. The city's share would be negotiated by means of a comparison between the city's risk capital to the developer's risk. In the example above, a developer with ten percent equity in the project would be risking $450,000 at the outset. The city's risk would be the discounted value, over the ten-year period, of the $75,000 annual tax abatement. Strecker would use the interest rate at which the city could borrow in computing the discount rate. A ten percent rate would result in a present value of $300,000 for the ten-year tax abatement and would be the basis for negotiating approximately a 40 percent city share in the project. Strecker estimated that the terms of the tax abatement legislation and prevailing city borrowing rates would produce an equity share in the range of fifty percent for the several major projects in which the city would share.

The city would get return on its equity both through shares of annual after-tax net income and through a share of the capital gains realized after the project was refinanced. Thus, the city was trading off immediate tax returns for future shares of profits and capital gains. Modern developers, on the other hand, sought immediate gain and limitations on their risk. This was the financial basis of the city-developer relationship. But the political aspects of such deals may have been at least as important to Carbone. He was putting the city into a partnership relationship with private developers. The tax and lease arrangements together gave the city a measure of control over each project. Each specific lease provision gave the city something it could trade off for something else, a little more leverage.

The legalities of these arrangements would have meant little in and of themselves. This kind of a partnership, to be successful, also required a level of expertise on the part of Strecker and Carbone that was equal to that of the developers, and it also required of them a willingness to enter the city into risk situations. This they did, in a series of projects that followed the Civic Center: One Corporate Plaza, an office complex immediately to the east of the Civic Center; the conversion of an abandoned Korvettes store into an American Airlines reservations center, with an agreement to hire and train a specified proportion of minority Hartford residents; and some nine other projects. Strecker estimated the total private investment in these eleven projects at $350 to $400 million through 1981.

Carbone later claimed that many other policies had also been organized around the principle of maximizing the value of city land: a policy of advocating city interests relative to the suburban towns, a policy of expansive public enterprise, an affirmative action policy, and a policy restricting transportation access to the suburbs.[21] In 1971, the city filed a complaint against the state highway department, which had proposed building a beltway that would have facilitated the growth of suburban shopping centers. Since this would have taken businesses away from Hartford, the city opposed the road. They managed to stall the construction until economic crisis and energy shortages killed the project. This, in Carbone's view, helped maintain the value of city land: " . . . all of a sudden, the real estate that was in the city became more important." The city also lobbied the state to develop an urban policy statement denying state funds to places that did not have affirmative action programs. This curtailed state grants for industrial parks and sewer and water system improvements in Hartford's outer-ring suburbs. The city also attempted to limit the flow of federal funds to the suburbs; at one point it sued the federal Department of Urban Development to prohibit the distribution of Community Development Revenue Sharing Funds to six towns that did not have plans for low-income housing. Carbone said:

> What we were advocating was to keep the suburbs suburbs, so that they didn't become city. We wanted to keep the rural areas rural . . . and we wanted to protect the open spaces of the farmlands. And we wanted to keep the city from becoming wasteland. What we did was to start enhancing the value of the land in the city. So, we created value and that's what you've got to remember. You can create value through land use planning, if you look at zoning . . . transportation . . . sewers and water.[22]

POLICE REORGANIZATION

The real estate strategy developed by the city demonstrated Carbone's business side and the willingness of the City Council to operate in an entrepreneurial way on behalf of public objectives. But, early on, even at the beginning of the 1970s, there was a social side to Carbone's concerns, and the first such concern was the police department. Carbone and other members of the City Council had tried several measures for controlling the police, including new gun regulations that stipulated the conditions under which a police officer might use his weapon. There had been discussion of establishing an external police review commission, a measure that had been instituted in many communities by the end of the 1960s. But what they did had a more permanent effect. They established the Hartford Institute for Criminal and Social Justice in 1968.[23] The institute was initially set up under a Ford Foundation grant, but soon got local corporate and foundation backing. It was to be a research facility to help spur innovation and adaptation within the operating units of the criminal justice system. By the 1970s, it had hired several staff members and, in addition to its local financial base, had a contract with the federal Law Enforcement Assistance Administration.

The institute, at Carbone's and the council's request, released a study of Hartford's police department organization that described a new approach: a shift from a centralized to a neighborhood police organization, including increased training for police and increased community involvement in neighborhood crime prevention. In early 1974, an opening for police chief arose, and the city — in a controversial move — brought in an outsider, Hugo Masini. Masini had a mandate from the City Council to reform the police organization, according to the model already conceptualized by the institute. The problem then was to implement these changes, in the face of a history of centralized police operations and what was sure to be police department resistance.

The institute started by surveying the Asylum Hill Neighborhood. Masini assigned a lieutenant, Neil Sullivan, to be part of the survey team (and later, district commander). The team's prime objective was to explain the neighborhood team-policing concept, to get a sense of neighborhood perceptions of the crime problem, and to establish a base for their own operations after the survey was done. Their focus was on robbery, purse snatching, and burglary, crimes that they thought offered a practical chance of reduction and that they saw as contributing to a climate of fear. They employed a physical planning consultant to design neighborhood alterations that might deter crime by cutting off escape routes. They interviewed some forty persons who had been apprehended for crimes in the area, to determine what kinds of targets were picked for crimes and for what reasons. They sought ways to get greater resident involvement in crime prevention.

The city began operating according to the neighborhood-policing design during 1975, and later extended this design to five other areas, so that it covered the entire city. The institute continued its research over several years, ending in 1979. The changes made touched on several aspects of police organization. First, police personnel took neighborhood assignments, instead of ranging over the entire city. Being stationed in a neighborhood for a long time, they got acquainted with its people and business proprietors. Second, police authority was decentralized from headquarters to the district commander, Sullivan. The Asylum Hill district was expanded to cover Clay-Arsenal, in the city's North End, and separate deputy commanders were assigned to that area and to Asylum Hill, working under Sullivan. Third, the police encouraged the community to become more involved in policing. One resident innovation, for example, was a street observers program; another was an Explorer Scout program, which involved its members in traffic control and other duties. Neighborhood team-policing, as it developed in Hartford, was not the extreme power devolution proposed in some cities. There was no neighborhood precinct house; at most the police managed a storefront office, where police officers would sit and write reports, be available for contacts with neighborhood people, and hold meetings related to community involvement. The effects of the program, however, were positive and these could be measured in evaluations published by the institute. The institute and the police succeeded in creating two community organizations; there were reductions in burglary and robbery, and as crime subsided, so did community fear of crime.

The neighborhood police measures had a profound impact on the police administration. The idea of involving lieutenants and district commanders in the survey and design phases of the project made them converts to the concept; contact with the community, while it involved some strain, created a solidarity not dependent on police headquarters. Masini supported the neighborhood concept and later implemented it throughout the city in four additional districts. Police resistance remained, however, particularly at headquarters, and the system was changed again upon Masini's resignation in 1980.

THE SHIFT TO SERVICES

The Hartford city administration shifted from a "bricks and mortar" to a services emphasis after approximately 1974. The reasons for this shift included a steady deterioration in city conditions, a shift in federal grants formulae, and Carbone's response to staff and neighborhood arguments.

First, city conditions in general deteriorated throughout the 1970s, and it became obvious to more and more people that capital investment projects had to be supplemented or replaced by direct efforts to sustain or raise local personal incomes. Decline in Hartford intensified in the early 1970s, even as such projects as the Civic Center and the Hartford Process plans for new towns moved ahead. Part of the shift in city perceptions came of the Greater Hartford

Process itself, and these shifts affected Carbone. After the failure of its new town construction scheme in 1974, Greater Hartford Process changed direction. A new director, Maurice Coleman, took charge and turned the organization toward social services. Coleman hired Sidney Gardner, a social services planner, who had worked at the U.S. Department of Health, Education, and Welfare under Elliot Richardson. Gardner began to make an impact on city policy.

Gardner's analyses, which were published in April 1975, documented drastic deteriorations in the living situations of the city's population.[24] He showed that welfare and unemployment had doubled in ten years. By 1975, 44 percent of Hartford school children were coming from welfare families, and almost half of the total population lived on fixed incomes—welfare, unemployment insurance, or social security. Meanwhile, the dollar gap between city and suburban median incomes had increased. The result was a double impact on the city budget. The costs of fire, police, and social services were rising, while the local tax base was declining. An ever-increasing tax burden was falling upon an increasingly poor population; as the population got poorer, rents went unpaid and houses were abandoned, which further decreased both the housing stock and the tax rolls. Further, Hartford property taxes were very high compared to other towns in the state. And the state was not carrying its share of Hartford's costs. The city estimated that the state took $135 million in tax revenues from Hartford in 1974–1975, and only disbursed $22 million to the city in grants-in-aid. Welfare payments lagged far behind cost-of-living increases.

Two other factors affected the city's policies. Changes in federal grant policies were putting constraints on the city's ability to initiate physical development projects. With the passage of the Housing and Community Development Act of 1974, the urban renewal program was to be phased out in favor of Community Development Block Grants (called CDBG), but the total funds available to the city were reduced. The reality of these cuts began to be felt. Later, local neighborhoods began to exert additional pressures on the city. Neighborhood residents became much more organized and their groups more autonomous: the presence of these organizations, originally a consequence of the community action program and a generalized response to urban disorder, became a wider phenomenon, and extended into the South Hartford ethnic neighborhoods. The real impacts of community organizing came at the end of the decade, but neighborhood voices were heard earlier and had an impact on city policy.

Carbone, who had always seen Greater Hartford Process as a resource for his own analysis ("They gave me a three-million-dollar education," he said) and who was attentive to the changing federal funding climate and the changes in neighborhood constituencies, listened to Gardner and began to change and expand his conception of appropriate policies. Gradually, a new city policy emerged. Its elements included (1) an increased administrative and fund-raising capacity in City Hall; (2) a policy focus on raising local incomes and lowering inflationary cost increases; and (3) lobbying to change the character of outside funding authorities to suit these purposes.

Carbone added new staff advisors and greatly altered the character of the city's administration. In 1969, the city manager had held the most important administrative position in the city, and through his use of the budget function, he had exercised some of the policy functions that had formerly been the prerogatives of the City Council. After Eli Friedman resigned as city manager in 1972, the city never restored a strong city manager. A succession of city managers functioned fairly much in Carbone's shadow. But the main administrative changes were made in the appointments just below the level of the city manager. These included Jonathan Coleman, who ran the city planning department, Michael Brown, the finance director, and John Alschuler, who, as assistant city manager, focused attention on raising funds in the state capital and in Washington on several local policy and management projects. In general, these appointments involved a shift in city activities: important city departments had lost manpower throughout the 1970s, but new administrative positions had been added. Between the years 1971 – 1972 and 1979 – 1980, total workyears accounted for as "administration, developing programs and finance" increased from 118.5 to 144.9, while the overall city work force decreased by 195.5 workyears.[25]

The city administration produced a large number of policy initiatives in the latter part of the 1970s, all oriented toward the cost-cutting, income-maintenance imperatives that had become urgent. One theme that emerged was the restructuring of administrative budgets and service delivery systems. The city also paid greater attention to education functions, adding four hundred positions to the Board of Education payrolls, while subtracting one hundred thirty-eight from the police and fire departments and ninety-nine from public works. It initiated new dental, lunch, and breakfast programs in the schools—an indirect income subsidy—while replacing teachers with paraprofessionals subject to local residency requirements. It redirected $1.5 million of Community Development Block Grant funds, which had been used for capital investments, to the school system.[26]

A general purpose that seemed to underlie much of the innovations that took place in Hartford after 1975 was to substitute local organization for expensive bureaucratic and professional agencies. The City Council began to encourage citizen participation, not just in policy decisions, but in performance—in the actual delivery of services to residents. The neighborhood team-policing initiatives were one prime example of this substitution of local involvement for central staff positions, but the pattern could be seen in other areas as well. An effort was made to bring local residents into the process of providing recreation services. Over 40 percent of the city's part-time recreation leaders had been suburban residents, but Hartford created instead a neighborhood incentive program that allowed residents to plan and operate their own activities. If someone in a neighborhood wanted to teach a class in oil painting, for example, he or she could submit a proposal to a neighborhood planning group. If it appeared that the person was qualified and there was sufficient interest to warrant a class in oil painting, the resident would be paid to teach a class. This system involved far more people and offered a greater variety of recreational activities than the former, more traditional program had. Classes were given in cross-country skiing, squash, acting, weaving, guitar, vegetarian cooking, and many other subjects.

Toward the latter part of the 1970s, Hartford planners adopted a strategy to reduce the cost of basic necessities that was focused on Hartford neighborhoods. They realized that even the most optimistic forecasts of local job creation through infusions of outside capital would not suffice to provide jobs for every resident. They believed that if they could help reduce the costs of such basic necessities as food, energy, transportation, and health care, more purchasing power would be available for other local activities. There would be additional resources to purchase private market housing and to patronize neighborhood retail and service enterprises.

The city had the greatest success with food and energy cost reduction programs. The Hartford food system included five neighborhood food markets, a community cannery, community gardens, youth gardens, neighborhood buying clubs, solar greenhouses, rooftop container gardening, and a city-wide composting program. All these elements were planned to complement one another. The system was justified because it developed traits of self-reliance and cooperative consumption by residents and because it generated an environment for job training that could later be applied to private-sector employment.[27]

The energy program was initiated as a result of steep increases in fuel oil prices in 1978, which caused many owners to abandon rental units. Not only were many residents without heat, but these abandonments produced the drastic secondary effects of neighborhood economic deterioration and loss of housing units. In response, Hartford planners made surveys to determine why specific structures might be subject to abandonment due to energy costs and which buildings were likely to generate complaints of heating failure. They used a computer-based information system to determine what structures in the city were at risk and used the information to target outreach workers. They created a Coordinated Energy Response Center with a central "heat line" to allow for quick responses to heating complaints. They coordinated the distribution of weatherization kits according to the claim that these materials could save up to 20 percent of each tenant's fuel consumption. They established a rent receivership program as a last resort to maintain minimum heat levels in buildings and to reduce the likelihood of housing abandonment. The combined effect of the targeted code enforcement and rent receivership programs was reported for the winter of 1979–1980. Officials stated that the landlords of 217 housing units had corrected heat violations, and 51 units had been placed into rent receivership, requiring the city to pay the cost of correcting violations.[28]

These programs—mostly created after 1975—took hold not only because of greater staff resources in City Hall, but also because of qualitative changes in administrative style. One of the key persons providing the new style was John Alschuler.[29] While Carbone was able to generate the constituencies for new programs, Alschuler and others in City Hall developed policies, raised money in the state and federal governments, and created new organizations to implement these policies. Thus the team at City Hall expanded and attended to new topics. Alschuler's background made him particularly useful in this process. He had been prominent in the alternative schools movement as a Ph.D. student at the University of Massachusetts and had national connections. He came to Hartford in 1973 as a policy analyst for the school board and became an early board member of the Washington-based Conference on Alternative State and Local Policies. That organization was soon to become a network for liberal and left-leaning public officials, with Carbone taking a major role. Alschuler began to work with Carbone on school issues and by 1977 he had moved into the city manager's office. There, he had a "staff" rather than "operational" job description, which meant that no program formally depended on him; he was free therefore to range over all the issues of interest to him and Carbone. He would divide his time between acting as staff and initiator of local policy groups and going to Washington or to the state capitol to get funds and legislation to support the local projects.

> I spent a fair amount of time—because I had no operational responsibilities—a great joy. I could take a problem of particular importance and devote 20–30–40–50 percent of my time to it for six months. The three best examples were energy policy, economic development policy, and housing policy. And to be able to create an *ad hoc* working structure which brought together members of the community, members of the city government, members of the private sector, members of the city government across different departments and divisions to concentrate totally on problems that we thought were of crisis or near-crisis proportions. So I would spend a fair amount of time on those areas that were very high priority and I had the office and the latitude and the political backing so that if I—with Nick, with the manager—said okay we need to do a major revision and analysis and rebuild the way the city approaches housing, I'd have the latitude to go in.[30]

Alschuler also established an extensive data-processing and analysis operation in City Hall:

> One thing we spent much more time on than any other government I know—and it was extremely expensive, probably [cost] $700,000 over two years—was data collection. We used that computer . . . and it was useful in two or three different ways. It was useful for internal planning, so we knew what the hell was going on. It was useful in presenting our case to the corporate community and to the legislature and, finally, just the speed of what we were doing—for example, we had more data in our computer which allowed us to project the impact of various state aid formulas, so that our state delegation, in the last half an hour of a conference over a formula, our delegation had better and more accurate data than the state computer was turning out, on the various implications of various formula changes. I can't tell you how much money we got, simply by having faster data than anybody else.[31]

He had, he said, thirty or forty professionals working for him by 1979:

> We were willing to spend an enormous amount of money on what I think you would call planning. . . . We invested in infrastructure—bought the computer, staff, time. . . . At one time I had two people simply working on a regional transit issue. I had more people working on that than the entire region had. But it was an investment in things that we knew would lever much larger returns over time. And it was expensive. The school litigation probably cost us $300,000 or $400,000. Everybody criticized that at the time, but it returned the city $3 million a year in increased revenues. So, I think a lot of governments are too hesitant to commit time up front just going after basic, economic, structural decisions, made either by the government itself or by a higher level of government, and trying to impact those before they've done. You're going after symptoms, not causes. . . . Governments are always trained to deal with—something happens, then you respond to it. Well, it takes staff time, to mitigate that problem.[32]

Alschuler's staff created policy initiatives, but it was sustained by and exploited resources supplied at higher levels of government. Alschuler in fact spent the major amount of his time on intergovernmental relations. At the state capitol, he lobbied: preventing a shift of property tax assessments onto residential property, getting increases in welfare benefits, and stopping "some fairly draconian legislation, such as workfare." All this took up an enormous amount of staff time. He also spent, along with Carbone and other staff members, a great deal of time in Washington. Hartford was, he said, one of the "two or three most productive cities per capita in the nation in attracting federal funds, primarily for economic development."[33]

THE CITY AS ADVOCATE

After 1975, Carbone increasingly saw the city as being in desperate straits, impoverished by a structure that channeled the poor into it, while keeping a disproportionate share of resources in other places. This led him to take a combative stance toward the state government and the suburbs and, in some cases, the federal government. He was trying to generate support for redistributive policies by dramatizing the developing inequities. In 1976, the city went to court to stop the delivery of federal Community Development Block Grant allocations to six suburban towns, based on the argument that the towns had no effective plan for accommodating low-income housing. In 1978 a state-mandated property tax reassessment confronted the city with a shift in the tax burden from business to residential properties, and the city supported a citizens' lobby to press the legislature to adopt a tax differential favoring residences. Earlier, the city had gone to court to block construction of an interstate highway connector that would have stimulated suburban, not city, growth.

Carbone's relatively aggressive stance as an advocate of the have-nots in Hartford was complemented by the growth of his internal staff. They fed him the information and helped do the paperwork to follow through on the positions he took. It took competent legal staff work to pursue the lawsuits in court, and the top staff in the city manager's office spent time in Washington and at the state capitol negotiating the concrete outcomes of positions Carbone took in public. Jon Coleman told me about the effort to get federal Community Development Block Grant funds allocated to social services: Coleman ultimately spent time at HUD helping the federal agency rewrite the regulations so that Hartford could pursue its strategy.[34] Staff time completed and complemented the drama.

Afterwards, what most people remembered was the drama, and they were dubious about whether the city had gained more in understanding than it had lost in resentment. Carbone had used the lawsuit on the block grants to project the city's position into the suburbs. He did not intend simply to make a grandstand play on behalf of the city's constituencies, but to gain the attention of the suburbs so as to win support in the state capitol. In the wake of the lawsuit, he took on speaking engagements in hostile suburban auditoriums to present the city's cases, often winning new attention and support. But the situation as a whole was against the city. Tradition was on the side of suburban autonomy and a kind of privatism that could not only outvote Hartford, but, because of the way the city boundaries were drawn, could simply ignore it. Earlier, John Wilson of SAND had told numerous relevant corporate executives that it was in their interests to solve the race problems in the city, because otherwise they would have to confront them in the suburbs.[35] But in the end, Wilson was wrong, or at least those consequences were sufficiently delayed for those executives not to have to act.

The Growth of the Neighborhood Movement

History had a way of repeating itself. The remedial policies of Lumsden and the council-manager government of the 1960s were overtaken by social disorders that were too profound for that government structure to accommodate. The new City Council majority of the 1970s was installed because of the failure of administrative and political leadership to adapt to new circumstances. A parallel kind of challenge confronted Carbone toward the end of the 1970s. At least on the surface, the challenge came from the neighborhoods. Like other cities, Hartford experienced an explosive growth in neighborhood organizations after about 1975. They had been nurtured in the 1960s by the corporate community and its creation, the Community Renewal Team, encouraged by such various city actions as the neighborhood team-policing experiments of 1976–1979, and they had been given a strong organizing push by the Catholic Church's Campaign for Human Development starting in 1975. But one has to look to the slow evolution of neighborhood conditions to really understand the situation that emerged. Neighborhood organization in Hartford was a black problem throughout the 1960s and early 1970s. Blacks were central to the riots in North Hartford and provided dynamics for minority social action and politics. CRT established SAND, the South Arsenal Neighborhood Development Corporation, in the late 1960s and SAND remained the most successful neighborhood organization until the mid-1970s. Also, blacks were Carbone's main minority allies in 1970: Allyn Martin and Collin Bennett, for example, on the City Council. Other neighborhood interests remained quiescent. Puerto Ricans did not organize prominently until later. South Hartford and the ethnic Italian areas were quiet because they felt they were adequately represented in City Hall.

This pattern changed after 1975. The Puerto Rican population grew and became more vocal. And the South Hartford ethnic population—more numerous—developed as a base for organizers. This was the new challenge, and it was to cause Carbone and the City Council to lose support. Actually, the reasons for the problems in City Hall were complex. The conventional explanation in Hartford has been that Carbone had South Hartford's support for social programs and downtown development as long as he kept their taxes down. But the continued erosion of the tax base throughout the 1970s made this bargain increasingly more difficult to keep: the property tax base had been declining in real dollars since 1967, and staffing levels in police, fire, and public works had been cut back. Carbone's property tax campaigns had not successfully countered these underlying trends. The social programs, some of them highly visible, had gone to other parts of the city.

When, in 1975, the Catholic Church's Campaign for Human Development began to finance community organizers in South Hartford, block clubs and neighborhood groups developed fast. Jack Mimnaugh, who played the lead role as organizer, described this growth in this way:

> From July to October 1975 we went from a situation where we didn't even have an assurance of funding, to 15 block clubs which could produce an average of 30 people each. In the fall we surfaced a coalition of 300 persons at City Hall. By October 1976 we had 1,400 persons at a day-long community congress—it covered a third of the city in South Hartford.[36]

Mimnaugh's organization emerged as HART (for Hartford Areas Rally Together). Its method was to organize neighborhoods around immediate concerns and to try to build toward broader positions approved by the annual community congress. In the process it got into conflicts with the corporations and with the city administration. The most visible of these conflicts involved its opposition to a downtown project Carbone had backed, which featured "skywalks": a series of covered pedestrian walkways designed to channel people between the large office concentrations and the shopping facilities downtown. HART took these on as a symbol of City Hall's support for corporate and business interests and in the end managed to defeat the proposal. The skywalk defeat may have been the high tide for Hartford neighborhood organizations. It was a dramatic victory, and it reinforced opposition to Carbone that had developed in the City Council and outside. Robert Ludgin, who had been elected to the council in 1977, began to make attacks on the council majority and on Carbone, exploiting a climate of neighborhood dissatisfaction and a malaise that strained the teamwork that had characterized the council majority earlier in the decade. Later, in 1979, Carbone was defeated in a primary election bid for the mayoral nomination, bringing down his entire organization and a whole set of programs, including many that had benefited neighborhood groups.

Carbone's Defeat in 1979

Carbone had never been the top vote-getter on the City Council. His authority came from his abilities as an analyst and negotiator, and from his willingness to articulate the city's position. At times, these qualities had nearly cost him his council seat. At some point, early in his 1977–1979 term on the council, he decided to run for mayor. He later said the reason was that he could no longer afford to stay on the council, where the pay was only $4,000 per year. But there were also other reasons. While the position was weak in formal powers, the mayor was the titular head of government and the incumbent, George Athanson, had been a thorn in the side of the council majority. Moreover, there was a possibility that the city could pass a charter revision providing for a strong-mayor form of government, a shift that Carbone favored. Carbone challenged Athanson in the Democratic primary in September 1979. He had, however, accumulated many political liabilities, and it was clear to his supporters that the election would be an uphill struggle. The controversy with HART and other neighborhood groups over the skywalks had made him vulnerable. The corporate community that had, in the past, been at least partially supportive, now largely withdrew that support. The *Hartford Courant* played up the controversy and opposition to Carbone, featuring both the neighborhood organization's and Ludgin's attacks. Carbone lost in the primary by a substantial margin.

This defeat marked the end of most of the programs established by the coalition Carbone had led since 1969. Ludgin became the council majority leader and proceeded to clean house—with a thoroughness that surprised even his supporters. He forced the resignation of Masini as police chief and abolished the neighborhood policing efforts. He eliminated the energy programs and there were resignations of all the administrative people, including the city manager, Coleman, and Alschuler and many others. The scale of change made in the police department was typical. The Hartford Institute remained visible, but, after Masini resigned, there was little left in the police department. One participant in the neighborhood team-policing experiments said:

> I'd always been led to believe change would be incremental. We would gain ground slowly, and we might lose politically and then lose ground. But I never thought it would be like this.

I never expected a one-hundred-percent move back to the earlier central watch system.[37]

Masini took a position as head of security for a large private utility corporation, and other participants in the neighborhood team-
policing experiment took new jobs in the Hartford area. Similar
changes occurred in other parts of the city government.

The dismantling of the programs and organizations built up
over ten years shook the city. On all sides, the major actors groped
for explanations. Two years later, conversations about Hartford politics still tended to revolve around Carbone. Ludgin had become
deputy mayor in 1979 and the process of destruction had been the
main achievement of that council; the shock waves of reorganiza-
tions, firings, and resignations overshadowed all else. Ludgin's was
a negative program, shaped by the structure he was destroying. In
1981 there was another electoral turnover, with leadership moving
to black politicians led by a new mayor, Thurman Milner. But
people also measured that council against Carbone. So it was clear
that while the city had changed course, Carbone had left a legacy.
But there is much that remained unclear. Why had he lost? Even after he lost, why had the city programs built up over ten years been
so completely dismantled?

At one level, Carbone lost and his programs were dismantled
because the voters and certain key organizations lost their taste for
confrontations with interests outside of the city and began confronting one another. Neighborhood groups identified Carbone with
downtown business interests because of the skywalks issue, and
homeowners opposed him because he had said their taxes would
have to go up to pay for social services. They felt the the city was not
delivering on such basic services as public safety and public works.
Carbone had tried to mobilize city voters to extract tax and services
concessions from the state, pointing out that the suburban towns
were getting the lion's share of all resources and forcing the city into
poverty. But major suburban interests and opinion—to which the
city's one major newspaper, the *Hartford Courant*, had become increasingly oriented—successfully deflected this argument. The
Courant, endorsing Athanson, said Carbone was "knowledgeable,
hardworking, and willing to experiment. But he is also an angry
leader who believes in confrontation politics and who has managed
to enrage his suburban counterparts, the state legislature and the
governor—distinctly disastrous attributes for a city in need."[38]
Many people, including people who said they supported Carbone,

thought activism needed a rest. Carbone himself, looking back on his defeat, said, "I just made too many enemies."

It may be that Carbone lost because he tried to do too much. The broad array of policy initiatives that were begun under Carbone far exceeded—in the substance of what the city intended—the goals of the liberal and conservative regimes more common in American urban politics. Because of this range of purposes, Carbone became vulnerable. His burden was that while he was widely regarded as a superb "street politician," he was also a synthetic thinker who cared about moral issues. His clear-headedness and willingness to act was what gave him control of the City Council, but it also resulted in policies and projects that, as time went on, drew attacks. The Civic Center and subsequent real estate projects may be the best examples of this process. As these projects developed, they became more and more complex. Almost no one in Hartford fully understood them. Newspaper coverage of them was superficial. In most people's minds, they were simply tax abatements. The skywalk plan required explanation. But because it was graphic, it was attackable as a needless luxury, when people in other parts of the city needed housing immediately. Other projects also became vulnerable to attack in the same way. The neighborhood policing policies implemented by Masini had annoyed the people at police headquarters and when crime rates contined to run high through the late 1970s, Masini became a target of attack. Various other projects initiated by Carbone were also vulnerable.

An even more prominent theme of those opposing Carbone was City Hall's administrative style. Overtly, Ludgin articulated few if any substantive policy concerns in 1977—1979 as a minority city council member. He seemed to be motivated by process problems: by opposing the "machine" he said Carbone had built in City Hall. Upon his election, the *Hartford Courant* reported him as saying "he would keep his election promises, including investigating what he called the 'cozy' activities and relationships of the Democratic leadership of 'this boss-ruled city.'"[39] In order to attack the machine, Ludgin attacked its projects. His tactics annoyed and exasperated both Democrats and Republicans on the council, but he got good press. He attacked the city's administration of the CETA program, the council's support for a community energy corporation that had failed when federal CETA funds proved unavailable, and the council's dominance over the city manager. The *Courant* featured him as "Grit in the Face of a Well-Oiled Machine," and reported that:

accomplishing specific projects or winning particular votes seems to be less important than making certain the democratic process works, that government does its business in the open and that there's a counterweight to Carbone in City Hall . . . he . . . tapped what appears to be significant community-wide anger focused on Carbone and those who control City Hall.[40]

During the 1979 campaign, George Athanson, against whom Carbone was running for mayor, successfully attacked Carbone for his "arrogance" and argued that he would create a "dictatorship" if he became mayor. The "arrogance" issue was raised repeatedly, both before and after the election. Many Hartford liberals, two years later, expressed their annoyance and outrage at Carbone. One said "Nick Carbone destroyed liberalism, because he subverted the council-manager form of government." Others recounted their efforts to participate in city decision making and told of their being ignored or pushed to the side while an inner clique made the most important decisions.

Jack Mimnaugh, HART organizer, took exception to Carbone's style, not to the substance of his policies. For him, it was a problem of getting an independent base of power for the neighborhoods and a legitimate voice for them in city policy making, something in which they had felt frustrated with Carbone. He said:

> The main struggle was between the neighborhoods and the corporations. Nick fell through the cracks. Nick's obvious problem was that it was *his* agenda. He didn't necessarily badmouth the neighborhood agenda. But he didn't feel accountable to the neighborhoods.[41]

For Mimnaugh, it seemed to be paramount to change the system of power. He found Carbone's government to be like a benevolent dictatorship. He liked Carbone personally and liked his objectives, but he did not like the relationship between the two. He said:

> I liked Nick, but I helped bury him. . . . Under the old machine, at least each interest got something. Now, it's become a monster. Instead of city officials asking neighborhood people "what do you want," you had them telling them what was good for them. It happened in the police, in education, in planning. Everybody had a degree. Everybody was a professional. And the politicians mimicked that.[42]

Mimnaugh may have overstated the education levels of Carbone's people—Carbone had hired many nonprofessionals—but the "non-responsive" tag on the administration came to be perhaps the consensus in Hartford and was picked up and repeated over and over in the press.[43]

Against all this, Carbone posed his own analysis:

> This is going to be the first time the least popular candidate wins the primary. . . . It's time for Hartford to decide what kind of leadership it wants. I'm an activist, and I am angry about what I see when I walk through this city, and I do want change. We'll see if that's what people want now or not.[44]

While the opposition successfully exploited the issue of administrative style, "arrogant" is not the word Carbone's supporters would have used to describe his flaws. They saw the situation in a more complex way. They described him as having a kind of quiet charisma, and they thought that it was his commitment to social issues that got him into conflicts. Mildred Torres-Soto, a Carbone ally who had been appointed to fill a vacancy on the City Council for several months in 1979, said:

> Nick was a good guy. But he had an awful image problem. People didn't like him at first, especially when he was first on the council. Later, he changed. He started running, lost weight. . . . People thought he was aloof. I remember once he was at a big party, and he stood off to the side, waited for people to come up to him. People didn't like that, thought he was too much of a big shot. What it really was, Nick is shy. . . .[45]

Carbone tried to deal with what people saw as his image problem, but he continued to be impelled personally by what he saw as the need to handle the city's substantial problems. This led him to make many alliances, to start many new programs. Alschuler, who had been as responsible as anyone for the administrative proliferation that occurred in City Hall, later looked back and thought it would have been better to have involved more people:

> Well, put it this way, what was clear at the time is you had people—like myself—who felt we had this remarkably sensitive, powerful, creative tool of local government. And what we wanted to do was use it as many times as we could to help people who had been victimized by various parts of the society.

And that's what drove us. And the fact is that we weren't necessarily spending as much time as we needed involving people so that they felt they were controlling the process.

Had I to do the situation in Hartford over again, I'm inclined to think I would have spent less time, would have limited the numbers of issues in which the government itself was involved, and spent more time involving other people in those things we were capable of performing.[46]

Certainly there are indications that the City Hall organization had been pushing itself at an ever-increasing pace between 1977 and 1979, and that it was facing increasing external pressures. The council majority was under constant attack from Ludgin, while such problems as police department morale, the city's administration of the C E T A program, and the skywalk program got increasing outside attention. Carbone felt the structure of local government was working against him.

I was only a City Council member and had the limitations of that, but I was getting attacked for everyone's mistakes. That's why I wanted to go to the strong-mayor charter. I was spending days of every week on the road—in Washington—because I had to raise money for the city. I couldn't give enough time to things in Hartford. I was going crazy.[47]

Strecker recalled urging Carbone to spend more time in the city. He thought it unfortunate that a superb "street politician" had to spend so much time away from his constituency. He remembered saying: "Nick, why are you doing this? You are out raising money for the same people who are going to kill you."[48]

The cohesion of the council and City Hall's administration began to unravel. Richard Suisman, a prominent member of the majority group on the council, thought the turning point was Carbone's decision to run for mayor. "After 1977, Nick decided to run for mayor. Up until then, the council was pretty much a team concept. Later, Nick started judging issues for what they would do to help with the election."[49] Council members began to feel that they were being left out of decisions. Carbone thought he could get anyone's support on any issue if he could just sit down and persuade them, but the evidence is that there wasn't enough time for that. Suisman resigned from the council during the summer of 1979 and other members became less cooperative, if not openly opposed to Carbone.

The Endemic Tension between Carbone and his Base

Most discussions of City Hall organization during the years 1969–1979 present the case as if there had been no external forces pressing on the administration, or if they concede that these forces existed, they argue that a different leadership could have handled them more effectively. They rarely mention the grinding poverty in the city, the increasing disparities between the city and the suburbs, the withdrawal of federal government support. Thus, the attacks were made on Carbone as being personally arrogant and dictatorial, without consideration of the context of his actions.

But there were external forces. No city is an independent power, and a further perspective needs to be considered: the perspective of the business community, which may subsume both the concerns felt by the voters over policy issues and the widespread annoyance people felt about the administration's style. Most businessmen simply got tired of confronting the city through Carbone. He did see it accurately when he said that he had "just made too many enemies." But it was not simply a question of Carbone wearing them out, or of his administration developing an obnoxious quality it didn't have earlier. The structure of business in Hartford was itself changing.

In the 1950s and 1960s, Hartford's corporations had created an edifice of liberal politics around the newspapers, the city-manager form of government, corporate philanthropy, and support for social programs in government. They tried to use the city as a magnet for their own social interests, to counterbalance their own tendencies to move to suburban locations, to accommodate the influx of blacks and Hispanics. Lumsden and the Chamber of Commerce were central to these efforts, organizing collective support for community action, urban renewal, and Greater Hartford Process as the backdrop against which Carbone was to develop his own programs in the 1970s.

But all that changed after about 1975. In the end, it was the corporations themselves that pulled back from Hartford. They became larger and more diversified, their traditions of family control eroded with time, their executives and to a lesser extent their employees moved to the suburbs. In the 1950s, when Connecticut General made the first major move from the city to a suburban location, there was still a feeling that in some sense the companies needed Hartford. The Travellers decided to stay because its employees wanted to stay. But even that tenuous link had weakened by the end of the 1970s. By then, Lumsden had retired, and he felt the era he had helped create was over:

> These companies don't need Hartford. Aetna could lose the entire Hartford city budget in a year and it wouldn't affect its operations. . . . Cities tend to go in cycles. It will take this crowd a while to run out of steam, and then in ten or twenty years the city may make a comeback.[50]

By 1981, corporate disinterest in the city had become evident to many observers. Lumsden thought the reason was Carbone's conflictual style, and so did many other businessmen and liberal leaders. But even with Carbone out of office, there was no particular evidence of a resurgence of civic spirit. The Ludgin-Athanson council of 1979–1981 turned into as much of an anathema as Carbone had been. The new administration of Thurman Milner and Deputy Mayor Rudy Arnold did not make corporate eyes light up either. In 1982, Aetna announced plans to relocate part of its operations outside the city, a move widely seen as ominous. Others pointed out that the major insurance office concentrations still in the city were less permanent than they looked: many had leases that were due to run out in the next few years. There was no grand corporate plan for the city in evidence, as had been suggested by Lumsden's efforts of the previous decades.

The corporations could afford to get tired of conflict, but the local people, for whom Carbone thought he was fighting, also got tired of it. Thus there was a reverberation of corporate tiredness — perhaps as relayed through the *Courant* — in local exhaustion, though the stakes were vastly different. Alschuler, Mimnaugh, and others thought Carbone could have staved off local exhaustion by cultivating local participation more carefully. But most agreed there had always been an endemic tension between Carbone and his base. Increasing poverty made it harder and harder to deliver as a political leader, and finally governance became impossible.

The Residue of the Policies of 1969–1979

Hartford city government cleaned house after 1979, and no one who was very high in the administration remained. Masini and the lieutenants who had done the neighborhood policing experiments left the city, most for private-sector security jobs. Mildred Torres-Soto became a grants administrator for the Aetna Foundation. Jonathan Coleman became director of Hartford Ride-share, a quasi-public organization. Paul Strecker stayed on for two years as development administrator, then took a job with a real estate development firm. Several others became consultants or took jobs outside of Hartford.

Carbone and Alschuler established the Hartford Policy Center and did contract work for foundations and federal government agencies for a long time. At the end of 1981, Alschuler became city manager of Santa Monica, California. Carbone, who had been consulting with the American City Corporation on large development projects, went on his own as developer of a large project in Hartford, in relation to which he found himself instructing the new City Council on the nuances of the city's equity-sharing development agreements.

By 1983, neighborhood activism was reviving in Hartford, and a series of proposals had been made to tie downtown office development to a neighborhood development fund. It was a scheme that was almost hauntingly reminiscent of Carbone's policies, but Carbone himself was not involved.

CHAPTER 3

Cleveland: Planning and Urban Populism, 1969–1979

In Cleveland, the survival of a minority liberal agenda in the 1980s came after a decade of analysis and the formulation of ideas in the City Planning Commission during the 1970s. Planning was not the only factor that led to the establishment of this agenda; so did developments in the neighborhood movement, in public interest organizations, and the city's polarized and ambivalent response to overtly populist politics under the 1977–1979 mayoralty of Dennis Kucinich. But planning was of key importance in making this agenda live, because a liberal planning director found ways to use his piece of official turf to promote a vision of the public interest, while "politics" effected a kind of mundane populism, despite swings between white and black, Republican and Democratic leaders.

Background

In retrospect, the planners' insights were straightforward—city policies ought to be pursued in the interests of the people who live in the city. This insight was deepened by the understanding that these people were relatively poorly off compared to their suburban neighbors or to the corporate entities that did business downtown.

By all the objective indicators, Cleveland was a good place for such ideas to take hold. The city's population, after reaching its peak at 914,808 in 1950, had declined to 750,903 by 1970. The city lost nearly 100,000 jobs during the same period and its population changed character: Nonwhites, who had numbered 149,544 in 1950, had increased to 292,819 in 1970. Along with this demographic change, the city became relatively poor compared to the rest of the Cleveland metropolitan area and to the nation: median family incomes in the city had been equal to 96 percent of those in the Cleveland Standard Metropolitan Statistical Area (SMSA—consisting of Cuyahoga and Lorain Counties) and 115 percent of the U.S. median in 1950. By 1970, these proportions had dropped to 80 percent and 95 percent, respectively.[1]

This double shift, in ethnicity and wealth, meant a profound change in the kinds of problems the city would have to solve in its economic and political life. In 1950, Cleveland was still predominantly a white working-class city whose economy was dominated by manufacturing. This population had had its greatest growth between 1880 and 1920: 100,000 in 1880, then 120,000 in 1890, 180,000 in 1900, then 210,000 in 1920, new people in each of these decades. Mostly, they came from eastern Europe. But after 1920 immigration was cut drastically, and the history of these new people up until 1950 was one of gradual assimilation into the American and the Cleveland economy.

During this period a pattern of economic and political life became established. The economic pattern was industrial. Old families, who had led Cleveland to industrial prominence in the nineteenth century, maintained economic control. Cleveland had long been a citadel of concentrated economic power. Starting in the middle of the nineteenth century, the steel industry had dominated the economy. Rockefeller began Standard Oil there. The city was a leader in heavy manufacturing, food processing, textiles, shipbuilding and auto manufacturing enterprises. Fortunes were made by Mark Hanna, Cyrus Eaton, the founders of Standard Oil, and by the founders of the National City Bank. Cleveland became the headquarters of many of the world's largest industrial corporations, third in rank after New York and Chicago.

The city's political life evolved from these economic foundations. For a long time, Cleveland's politics had been controlled more or less directly by these industrial interests. Mark Hanna, himself a major industrialist, came to national prominence at the end of the nineteenth century as the leader of a Republican political machine, which—despite a populist period under Mayor Tom Johnson in

1901–1909—successfully incorporated working-class, immigrant voters. This industrial control continued until 1941, when Frank Lausche became the first ethnic mayor, establishing a pattern that has persisted. But the shift in the ethnicity of the city's political leadership (which tended to coincide with control by the Democratic party) did not result in any relinquishing of power by economic elites. The new ethnic mayors, although they often used a populist rhetoric, generally followed the dictates of the business community once they were in office.[2]

ETHNIC POLITICS

Cleveland's white population seemed to adapt rather easily to the new ethnic pattern. That a succession of white ethnic mayors ran the city without apparent distinction or disruption for several decades implies that the most important political constituencies were getting what they most wanted, if not from politics, then from the economy. First, white families were doing well economically. Median incomes for the city were comfortably above those of the nation as a whole until after 1950, and Cleveland's suburbs, which were getting increasing amounts of migration from Cleveland, continued to do better than the nation as a whole after 1950. Suburban migration itself, which increased significantly after 1945, forged a connection between the objectives of the Cleveland elites and those of white ethnics, who followed them. Not only families but jobs were migrating to the suburbs. Major highway building programs were connecting the city with the suburbs, making possible easy movement between the city and the outer locations and among the suburbs.

Within the city, white families continued to manage well economically, at least through the 1950s. The neighborhood social fabric was maintained; church and other ethnically identified institutions flourished.

The political rhetoric and the programs adopted by Lausche and the mayors who followed him—with notable vote-getting success—emphasized small business values: independence of any political party, opposition to unions, low taxes, and low levels of service. Lausche and most of those who followed him ran as Democrats, but ruled as Republicans. The result was to diminish the leadership role of the mayor. Even with a strong-mayor form of government, the City Council became the main locus of political exchange, with power dispersed rather than centralized and fastening on small rather than large issues. Carl Stokes, after his term as mayor in 1967–71, said:

> Membership in the City Council repelled me. The only inter-
> ests I could see being served by councilmen were petty and pecu-
> niary. They counted their success by whether the office brought
> them money—so much for allowing a new gas station, so much
> for a zoning change, so much for allowing a cheat spot to oper-
> ate. Being elected to the council wasn't a mandate to legisla-
> tive responsibility, it was a ticket to a bartering system.[3]

Pluralist theorists might look at this system—given to petty rather than major graft and presided over by honest mayors—and see a kind of surface democracy; for the large council system was quite open to neighborhood representation. But it was also quite congruent and compatible with the interests of economic elites. Major industrialists, who were not eager to make large reinvestments in their own operations, at least within the city limits, did not want to be taxed for public improvements either.[4] When the city tried to alter its low-spending, custodial approach to government after about 1950, the results were disappointing and seem now to reflect a deep underlying ambivalence. Anthony Celebrese, who was mayor from 1953 to 1962, initiated a large-scale urban renewal project in the downtown area. As a plan, the project, called "Erieview," was quite magnificent. But the city seemed unable to follow through. At one time in the 1960s, Cleveland had going the largest urban renewal program in the nation in terms of dwelling units demolished, but at the same time it had built almost no new housing. The city could not attract local financing for development because of the extraordinarily conservative nature of Cleveland's business establishment, which refused to experiment with such public-private partnerships as urban renewal. Thus while leaders in such cities as New Haven, Pittsburgh, and Philadelphia supported liberal reform movements focusing on the renewal of their central cities, Cleveland money remained aloof. Stokes tended to focus on the tight control of investment capital, historically in the hands of George Gund, president of the Cleveland Trust:

> Gund was an extraordinarily conservative man; the effect this
> had on the use of risk capital in Cleveland is only too clear. The
> old industries were carefully protected from any new, compet-
> ing interests that wanted to come in from outside. Young busi-

nessmen within the city with ideas for new development found that venture capital was held intractably within Gund's marmoreal fist. At a time when Cleveland should have been growing and shifting away from its old reliance on steel and oil industries, Gund held back, protecting the old, fat, but increasingly impotent interests; these men drew closer together, ignoring the need for vigorous competition. This is a form of dry rot.[5]

This entrenched attitude in relation to city politics did not, however, produce a clear-cut and monolithic structure of policy. Instead of providing a consistent business position against development, what came about was a pattern of initiatives and failures, projects proposed and sometimes (like Erieview) started, but seldom followed through to completion. This resulted in a climate of conflict. There were *some* business interests that wanted to promote a public-private partnership for city development. The private utility, the Cleveland Electric Illuminating Company (CEI), became worried that the levelling off of manufacturing employment would cut electric power sales, and it began an economic development campaign in 1944.[6] Its efforts later on helped to establish the Greater Cleveland Growth Board in 1962. Gradually, a business position on the desirability of a transition from manufacturing to central city office activities, accompanied by public urban renewal policies, has developed in Cleveland. But this remained a minority position in the business community at least through the 1950s and early 1960s, and Stokes cited the unwillingness of the Cleveland Trust to invest in the Erieview project as the crucial barrier to its implementation during his term from 1967 to 1971.[7]

BLACK POLITICS

With the buildup of the black population after 1950, black politics seemed like it might follow the same pattern that other ethnic groups had in Cleveland. Many of the city's black leaders had pursued the same values as Lausche and the other Cleveland ethnic mayors. A substantial black middle class had developed and had gotten a foothold in the suburbs. The representative structure of the City Council had provided at least minimal black representation and given blacks access to some of the entailing small-scale favors and patronage that were available. In the 1960s there was some prospect that a black middle-class political strategy might become viable. What happened, though, was not so straightforward.

Most important, black participation in the national civil rights movement, a movement that enlisted significant white liberal support, created a context quite unlike that within which the white ethnics had sought political office. There was more fervor and idealism, perhaps, at least on the part of some black leaders, and this increased the possibility that blacks would hold out for substantial economic and political gains once they got into office. But in Cleveland, as in many other Northern cities, black politics came to be overwhelmed by civil disorder: riots took place during 1966 in the Hough neighborhood, which caused extensive property damage and created a series of shocks from which the economy and political system did not soon recover. Carl Stokes had run for mayor in 1965 and had come within three thousand votes of winning. He had had little business backing and almost no media support, but he had created a massive grass-roots campaign. Two years later, the Hough riots had occurred, and the incumbent mayor, Ralph Locher, came under constant media attack for his failure to manage the city or to keep control of racial conflict. Under these circumstances, business and communications institutions rallied to Stokes. His campaign received large infusions of funds and professional management. By many accounts, Stokes came to be seen as an attractive, even a charismatic figure, who could keep the peace. The 1969 campaign, which was smoother and more professional than his first, resulted in a close victory for Stokes over Seth Taft, the Republican candidate.

Stokes's program marked an attempt to move out of the old ethnic patterns into active, interventionist government based on an alliance with progressive business leaders. His victory had been a huge event in the consciousness of black and white liberal constituents. He had charisma and was intelligent, and he attracted national attention because he was the nation's first black mayor of a major city and had won where blacks were not even an absolute majority. His administration was immediately exposed to intense media scrutiny, and external relations took up a large amount of his time. Anything he did would have symbolic importance, and the time left for day-to-day administrative matters would be limited. Under the circumstances, and particularly in light of the limited capacities of the political machinery he inherited, Stokes did rather well. In combination with other political and economic leaders, he changed the course of city government; but his immediate accomplishments were rather small, and the general stalemate between competing political forces within the city continued.

Stokes's biggest achievement was in mobilizing a black, liberal, and—for a time—business constituency, which he then converted into a series of black appointments to major department head positions and into contracts for black businesses and professionals. Stokes also attracted a number of white liberals into his government and he gave them staff appointments and made them department heads. Overall, the impression ten years after he left office was that these shifts in personnel were his main accomplishment. He had attempted other substantive program changes and initiatives, with little success. His biggest difficulty had been with the police department. Crime and violence on the city's East Side was the most explosive issue the city faced, and the police department, largely white, lacked the legitimacy to deal with it. Stokes's efforts at police reform, however, met with great resistance. A succession of safety directors and police chiefs caused continual turmoil within the police department. These continuing problems in the community made Stokes vulnerable on all other issues.

Stokes had received the support of a major segment of the Cleveland business community because he was seen as a better bet to manage the city and keep racial peace than his predecessor, Ralph Locher. In March 1968, after the assassination of Martin Luther King, Stokes seemed to bear out this promise, when he walked the streets of ghetto areas, imploring black leaders to keep the peace. But he also had more substantial aims for fundamental programs to get at the economic roots of Cleveland's racial unrest. In a departure from previous administrations, he hoped to get business and neighborhood support for employment, education, and capital construction programs. After a nationwide search conducted by local businessmen, he had hired Richard Green as director of community development in hopes of doing a more effective job in housing and urban renewal. Later he hired Norman Krumholz from Pittsburgh to be city planning director.

But it was after Martin Luther King's death that Stokes's most comprehensive set of plans emerged: the "Cleveland NOW!" program. He held meetings with community and business leaders saying that the prevention of violence was only a part of the problem, that investment was needed to change the conditions that led to violence. He asked for, and soon got, a commitment of $11.5 million in individual and business contributions for the Cleveland NOW! program, which was to be seed money for what was billed as a $1.5 billion program over ten to twelve years. The program identified several areas of activity. There were to be 11,000 full- and part-time jobs made available in cooperation with the city, community organizations, and the National Alliance of Businessmen, with training funds available from federal and state governments. Some of these funds would also be used to stimulate the growth of small businesses within the city. A youth resources program would be established, employing young people in neighborhood cleanups, recreation, and other projects, with the federal government providing funds for new open-space and recreation development. There would be established a series of neighborhood child care centers, and decentralized health and welfare service centers. There would be a neighborhood housing rehabilitation program involving the construction or renovation of 4,600 units, to be carried out by a new Community Housing Corporation, involving private developers, nonprofit housing organizations, and the Cleveland Metropolitan Housing Authority; mortgage guarantees and rent supplements would be supplied in areas designated for concentrated code enforcement. Finally, plans were made for downtown economic development including six existing urban renewal projects, the city's provision of capital improvements and services, and federal loans and grants.[8]

As it happened, the law-and-order issue vitiated Cleveland NOW! In June of 1968, a gun battle occurred between white police and a group of black nationalists in the Glenville neighborhood, and rioting broke out afterward. Stokes, in order to avert further violence, pulled white police out of the area and replaced them with black police and civilian volunteers. The ensuing outcry by the police and the media convinced many businessmen that racial unrest was a permanent problem for the city, with or without Stokes, and business support for Cleveland NOW! crumbled. After 1968, with a Republican in the White House, Stokes's leverage was weakened further and a stalemate persisted with the City Council. In the end, less than half of the $11.5 million pledged to Cleveland NOW! locally was ever delivered. Stokes's own evaluation was that:

> Cleveland NOW! was instrumental in building housing, creating jobs, building day care and recreation centers, establishing a multitude of summer recreational activities, new drug treatment centers, and a number of other positive things. But the really important achievement was in solving a problem no other city has been able to solve, that of getting people totally involved in an effort to do something for their city.[9]

In retrospect, Cleveland NOW! seems to have justified the characterization Stokes gave it: it was a public relations coup in City Hall, both stimulating and responsive to a short-term outpouring of collective sentiment. It was a collection of "Great Society" programs pulled together at the very end of the Johnson administration, very expensive, yet not expensive enough actually to cope with the problems that were about to overwhelm the city. Similar programs, which were much more cohesive, were already failing in other cities, after much longer experience and greater expertise had been devoted to them. In contrast, Cleveland's fragmented City Hall was unable to develop enough unity to bring off such a program. Cleveland's business elite had only tentatively gotten its toes wet in central city public-private ventures. The administrative strength to allow city government to play its necessary role in such programs was only just being gathered. The forces set in motion by Stokes's election were apparently making the transition to the problems of the sixties, but tentatively, and at least a decade late.

Within the period in which Stokes was in office, however, a number of programs were started that were to flourish through the 1970s and did much to shape that decade. City Planning Director Norman Krumholz, appointed by Stokes in 1969, created an organization that was to fill a conceptual vacuum in programatic thinking throughout three administrations over a period of ten years. Roldo Bartimole began publishing the bi-weekly *Point of View* in 1967, offering a critical dissent from the uniformly establishment-serving line put out by the ordinary press. The Catholic Commission on Community Action began operations in 1969 with a series of adult education seminars that later resulted in the development of a strong neighborhood movement. And Dennis Kucinich, then a newly-elected city councilman, initiated a breakaway election campaign in 1971 against Stokes's chosen successor, which helped put a Republican in the mayor's office, erased many of the gains in black office-holding that Stokes had established, and set the stage for his emergence as mayor espousing "urban populism" at the end of the 1970s.

Krumholz and the City Planning Department

The most promising time for the Cleveland City Planning Commission was in the 1940s. It was created in its present form with independent authority in 1942 by Charter Amendment. It had commissioners, appointed for six-year terms by the mayor, charged to "take the initiative in planning for the city."[10] It was given the

job of passing on all city council ordinances and all administrative
rulings that affected the city plan. As director of planning, the commission hired John Howard, a leading professional planner and
later chairman of the Department of City Planning at MIT. Howard
produced a master plan in 1949 and maintained something of an independent posture relative to the city administration. As its charter
intended, the commission was to be a formulator of plans and, based
on those, a critic of administrative actions. But the actual development was to be left to others—according to the charter, a "Coordinating Board," made up of the mayor, the directors of line departments, and other agency representatives. Howard later elaborated a
theory of the function of the independent planning commission.[11]
He stressed the value of city planning based on long-range thinking,
not constrained by current political realities; he then argued that the
way to get this kind of independence was to limit such a structure to
an advisory capacity, instead of involving it in implementation. A
direct role in policy implementation, he thought, would necessarily
compromise the long-range foresight function of the commission because of the immediate pressures such a role would entail. Without
having to worry about implementation, the commission would be
free to cultivate a constituency for its wise foresight, and it could
pressure and bargain with the political leadership.

By the 1960s, this view had faded in U.S. city planning circles,
and most agencies were avidly courting an active role in plan implementation. They were getting in on urban renewal and downtown
development projects and were bent on establishing prominent roles
for themselves in the executive departments of liberal big city mayors. But in Cleveland, planning evolved differently. There were no
liberal mayors, and the mayors there were had not established coalitions around executive leadership. Anthony Celebrese did not
launch his ambitious downtown development plans until the late
1950s, and he was unable to get local backing. Meanwhile, the planners had not been able to influence the thinking of those who might
be willing to invest in the downtown. After 1959, Celebrese turned
to private consultants and the Cleveland Development Foundation
for downtown planning. The City Planning Commission was forced
aside, despite its formal review powers. Faced with proposals that
had been derived in secret, but lacking a credible set of alternatives,
the commission began simply rubber-stamping proposals put before
it. In 1960 the commission approved the major urban renewal plan
for downtown, Erieview, only three days after it had been made pub-

lic, having been bypassed in the planning stages. The staff of the planning commission, which had numbered forty-five in 1959, was cut down to thirty-two in 1966.[12] On being questioned, the commission chairman, Ernest J. Bohn, admitted that:

> In recent years the planning commission has not been paid much attention. . . . We've been without power . . . because there has been no money to hire adequate staff. . . . Here was a dramatic thing. What are you going to do? Stop it, when we had no money to do it ourselves?[13]

When Stokes took office, his first priority was not planning. The first planner he hired was Richard Green, whom he placed in charge of urban renewal and community development, not planning. Like others before him, Stokes saw the main problem as one of getting development moving, as in the Cleveland NOW! program. But Stokes's emphasis on hiring the best people extended as well to the Planning Commission. Bohn had resigned as chairman of the commission in 1966; Stokes had been able to make some new appointments; and by 1969, the commission, with Stokes, was able to move to appoint a new director. The search was made by a committee consisting of Allen Fonoroff and Robert Storey of the commission and Sidney Spector from the mayor's office. Krumholz was hired and he was on the job by November. His coming to Cleveland was to have a major impact.

Norman Krumholz was a liberal, a man both profound and intuitive.[14] He came from a modest family in Passaic, New Jersey, where he grew up, the youngest of three brothers, in the 1930s and 1940s. His father, a foreman in a woolen mill, died when Krumholz was four years old, and his mother made ends meet by cleaning houses. One of his frequent memories was of moving out of apartments because they did not have the rent; his job as the youngest son was to sit on the furniture to make sure no one stole it, while the older brothers started the move to the next apartment. But his mother worked hard, he said, to make sure that all the boys got their education. Krumholz finished high school in 1945, then joined the Navy, and later attended the University of Missouri, where he got a degree in journalism. He held a succession of jobs in New York City and then in the Buffalo area. By the early 1960s, he was running three businesses: a travel agency, an advertising agency, and a rug franchise in a local department store.

Krumholz was an entrepreneur, but one with liberal ideas.

While growing up, he had become committed to the New Deal for its goals of redistributing wealth and constructing a safety net for those in poverty—people he felt immediately close to. In the first presidential election in which he could vote, he worked on the Henry Wallace campaign. He did not pick up the anticommunist line of many liberals during the 1950s, perhaps because he was not aware of its more sophisticated variations. He found McCarthy's anticommunist vendettas an anathema. He supported Stevenson. He was moved by the civil rights struggles that began in the South in the 1950s.

After 1960, Krumholz began to feel that life as a businessman was not all he wanted; it was boring him. He read a series of articles in the *New Yorker* by Lewis Mumford and Robert Moses, an exchange of sharply contrasting views on city development and planning. He began to fasten on planning as a way of engaging with the issues that appealed to him. In 1963, he enrolled at Cornell, where he got a city planning degree. He was impressed by courses taught there by John Reps, A. Miller Hillhouse, and Alan Altshuler. He did well there, particularly in politics and administration, and was invited (by Altshuler) to consider working on a doctorate. At that time, however, because he was already in his late thirties, he felt he should get back to professional work. He took a job as assistant director of the Pittsburgh City Planning Department, where he worked from 1965 to 1969.

In Pittsburgh, Krumholz was inserted into a situation typical of many city planning agencies in the 1960s. A wave of analytical sophistication had hit the city planning operation: the use of computers, the emergence of a corps of methodologically ambitious technicians, the development of sophisticated planning models that purported to vastly increase the city's capacity to decide what policies to follow in such areas as housing, economic development, transportation, and land use, all were seen as the key to the future. At the same time, local political decision makers were facing rapidly escalating demands for participation from people in the city's neighborhoods. Procedurally, the new models were exactly wrong for the situation, and at times their projections were also wrong. Soon after Krumholz arrived, politics overcame technology in Pittsburgh, the planning director was fired, and a new director, John Mauro, took over with a program dedicated to political expediency. Krumholz soon began a series of meetings with neighborhood groups, predominantly those from black ghetto areas. Later, he reported that these meetings greatly affected his outlook. He was skeptical of some of the rhetoric and ideology, but thought he could see clearly that poverty and people's needs were not being met by the formal planning procedures he had been trained in or by the technicians who had recently populated the Pittsburgh City Planning Department.

In 1969, Krumholz was contacted by the search committee in Cleveland. He was strongly attracted by the chance to work for Stokes. As the first black mayor of a major American city, Stokes projected a purpose that Krumholz was ready to serve. For his part, Krumholz impressed the interviewing committee. He came well recommended and had a pleasing, if forthright and irreverent, manner. He had a striking appearance, he was straightforward and intense, and he had a devastating wit.

When Krumholz began work in Cleveland in November of 1969, he had only a little foreknowledge of the kind of situation he faced. He had made only two previous visits, one for an interview with the commission's personnel committee, the other to meet Stokes. He inherited a staff of about thirty-five, of whom perhaps ten had professional titles and only two had professional degrees in planning. He had only the vaguest idea of their capacities when he arrived, but he quickly formed the opinion that, aside from zoning and land-use controls, which the department administered but mainly as a service function for the council's log-rolling politicians, he did not have too much to work with. He did not have a detailed program. His first day on the job he spoke to a reporter about the need to update and complete the downtown urban renewal plan, and later he developed the general goal of updating and revising the city's plan, which had been revised only once since its original formulation in 1949.

His most important initial move was to hire a core of professional staff people. He first hired Ernest Bonner. Bonner had been a colleague of Krumholz's in Ithaca, where he worked at the City Planning Department downtown; later he got a Ph.D. in economics in Pittsburgh and moved on to a faculty position in the planning department of the University of Wisconsin in Madison. Krumholz valued Bonner for his analytical capabilities and saw him as playing a complementary role to his own, responsible for the technical work, while he himself would play the public role. He soon hired additional professionals to supplement Bonner and assigned them the task of working on the Master Plan. It was a situation where there were few egos and little entrenched power to fight against within the department. Krumholz simply left the staff he had inherited alone to do what they had been doing, and even found some of them useful:

> There were a few old-timers who knew their jobs and kept their eyes open and, with proper recognition and encouragement, could (and did) provide invaluable links to the past and to the other departments with which we would have to work. But it was obvious that much staff rebuilding needed to be done.[15]

The regular staff already occupied about half of the top floor of City Hall, and he left them there with his own office among them. But there was an attic, with vast skylights, that Bonner adopted for his master plan staff. Krumholz adapted to a bifurcated staff. His idea people were upstairs, the regulars with him, below. There was a minimum of friction, and Bonner's group began work on studies and analyses.

For about six months, Krumholz simply went around the city, going to meetings and playing his public role. It was clear to him that he had to put a priority on gaining visibility. Visibility was a precondition of influence. He attended the mayor's cabinet meetings. Previous planning directors had avoided the cabinet, perhaps acting out the "independent" planner role, and no notification or invitation to the meetings came to his office. Krumholz found out the time and the place of the first meeting after he arrived and simply showed up. No one objected; he became a regular fixture and thus served notice of the Planning Commission's willingness to take part in the political decisions of the administration.

His best vehicle for becoming visible during his first few months, however, came with his role as Stokes's alternate on the board of the Northeast Ohio Area Coordinating Agency (NOACA). Stokes never attended these meetings, but they were of a certain significance because NOACA had the formal authority for approving or disapproving federal grants in the city and region. Many of these were of great importance and a cause of conflict between the city and the suburban interests that made up a large majority of NOACA's membership. The issue that immediately got Krumholz's attention was a proposal to build a part of Interstate Route 290, called the Clark Freeway, through a residential neighborhood of Cleveland's East Side. The proposal was made at one of the first meetings he attended, during his first week on the job. It would have displaced 1,200 families, destroyed three stable neighborhoods in a city already suffering decline in many other areas, and removed millions in assessed valuation from the tax rolls. Speaking for Stokes, Krumholz immediately raised objections. He was one of only three Cleveland representatives on a board dominated by suburban interests, but the freeway proposal had been opposed by NOACA's own technical staff and by its steering committee. He was shocked when, after hearing the city's objection, the board voted overwhelmingly, almost casually, to approve the proposal. Later, he described his feeling as rage, brought on by a sense that, in Stokes's seat, he was experiencing collective racism directed at him personally. He came away with the view that the coordinating agency, instead of simply rubber-stamping noncontroversial grant requests, had become the instrument of surburban exploitation at the city's expense. He presented this view to Stokes, who accepted it, as did the City Council leaders. Together they made an issue of NOACA.

Over the next two years, they forcefully articulated the city's positions on regional issues, not only in relation to the freeway, but also in relation to housing, proposing that suburban towns accept a proportionate share of needed public housing units, and in relation to the constitution of the board, in which Cleveland, with 25 percent of the affected population, had only three out of forty-nine votes. The conflict escalated when these city proposals were rejected by the board. NOACA, which had review authority, rejected a Cleveland grant proposal to the federal government for funds for inner-city parks. The city refused to pay its NOACA membership dues. NOACA turned down more requests. The city went to HUD in Washington, which had jurisdiction over the agency, and finally, in the summer of 1971, HUD decertified NOACA's grant-review powers. The situation was finally resolved after Stokes left office through a reconstitution of the NOACA board with somewhat greater city representation (eleven votes out of fifty-six). In relation to this conflict, Krumholz inserted the Planning Commission strongly into the city's political processes, at the same time articulating a strong city position vis-à-vis the region. Stokes began to ask him to write speeches and Krumholz and his staff began to sense the potential for speaking to national as well as local audiences.

The staff in the loft—formally, the Comprehensive Planning Division—meanwhile began to consider the kinds of analyses they might want to make. Bonner was the key person, both in hiring staff and in establishing conceptions of what might be produced. Bonner's consciousness had developed at Pittsburgh and Madison. Student activism had stimulated various creative responses from the faculties of many professional schools of planning. Students in the sixties in general reacted against hierarchical and professional prerogatives in universities, but in planning departments, these pressures were intensified by student awareness of and experience in emerging urban conflicts. At Wisconsin, Bonner had been at the margins of such debates and conflicts within the faculty, where issues of equity were given prominence. His move to Cleveland was part of a general desire to bring these concerns into the real world. He was able to use his academic contacts to bring similarly motivated students to Cleveland. Janice Cogger came from Madison. A colleague on the Wisconsin faculty, David Ranney, had moved to Iowa, and through him they got Douglas Wright. Two other people also joined the comprehensive planning group.

This group, informed by Bonner's economics, began to consider program formulations. They interacted with Krumholz's liberalism. They held seminars with Krumholz on Thursday afternoons for six months; after a while he decided to leave them alone. Later he spoke of them as "coming down from the loft" with a set of principles that would guide the agency's work. In reality, they were busy on a number of other projects, like capital budget reviews, from the beginning. The general ideas that were to guide the group emerged out of the projects and seminars. There were two central themes in their work: opportunism and equity. Since these themes are central not only to the problems of Cleveland, which immediately stimulated them, but also to shifts in outlook in the planning profession as a whole, which occurred elsewhere also, I will describe these themes in detail.

The attraction of opportunism really began with Krumholz's concern to become politically visible. By "opportunism," he meant not the lookout for personal gain, but rather an awareness of the necessary centrality of politics in the planning process, in contrast to the remote idealism that had often characterized planners in the past. Later he described the transition in his thinking in the most systematic terms in connection with the Planning Commission's capital budgeting function.[16] As the charter mandated, and as he had learned about the budgeting function from Hillhouse at Cornell, capital budgeting was a wholly rational procedure, one of the major means of implementing a comprehensive plan. Theoretically, the planners were to obtain detailed capital budget project requests from the operating departments; they were then to review them in light of the resource estimates prepared by the Finance Department as well as those described by the general plan. Then they could hold public hearings, formulate priorities, and recommend one-year and five-year programs to the mayor. The mayor would then submit a capital budget to the City Council; if adopted, it would guide the city's action. These procedures were mandated by the city charter, and they were prescribed in professional doctrine.

Krumholz and his staff came to understand that reality did not match the theory in Cleveland. The list of projects in the commission's Capital Improvements Program, which it was required to publish each year, always far exceeded the city's capacity to finance them, and the annual publication had become known derisively as the city's "wish book." At first they thought that the fault lay with a lack of initiative and expertise on the part of the planning staff, and so Janice Cogger was assigned the task of redesigning the process. She found that the operating departments did not share the notion of capital budgeting implied by the theory. They lacked analytical capacity and tended to work in a crisis environment. Lacking good information about future project possibilities, they simply resubmitted, from year to year, the same wish list of projects they had the year before. The Finance Department did not keep up-to-date information on the city's capacity to fund projects. The major did not propose a capital budget and the council did not adopt one.

For a while, the planning staff thought that if they supplied the technical expertise, the city government would be able to think through its actions more carefully; ultimately, they decided this was an impossible task. Krumholz said they figured out that what was at stake was not a technical problem at all, but rather that "the city's elected officials and department heads had found that their interests were better served by the political process than by the planning process."[17] That is, operating in a crisis atmosphere, they had found that the process that paid off in actual capital investments was one whereby a problem, perceived as having reached crisis proportions, finally got the support of the council or of a council person in a particular area. Examples of this process of problem-solving could be found in localized street-paving projects, the building of a new firehouse or medical clinic, or the city's investment in support of a particular private investment that would provide jobs or other benefits.

But these procedures could not be programmed in advance. Advance notice might defeat the psychology involved in mobilizing the necessary support. So the operating departments, while giving lip service to the capital budgeting process as the charter required them to do, ignored it in practice, and technical help from the city planning staff made no difference. The planners finally wondered whether they shouldn't simply abandon the whole procedure and go back to the "wish book" charade. What they did instead was drastically to reconceptualize the problem. They made the list of projects because they were required to. But they cut back on their efforts in this area and presented the report quite differently. They dropped the pretext of this list being a plan and instead discussed the issues of city investment generally: the general shortage of capital, and the city's future problems caused by deferred investment in the less visible projects, such as bridge repairs. Following this rationale, the planners decided their approach to capital investment problems would be more pragmatic:

> We also began efforts to influence capital investment decisions which were not oriented to the preparation of the [Capital Improvement Program]. They took two forms: (1) providing operating departments with staff assistance in analyzing their capital needs and finding means to finance priority projects, and (2) active involvement in the highly political process by which individual projects are financed or tabled.[18]

This thinking came to permeate all the efforts of the comprehensive planning division: a tendency to focus on decisions that were politically important at the time and to organize their analysis around these, rather than organizing their analysis around the needs of a long-range plan regardless of what was politically important at the time. Thus the planners postponed the revision of the 1949 plan in favor of a series of other studies. They prepared an analysis of the Clark Freeway route location, illustrating its costs and benefits, and proposed an alternative route. They did a series of analyses of housing issues. In one case, they proposed a "fair share" public housing scheme, which would distribute these units throughout the suburban area of Cleveland according to population and the number of low-income people in each place.

Political opportunism came to the Cleveland planners out of experience and in the context of their need to get visibility, but it did not solve another problem that planning agencies (and chief executives) have and which the comprehensive plan idea was supposed to solve: the organization of planning studies and city decisions around more general themes. The supposed function of a comprehensive plan was to set long-range goals embodied in a picture of the future, so that other goals and decisions (such as the capital projects) could be given priorities and assigned their relative importance. One of the great dictums of the planning profession has been: "Make no little plans, for they have not the power to stir men's blood,"[19] the point being that political opportunism alone will not motivate action, at least not major action, unless it is placed within a context of principles and goals. The counterargument, which runs deep in the American pragmatic tradition, says that plans stifle initiative; where there is a choice to be made, spontaneous initiatives should be favored. Political opportunism in the City Planning Commission in fact acted to support initiatives with analysis. Thus it was not simply a way to achieve visibility; it provided a real service in a constructive way. But there was also a need to organize the commission's opportunism, to project larger values.

A larger system of values did in fact emerge from the comprehensive planning section, an approach Krumholz later began to call "equity planning." The group produced, in October of 1971, a remarkable document, "Toward a Work Program for an Advocate Planning Agency," which they presented at the annual meeting of the American Institute of Planners.[20] In it, they laid out their argument rationalizing their values. On the one hand, they said their vision was that "individuals choose their own goals and the means to pursue these goals"[21] and society's values and institutions must further the pursuit of individual goals. This amounted to a justification for political opportunism: Planners, by inserting themselves into politically visible decisions, were able to be closer to the interests of individuals pursuing individual goals; on the other hand, the abstractions of the comprehensive plan would tend to assert broad values and to further institutions (the capital budgeting process, for example), without providing systematically for the furtherance or even for the awareness of individual goals.

On the other hand, they also inserted, at the end of their introductory statement, an equity position: "In a context of limited resources, first and priority attention should be given to the task of promoting wider choices for those individuals and groups who have few, if any, choices."[22] This statement came to reflect a central theme of the Cleveland planners. Its derivation was important, because the emphasis on individualism and opportunism for the selection of planning analysis topics became widespread in city planning practice during the 1970s, while the equity theme did not. The equity argument *may* have followed from the individualism argument, but the derivation was not explicit in the planners' writings. There is an argument in welfare economics, which some of the Cleveland planners may have used, that individual choice, to be generally enhanced, requires that the least-well-off (in choices) be given the greatest government priority. But the Cleveland planners don't cite this argument. Instead, they treat the equity argument as one that can stand on its own. Krumholz tended to think of equity as a principle that opposed efficiency and for which his agency ought to be a special spokesperson. In later statements of the equity principle, he tended to justify it by reference to statements of the American Institute of Planners and to the Bible.[23] Very clearly, the equity position, like the principle of opportunism, came to the Cleveland planners out of their personal experience of the place. Krumholz's experiences with the Northeast Ohio Area Coordinating Agency drove home the equity issue in clear, spatial terms, and in racial terms.

The Cleveland City Planning Department pursued these concerns throughout the 1970s. Three of the issues with which they were concerned and which later greatly affected city policy were public power, downtown office development subsidies, and public transit. The planners' concern with public power began during Stokes's term in office when, in 1971, they made an analysis of capital needs for the city's municipal light plant, called MUNY Light.[24] The study was part of their annual Capital Improvements Program and was occasioned by a series of power blackouts. They found that the private utility, Cleveland Electric Illuminating Company (CEI), which served the largest part of the city and the surrounding region, had for years been trying to buy MUNY Light, motivated presumably to eliminate some of its competition. Furthermore, CEI had consistently refused to allow MUNY Light to tie in to supplementary power sources. Since utilities customarily need such tie-ins to handle periods of peak demand or to cover periods when their own equipment needs maintenance, this constituted a severe handicap for MUNY. The power outages led to complaints about the service and caused many councilmen to push for the sale of MUNY to CEI. The planners concluded that the sale, even though it would solve the blackout problem, would lead to a rate increase for utility customers and, perhaps more important, would mean the loss of MUNY as a public yardstick on power pricing, because it held down private utility rates generally. This, they concluded, would place a serious burden on the city's poor. As an alternative, they proposed that MUNY Light use state law to condemn and purchase CEI's property within the city.

This proposal was not taken seriously by most people, but it would eventually have long-term impacts. Stokes had wanted to sell MUNY Light, but his term ended soon after the study began. Ralph

Perk, Stokes's Republican successor, saw the MUNY Light customers as a special constituency and supported MUNY Light until late in his term, too late to consummate a sale to CEI. In 1975, the city filed an antitrust suit against CEI and some other power companies for anti-competitive practices, a suit that generated a supporting brief from the U.S. Justice Department. The U.S. Nuclear Regulatory Commission also found against CEI in a separate decision, following the line initially argued by the planners. After 1977, Dennis Kucinich made retention of MUNY Light a major political issue, and his successor George Voinovich continued the policy and vigorously pursued the antitrust case. So the arguments made by the planners at the beginning of the 1970s bore fruit later.

Perk's election in 1971 had seemed, at first, the worst possible outcome for the planners and for their equity strategy. Krumholz had originally established himself under the umbrella of Stokes's liberal administration, and he had made the planners visible by means of the NOACA issue. He had identified himself with a black mayor, and the planners had worked well with both of the unsuccessful candidates whom Perk defeated. Perk, in contrast, represented the resurgence of the white ethnics and opposition to tax increases and big spending programs, and to the social engineering then in vogue with many intellectuals. Krumholz was not sure how to approach Perk, but he met with him and said he wished to identify the planners with a constituency of the people, not a political faction or a politician, and offered in effect to be a constructive part of Perk's administration. He became the only holdover department head. He thought this was partly because Perk, a white who had fired many of Stokes's appointees, needed to do something to keep the support of Cleveland's blacks. It also was a matter of Perk taking a Jacksonian view of city administration: he favored local appointees with no particular administrative credentials, in contrast to Stokes's practice of instituting nationwide talent searches to fill administration positions such as those that brought Green and Krumholz into the government. In dealing with the complexities of administration, however, particularly in the fields of housing and community development, Perk found the planning staff useful to him. As a result of this political and technical complementarity, Krumholz looked back on his six years under Perk as those when the planners had the most influence in the city.[25]

The planners' interest in public subsidies to downtown developers began under Perk, when in 1974 a local developer approached the city with plans for a development called Tower City. This was to be an office complex built over an extensive city-owned bridge structure near the rail terminal. The developer estimated his total investment at $350 million, and the local newspapers were strongly supportive of the proposal as a way to start the economic revitalization of the downtown. But the planners found the project, as proposed, of questionable value to the city. It turned out that the developer wanted a $20 million tax abatement, and the bridges, which had been constructed fifty years earlier, were in need of repairs, the cost of which could not easily be estimated, but which might amount to another $15 million, a cost the developer did not want to assume. The planners then got the Planning Commission to refuse to approve the needed enabling legislation unless amendments were made. They wanted the developer to guarantee a number of new jobs to city residents and to forego the tax abatements. This position resulted in a storm of criticism in the City Council. George Forbes, the council president, called for Krumholz's resignation. The planners, accused of obstructing downtown development, responded that development meant not office buildings and hotels, but jobs and services for residents.

The council voted overwhelmingly in favor of the project, and it would have gone ahead with it except that the developer went into bankruptcy in other dealings. But the planners had succeeded in drawing public attention to the problem. Later, in relation to other tax abatement or subsidy proposals, their arguments were repeated by others. The Ohio Public Interest Campaign argued the tax abatement question locally in 1977, and then Dennis Kucinich made it a major issue in his successful run for the mayor's office that fall.

Krumholz and his staff became very involved in the issue of the terms of sale of the city's transit system to the Greater Cleveland Regional Transit Authority (RTA) in 1974. The sale stemmed from the financial crisis and the unprofitability of the city's transit system and from the desires of regional planners to create an integrated transit system combining bus and rail services. Krumholz had worked on a five-county transit study begun during Stokes's administration, and the Cleveland planners had concluded that regional rail service would be of little benefit to the city's transit-dependent population. Instead, they emphasized the need for low bus fares, frequent bus schedules, and closely spaced bus routes. Thus, when the city went into negotiations with the RTA, the planners were able to present Perk with a carefully thought-out negotiating position. Perk was responsive. Dennis Kucinich, then a council member, was an early supporter of this position, and Krumholz and the city's law director, James B. Davis, became major negotiators for the city. They argued for service and fare guarantees, while the regional representatives argued for RTA flexibility to create a system emphasizing rail services. The outcome of the negotiations guaranteed low fares for three years, prohibited the RTA from spending funds on developing a downtown rapid-transit line for five years, and provided other service guarantees, including bus route coverage and service frequencies.

These were limited gains, and after the time limitations ended, the RTA began raising bus fares and cutting services, meanwhile spending large sums on other rapid-transit improvements. But Krumholz thought that the other guarantees, such as the Community Responsive Transit program—a door-to-door, dial-a-ride service initiated as part of the agreement—had developed a constituency of support during the period in which the guarantees were in effect, and this support could possibly make the city's gains more permanent.

The Late 1970s: Neighborhoods, OPIC, Kucinich

Cleveland's politics changed and developed after about 1975. Perk's regime represented, on the surface, a return to the pattern of ethnic, caretaker mayors that had begun with Lausche. But the underlying conditions making that kind of government viable no longer existed. With George Forbes as council president, the superficial appearances of a return to the nonideological, pragmatic, distributive politics that had evolved under the ethnics emerged again, this time with much greater participation by the black East Side. But the basic economics underlying these appearances were different. Throughout the 1950s, most of Cleveland's population were doing better and better and suburban migration was a believable way to gain upward mobility. After 1970, this sort of opportunity was largely a memory for most Clevelanders. Forbes and the council continued to play on the memory and to make it real when they could, but a different competing reality came to be an increasingly powerful motivation creating challenges to the Perk-Forbes view of the world. This reality led people closer to the equity argument that Krumholz and his staff had developed in 1970: Cleveland's people continued to become poorer, relative to the suburbs; city services became progressively less viable; the concerns of the business and the middle classes, who had historically offered support for the poor, narrowed as these classes moved away from the city. Gradually, the idea developed that local people had to take hold of their problems themselves.

THE NEIGHBORHOOD MOVEMENT

Perhaps the leading role in this shift belonged to the neighborhood organizations that grew stronger throughout the 1970s. There was perhaps one viable neighborhood organization in 1970; there were ten or more by 1980. How did this happen? Most people in Cleveland could not say for sure, but all suggested the importance of the Commission on Catholic Community Action, located in the Cleveland Diocese. The CCCA was initiated on a modest scale in 1969 when its director, Harry Fagan, led some adult education seminars in some of the city's parishes. Fagan had given up on ten years in the advertising business in Cleveland and had taken the CCCA director's position in order to get his working life more in line with his values, which had become strongly oriented toward such issues as civil rights, the antiwar movement, and urban poverty, which infused parts of the Catholic Church at the time. He initiated neighborhood discussion groups along with Dan Reedy, a priest who had moved to Cleveland from Pittsburgh. For the first two years, he said, "I remained about two feet off the ground . . . with a fervor to do good that would have made Joan of Arc proud."[26] The discussion groups moved from general issues, however, to the consideration of specific and local actions and advocacy strategies, and ended up focusing on organizing the neighborhoods of Cleveland.

It would be interesting to know the exact contents of these discussions. The neighborhood movement in the United States generally took on a confrontationist, pragmatic, and unprogrammatic style, which maximized initial organizational gains, but often failed to develop basic political consciousness about fundamental issues. This style was associated with Saul Alinsky, the pioneer organizer who began the Industrial Areas Foundation in Chicago. For Alinsky, pragmatic conflict tactics around a highly visible target were primary; he thought that discussions of values were a distraction. This was not Fagan's style. For him, conflict, if it came, came from deep thinking about values. His major evolution, though, was toward a more focused, localist strategy, whose key concept was "empowerment." Later he said,

In 1969 we started with adult education on justice issues. Then we became advocates. But about 1973–1974 we saw all this was still doing it for others. And so we adopted the idea of "empowerment." When I first talked to organizers I heard them saying organization itself was the output. For me, what counted was for people's lives to develop. I saw women who couldn't express themselves learn to stand up and argue with bankers.[27]

In his 1979 organizing manual, Fagan tried to convey the inner shifts in approach that the CCCA went through.

The problems we faced were extremely serious. There was absolutely nothing worthwhile in oppression and the plight of powerless people was awesome, but the dullness of our intensity was being matched only by the intensity of our dullness. Certainly, the notion of our being in ministry for the long haul would be dashed on the rocks if we didn't quickly find an emergency lever. The lever we found was simple.

We sat down, told our stories to each other, began to laugh, prayed like crazy, started to really care for each other, had a drink and got some fantastically expert skills training. We read everything available, listened to everybody, sat through every training session imaginable, actually tried a few things and finally we began to learn.[28]

What Fagan and his associates did was to develop a strategy for a neighborhood organization that they hoped would avoid some of the pitfalls of previous efforts. They drew their boundaries so that the organization would be heterogeneous rather than homogeneous. CCCA had begun as a city-suburbs coalition, with elements of rich and poor, black and white, young and old. The first community organizations were to reflect that kind of diversity. One was begun in Cleveland Heights, a suburb that had had a large influx of blacks; the other was begun in the Buckeye-Woodland neighborhood of Cleveland. The CCCA provided organizers for them both.

The Buckeye organization moved ahead faster than the other. Its base was the Catholic parishes and the East End Neighborhood House. Tom Gannon became its first organizer. Buckeye began to take political positions on issues facing its constituency. A community congress was formed, a coalition of organizations in the neighborhood by means of which people's consciousness of the issues they faced and how they could be approached was raised and deepened. In

1974, senior citizens were organizing around the transit negotiations and the Community Responsive Transit System (dial-a-ride), issues that were being argued for the city by Krumholz and Cogger. The outcome of those negotiations was seen as a "win" for the senior citizens and for Buckeye-Woodland. Later these same organizers got involved in a controversy over the city's proposal to purchase the Cleveland Arena for $1 million, after the city had told the community organization that there were no funds for housing. That was a win, too, establishing Buckeye-Woodland as an organization that could deliver.

After that, other neighborhood organizations developed. Tom Gannon went back to CCCA to help start the St. Clair-Superior Coalition, and the Coalition to Bring Back Broadway. By 1981, there were six to ten viable neighborhood organizations in the city, depending on how one defined "viable." Some, like Buckeye-Woodland, were thoroughly participatory; others, less so, were vehicles for business entrepreneurs to get investment funds from the city. This price of success may have been inevitable..

Krumholz and the City Planning Department were important to the development of Buckeye-Woodland and the other neighborhood groups. At the time of the transit negotiations, Krumholz's relationship with Fagan had developed and his staff developed contacts with the CCCA staff. The Krumholz staff carried information from City Hall to the neighborhoods, information that told them when to show up at what meetings so they could influence their outcomes. A Buckeye organizer said: "Norm gave us information. Without that, we could never have negotiated effectively on dial-a-ride." Fagan said:

> The biggest difference in this town was not Norm's programs, but that he would talk to us. He was a piece of the system that committed truth. . . . He would tell us when to strike. He'd say, "If you want these mini-buses, now's the time to get down here."

According to Fagan, the complementarities between the planners and the organizers were partly personal:

> We backed into most of our things. We backed into our relationship with Norm. We liked each other. . . . We had kids working for each other, who dated each other. . . . It was an instinctive feeling about being angry about the same things. Someone would say "that son-of-a-bitching RTA is going to go

to a buck" and we both know that blacks were likely to get screwed.[29]

As the neighborhood groups developed, CCCA was able to build an infrastructure, a supporting organization. They had started with Fagan and Reedy and some adult education classes. After Buckeye-Woodland's success, they got funding from some local foundations and this made it possible to hire more organizers. It got to the point where they had seventy-five young people working as organizers, sixty to seventy hours per week at $8,000 to $9,000 yearly salaries. Nurturing them became a CCCA preoccupation, and they established the Ohio Training Center. They also tried to meet the need for technical assistance for the neighborhoods. Krumholz, when he left the City Planning Commission in 1979, established a Center for Neighborhood Development at Cleveland State University, which was essentially a part of this neighborhood support network.

THE OHIO PUBLIC INTEREST CAMPAIGN

The other significant grass-roots organization in Cleveland was the Ohio Public Interest Campaign. OPIC was formed when a group of people linked by common experiences in the antiwar movement sought to turn their political energies to domestic issues. Ira Arluck from Columbus, Ed Kelly from Akron, and Jay Westbrook from Cleveland were among the early members of the group. They and a number of others came to face the impossibility of doing anything specific about the war, while at the same time they were developing an increasing awareness of the interconnectedness of the war with certain domestic issues. Ed Kelly remembered that they had all been interested similarly by Richard Barnet's and Ronald Muller's *Global Reach*, a book that in 1974 laid out the development of U.S. multinational firms and their ability to devastate U.S. communities by moving their capital and production operations to Third World sites.[30]

Looking around them, the OPIC founders saw that Ohio was as good a place as any to observe and fight the plant-shutdown issue. Arluck went around to the churches, the senior citizens, and the unions with the idea of setting up a public interest group. They got encouragement and then funding. They had the advantage of dealing with people they already knew from their antiwar work. In 1975 they established an office in Cleveland. Their first issue was a statewide campaign against a state referendum on tax abatements.

James Rhodes had won the governorship in 1974 partly by promising to bring jobs to the state. OPIC felt that while Rhodes was correctly diagnosing the problem (as industrial exodus), his solutions were wrong. Rhodes advocated tax abatements, authorized for Ohio municipalities for purposes of job creation, and the 1975 measure in question would have supplemented the tax abatement policy. OPIC advocated a different set of solutions, which emphasized local control of business and legislation to capture public business subsidies for public use. They felt that market factors would support such an approach, which, in any event, had some political appeal. They launched a campaign against the Rhodes-backed measure and won by a large margin.

The OPIC leaders saw themselves as distinct and different from the neighborhood organizers, although they worked with them on many issues. They wanted to organize people around relatively fundamental issues. Neighborhood organizing, they felt, tended to mobilize people around small localized issues and, moreover, was very labor-intensive—"You need almost an organizer for every block," Kelly said. But also they did not want to follow the example of another type of left organization, which involved talking about "global" issues without being able to organize real people. They wanted to organize in a popular way and also raise major issues.

After their initial success in combatting Rhodes' industrial proposal, OPIC set out in 1975 to do statewide organizing around the issue of plant closings. Ed Kelly wrote *Industrial Exodus*, a careful piece of research stating OPIC's arguments, and OPIC, with union backing, got involved in numerous campaigns around the state.[31] Meanwhile, OPIC established a Cleveland division in 1976 with Jay Westbrook as director. One accomplishment of Westbrook and his associate Paul Ryder was to stay on top of the abatements issue locally. They opposed (unsuccessfully) a 1976 measure to authorize tax abatements, but they succeeded in attaching amendments to it, limiting the measure to three years and requiring that half the jobs created be reserved for local residents. In 1977 they organized a much stronger opposition to individual tax abatements then under consideration in City Council: one for the National City Bank in June and one for Sohio in August, both involving large office developments. The abatements were passed, but the opposition had been very strong from the neighborhoods and from some of the citywide umbrella organizations that had been formed by that time. Dennis Kucinich, the underdog candidate for mayor who was soon to elaborate an "urban populism" theme during his two controversial years in office, picked up the tax abatements issue after OPIC's and the neighborhood groups' efforts and made it one of the major issues by means of which he attacked Perk in the November elections.

KUCINICH IN OFFICE, 1977–1979

Dennis Kucinich, who was elected mayor in 1977 at the age of 31, dramatized the concept of "urban populism" in the city and, because of his conflicts with the banks (leading to the first major city default since the 1930s), also in the nation. But the roots of the concept of "urban populism" and Kucinich's ability to win with it go back much further. The economic problems of Cleveland's poor and lower-middle classes became acute during the 1960s. Locher as mayor had represented the kind of populism that had a long tradition in Cleveland, but his somewhat simplistic approach to city administration would have had to change toward increased professionalism eventually, even if the Hough riots had never occurred. Stokes' administration marked a new departure. His opening up the administration to blacks was only part of it. He also represented a more rational approach to government: he conducted national searches for professional department heads, cooperated with major business interests to revitalize economic growth, and instituted larger welfare programs to serve those who did not immediately get the benefits of growth. These kinds of welfare programs may be thought of as a new local economic policy in Cleveland. The common judgment was that it failed, because, after the Glenville shoot-out, business pulled back from the Cleveland NOW! campaign, damaging Stokes's ability to get council cooperation and to generate the funds needed to keep the policy working.

The election of Perk, a white ethnic Republican, is usually represented as a racist reaction to Stokes. In part it surely was. But it was also a middle-and lower-class "populist" reaction to Stokes's economic policies, which were not working for those constituencies because private capital was not being invested in the city at the same rates it had been before Stokes, and because what was being invested was on terms that were not to the advantage of most of the people. There were other more fundamental reasons for the opposition to Stokes's program than racial conflict. Populism in Cleveland re-emerged because specific political factions began to see the adverse effects of Stokes's economics and sought different kinds of solutions—even short term ones—from those that had been tried by the Stokes-business alliance. Crucial support for Perk had come from

Bob Weissman, president of the United Auto Workers Community Action Program Council and from Dennis Kucinich, who led a "Democrats for Perk" campaign. Weissman was a close associate of Kucinich, then on the City Council, and later became his top political advisor in the mayor's office. At the time of Perk's election, Weissman had articulated "urban populism" as an alternative to Stokes's organization of a black-business alliance through what was called the 21st District Caucus of the Democratic party, after the Congressional District covering Cleveland's East Side that had elected Stokes's brother and law partner, Louis Stokes. Don Freeman, a black activist who published a newsletter called *Vibrations*, thought that Weissman's position was a step toward the "delegitimization" of Stokes. He said:

> Carl Stokes contained, pacified, and decimated emergent Black militance during his four years in City Hall. Consequently the 21st District Caucus dominates the political life of Black Clevelanders. Its reticence relative to socio-economic problems deprives Black People of a potent political *advocate*. The white populace is represented by the United Auto Workers C A P Council. The Black constituencies have no representative organization. Thus the 21st District Caucus inadvertently *maintains* Greater Cleveland's "Establishment."[32]

Whatever thoughts Kucinich and Weissman had for a positive economic strategy are not clear. Presumably they were trying to go a long step beyond attacking Stokes, even beyond "delegitimizing" Stokes (and putting the Democratic party into disarray) in order to achieve an "urban populism" that transcended race. Their populism could even have been a facade for racism, as was the case with the Wallace movement.[33] Perk, in any event, did not hold Weissman's and Kucinich's support for long. He accommodated the business interests, came to support tax abatements, and finally advocated the sale of M U N Y Light. In 1977, after O P I C had successfully generated great opposition to tax abatements, Kucinich made this issue, along with the M U N Y Light issue, the basis of his successful candidacy for mayor.

Kucinich laid out the fundamentals of his program of "urban populism" on September 28, 1978 in a speech to the National Press Club in Washington.[34] His basic insight was that private capital no longer formed the source of popular welfare in cities. Thus, the policies that had been used to induce growth—tax abatements, for example—would no longer be effective in helping city residents. The benefits that would trickle down to them from investments would not match the costs they would bear in lost tax revenues. As a result, the economic welfare of the mass of city residents was stagnant or declining, and such racial issues as busing and such social issues as abortion had become even more divisive than they had been previously; they got in the way of making policies for dealing with the more fundamental economic issues. From this analysis, Kucinich deduced that the proper direction for city policy was a shift in the agenda away from divisive race and social issues to deal directly with economic questions: most important, the redistribution of wealth from corporate concentrations to popular constituencies. City tax funds should be spent, not to induce corporate or private investment, but on direct neighborhood services and public works. Tax burdens should be shifted away from middle- and lower-class homeowners and toward businesses. The welfare bureaucracy should be replaced by a more basic redistribution of income. The private sector should be vigorously regulated. He thought structural reforms of political institutions would be a diversion, at best.

Once in power, Kucinich came under constant attack from the media and from business-oriented special interests. When he came into the mayor's office, he did not give business interests any special places on the advisory boards he appointed. He opposed tax abatements and supported MUNY Light. In 1978 he faced a recall election. He also faced the intransigent opposition of George Forbes, the black City Council president who supported tax abatements and a pro-business economic development strategy. In the fall of 1978, the banks struck back at Kucinich. The city's financial situation had been desperate for some time, a situation caused, first, by capital disinvestment and the loss of jobs and population, and second, by financial mismanagement on the part of the city's governments for over at least a decade.[35] Throughout the Perk administration, short-term borrowing had been used to pay city operating expenses. As these debts came due, the banks involved had routinely "rolled over" the debts, refinancing the city. For some time, the city had been in no condition to pay off these debts and had become dependent on the willingness of the banks to refinance them. In 1978, the Cleveland Trust, through its president, Brock Weir, announced that it would not refinance the city's debt that it held, unless the city came up with an adequate financial program, which in its terms included selling MUNY Light to CEI, dropping the antitrust suit against CEI and instituting a city income tax. Kucinich refused these terms, despite intense opposition from Forbes, and the city went into default in December.[36]

Kucinich might have survived these attacks had he been able to keep his neighborhood constituencies. To counter the banks, he proposed and put on a March ballot referendum a proposal for a city income tax, which he campaigned against, and a proposal for saving MUNY Light, which he supported. He lost on the first measure, but won on the second. There was at least a chance that he could have mobilized enough Cleveland people to match the moneys raised to defeat him and to counter the media. But this was not to be. Kucinich and Weissman ran City Hall with a small, tightly knit group of loyal supporters who had paid little attention to dissenting voices among the constituencies they claimed to work for. Kucinich sought to mobilize the neighborhood groups around his own campaigns, but they resisted. The St. Clair-Superior Coalition, whose membership was split on the issue, declined to work for Kucinich in the recall election, as did other such groups. Their conflicting tactics over some specific issues even provoked Kucinich to withdraw his support from some of them.

KRUMHOLZ AS COMMUNITY DEVELOPMENT DIRECTOR

The neighborhood organizations' conflicts with a populist city administration are revealed by a close examination of the city program most central to neighborhood concerns: community development. The Department of Community Development had been formed in 1969 with Richard Green as its first director, and it had inherited urban renewal, the Model Cities program, and other functions supported by the federal Department of Housing and Urban Development (HUD). In 1974, these and other federal programs were consolidated into Community Development Block Grants, whereby the city would be given a lump sum by the federal government each year, to be spent according to relatively loose federal guidelines. The amount was to be determined by the relative economic and social distress of the city, which worked to Cleveland's benefit. Within the city, the funds were to be spent so as to benefit low- and moderate-income families. In the program's first three years, the community development block grant funds, which totaled about $16 million per year, tended to be distributed rather widely, reflecting the high degree of participation on the part of the City

Council in the allocations. The major uses to which the grants were put were: neighborhood conservation, including housing rehabilitation loans and grants to local economic development corporations; public works improvements in the neighborhoods; and social services subsidies, mostly to neighborhood agencies.

After his election in late 1977, Kucinich made Norman Krumholz director of the Department of Community Development. Krumholz had credibility with the neighborhood groups and was attracted to the Community Development position because it was a way to distribute funds for maximum impact, using neighborhood groups whose capabilities he had come to know well. For the preceding two years he had served on a mayor's task force to consider means of neighborhood housing rehabilitation, and he had been a major proponent of the CASH program (Cleveland Action to Support Housing) which had emerged from the task force. CASH involved scrapping a three percent housing rehabilitation loan program, which covered twenty-eight of the city's thirty-three wards, and replacing it with a loan program targeted to about a third of the wards in six neighborhoods, with code enforcement and with Community Development Block Grant (CDBG) funds supplemented by private bank capital.[37] Krumholz wanted to target not only CASH but the majority of CDBG funds. He expected the city to get an additional $20 million more than its 1977 CDBG funds because of a new Carter Administration policy that favored cities with particularly difficult problems; added to earlier $4 million-per-year spending levels on housing rehabilitation and site improvements, he hoped for an annual pool of $24 million, available for a whole array of targeted neighborhood programs.[38]

Krumholz had evolved the targeting strategy earlier, and in some ways the idea was not unique to Cleveland. The idea was simply that the limited funds available would have more impact if they were concentrated in certain specified areas; if they were to be spread around the city, they would be lost in the more general disinvestment of private capital accompanying the movement of a large part of the population out of the city. The targeted neighborhoods were selected by criteria that included:

(1) apparent neighborhood deterioration, but not to such a degree that most problems could not be corrected;

(2) a relatively high rate of home ownership, with the average homeowner having owned his home long enough to have built up some equity;

(3) a strong sense of community, as evidenced by the presence of a community organization or churches active in neighborhood affairs;

(4) resident incomes not too far below the city average.[39]

Using the presence of neighborhood organizations as a criterion for targeting was a key political condition in Krumholz's program because it allowed him to build up constituencies for the program, which would force its implementation by the City Council. While "targeting" was a classic planning solution to a resource-allocation problem, it also incorporated a crucial political process. In a 1978 presentation, Krumholz described it this way:

> The City Planning Commission and the Department of Community Development will make the preliminary selection of the target areas. These areas will then be discussed with the Mayor, City Council, and the Board of CASH. . . . After the . . . Target Areas . . . have been agreed upon . . . planning teams would work with the citizens and community groups to identify the neighborhood's most urgent needs. This plan . . . should represent a consensus among the residents, the Administration, City Council, and the Board of CASH.[40]

Thus, both in the selection of target areas and later in the formulation of the program for expenditures within these areas, the decision making would go to the City Council. Krumholz would have a big hand in formulating the program, and the neighborhoods would have a chance to exert pressure in their directions.

This procedure might have solidified Kucinich's position in the neighborhoods as well as Krumholz's program. However, faced with a recall election in August and aware that his administration was providing more funds to the neighborhoods than had ever been done before, Kucinich sought to maximize his political returns. As was his pattern with all city departments, he had placed a loyal lieutenant, Betty Grdina, in the Community Development Department as "executive secretary" to Krumholz. Grdina sought to ensure that community development fund allocations were administered in a way that would help Kucinich's election. This put her in conflict with Krumholz on several occasions. Krumholz was tolerant of the community organizations' conflict tactics: He was willing to be attacked so long as this furthered the targeting strategy and may even have encouraged the attacks.[41] Kucinich and Grdina had different priorities. Faced with a recall election in August, they needed support. They asked the St. Clair-Superior Coalition to join the campaign against the recall election and were rebuffed; other neighborhood organizations also failed to cooperate. Krumholz held to his program as he had set it out, initially with Kucinich's backing. But after the recall election (won narrowly by Kucinich), the mayor concluded that he had to use Community Development in a more political way and put Grdina in charge as director, moving Krumholz back to the City Planning Commission. Under Grdina, the administration's relations with the neighborhood organizations deteriorated into open conflict, leading to Kucinich's defeat in November of 1979.

Krumholz never got into open conflict with Kucinich, and their relationship remained cordial, even when Krumholz, whose role as planning director had become increasingly less central during 1979, left the administration to head a foundation-supported neighborhood development program at Cleveland State University. In the spring of 1979, Kucinich said "Norm taught me all I know about city planning." Krumholz, on his side, understood the escalating pressures on the mayor. An opportunist when the chance came to implement the targeting program within Community Development, he was a realist when the opportunity began to slip away. Later, he said he thought that Kucinich's inability to work with the neighborhoods had been "tragic," as Kucinich had caused conflict unnecessarily and thus hurt his chances of getting his positive programs implemented.[42]

Some of Krumholz's staff found working under Kucinich exceptionally difficult. For them, the politics of the situation, which was conceived by Kucinich loyalists as combat, impinged on their identification as professionals. They were professionals, generally committed to the same kinds of goals as Kucinich. But they found the political demands being made on them intolerable. Mindy Turbov, who had come to work in the Planning Department in July 1978, described her introduction to politics on the job; along with two others who had recently started work, she met with Weissman and Grdina at Kucinich Campaign Headquarters:

> We were told to work on the [recall] campaign or else. They gave us reasons. They said this was an urban revolution. They said campaigns were good for your social life, that you owe us for this job. I said to Weissman, "Look, I've just moved here. Let me see what's what." And he said, "Look, if you're not with us, you're against us."[43]

Krumholz was unable to protect his staff from these somewhat over-bearing pressures, and disaffection with Kucinich grew both in the Planning Department and among those Krumholz had brought with him to Community Development. Many of those who were disgruntled left city employment; some went into the neighborhood movement, some went to professional positions in other cities.

Later, Krumholz reflected on his relative lack of influence with Kucinich: Kucinich's conflictual style was something he did not wish to join in because he saw it as a danger to some of the things he had been working for.[44] A comment he made about the Planning Department provides a sharp contrast with his experience at Community Development:

> One of the nice things about the Planning Commission is that we really didn't have programs to run, and so we could be cerebral. . . . Planners need turf they can control. The City Planning Commission was prize turf because it held few obligations. We could set our own agendas.[45]

Outcomes

In November 1979, Kucinich lost the mayoralty election to George Voinovich, a Republican who had strong backing from business and the press. For two years, Kucinich had withstood constant media attacks, but his own abrasive tactics and racist electioneering (particularly those policies associated with his lieutenants, Weissman and Grdina) cost him popular support. In the end, he was not able to maintain the focus on economic issues with which he had hoped to unite his black and white constituents.

Black politics in the city was represented in the City Council presidency of George Forbes—an apparent re-creation of the ethnic patterns that had persisted since Lausche. Forbes had maintained control of the City Council throughout the administrations of Perk and Kucinich. He was a staunch supporter both of business subsidies and of the sale of MUNY Light, he was the manager of the City Council's distributive pork barrel, and he was in a position to use race as a issue whenever he was attacked. Black militant leaders who had begun to emerge in the 1960s had generally been either repressed or co-opted. Black capitalism was popular among middle-class and professional blacks, who continued to consolidate the gains they had made under Stokes. Forbes continued to play the main City Council leadership role under Voinovich, cooperating with the new mayor.

Voinovich tried to cooperate with all sides and in this was remarkably successful. With Forbes' support, he gingerly approached the issue of downtown development in relation to a new Sohio headquarters, but he pulled back from proposing tax abatements or the sale of M U N Y Light, the two issues on which Kucinich had solidified community opposition. With Forbes' support, he pushed through a financial plan to get the city out of default, winning the cooperation of the banks by instituting an income tax increase. But he was also generally cooperative with the neighborhood groups, and in 1981 he was re-elected with no effective opposition.

O P I C remained healthy. Its Cleveland director, Jay Westbrook, won a council seat in 1979 at the same time that Kucinich was being defeated, and in 1981 Westbrook was re-elected. O P I C continued to raise issues in Cleveland and the state. In the council, signs of opposition to Forbes emerged, including a nearly successful move to unseat him from the council presidency, backed by Westbrook and led by a black councilmember, Lonnie Burten.

The neighborhood organizations also continued to flourish. Krumholz had established the Center for Neighborhood Development at Cleveland State University with funds from the Cleveland Foundation and was providing technical assistance to many neighborhood groups. Fagan and the C C C A had established the Ohio Training Center across the street from Krumholz's offices on Euclid Avenue, and this organization supported organizers in other ways. Local and national foundation support continued to come to this set of organizations.

Planning in Cleveland had again changed in character. It had been established in a unique form as a professional activity—in the City Planning Commission, by Krumholz under Stokes—and had been maintained in that form through the first part of Kucinich's regime. The important thing about this form of planning was not only that Krumholz maintained an advocacy role, but also that he established a professional basis for that role within the city government. Partly this role was a matter of his own leadership, but it was more than merely personal style. What he said was almost always based on well-prepared positions, which was made possible by his having recruited a strong staff. In most ways, he maintained a low profile; given the positions he took, the Planning Commission got remarkably little media coverage. His style was not abrasive, and people who disagreed strongly with his arguments generally took pains to point out his professionalism and his value as a critical element in city administration. Aside from his own leadership, he inherited an adaptable institution: the independent planning commission had a tradition of being kept apart from politics. He adapted that tradition to circumstances by joining the political debate, but he did not destroy it, for he always maintained his independence by having his equity strategy well developed.

Kucinich, who agreed with most of Krumholz's positions, destroyed much of that professionalism in the Planning Commission. When Voinovich became mayor, he selected a more traditional planner as director. The new director began by announcing that "there hasn't been any planning in Cleveland for over a decade," and set out on a program that emphasized downtown business development.

Homer Wadsworth, executive director of the Cleveland Foundation, had appreciated Krumholz's role. As director of the nation's largest community foundation, he had to satisfy a constituency of Cleveland businessmen while at the same time somehow keeping the city from falling into greater social and economic disrepair—perhaps an impossible assignment. He had used Krumholz as a consultant for directing funds within Cleveland and supported the Center for Neighborhood Development. He said the most important thing Krumholz did was "bring all those young people into the city." By nourishing the neighborhood movement, Wadsworth and Krumholz were continuing to do that. Many of the people Krumholz had hired at the Planning Commission had left the city. Bonner had left in 1974 to be planning director in Portland, Oregon, and then left planning altogether to join a business selling solar collectors. Linner took a position in Seattle. Doug Wright became a planner in San Francisco. Janice Cogger, after a time as a neighborhood organizer in Cleveland, moved to Boston. Others had stayed in Cleveland. Bill Whitney, who with Linner had held the Community Development Department together after Krumholz left, was working with Krumholz at the Center for Neighborhood Development. Others were back with the city government under Voinovich. Mindy Turbov was working in the neighborhood movement in Cleveland.

This liberal-to-left network had been pushed to one side, but they had been responsible for several tangible achievements. They had the pain of not having seen the political coalition of blacks and neighborhood organizations emerge that might have consolidated power; but they also had the sense that they were ahead of where they had been a decade earlier. First, Krumholz and the planners had the satisfaction of having given a rationale to a politics that simultaneously managed "advocacy" and "equity." They had made these arguments in professional channels for a decade and a half, and in 1985 Krumholz won the presidency of the American Planning Association largely on the basis of that record.

Second, they had co-existed with Kucinich's "urban populism" in an arena of intense dramatization of their themes, where they found the political leadership unable to simultaneously transcend racial and economic issues. Finally, though, their activist presence remained, despite its disarray and its loss of key city positions. The neighborhood movement was still in place and even stronger than ever in some respects. Krumholz, though out of the government, was still in the public eye and working in undiminished fashion. OPIC founder Westbrook and, after 1981, Kucinich himself, were on the City Council. In 1985, these forces were by no means finished, and it seemed only a matter of time before they or others like them found a winning political combination again.

CHAPTER 4

Berkeley: From Liberalism to Radicalism, 1969–1979

Berkeley, California, which adopted a city manager-council charter in 1923, developed in the businesslike, custodial style intended by the inventors of that form of government until the 1960s. After 1960, the city government was transformed by the coming to power of the liberal Democratic Caucus, and later by the social changes occasioned by the student and antiwar left. By 1970, the Democratic Caucus had split into liberal and radical factions. The result was a series of intense confrontations in municipal politics, and these confrontations also moved all political debate in the city further to the left. Republicans were no longer a major factor in city council elections, and many radical proposals had been absorbed into the city administration.

Planning was an important part of both the liberal and the radical programs that changed the course of custodial city government. Physical development planning issues provided some of the major programs on the basis of which the Democratic reformers ran for election in the 1950s and 1960s. Planning was also a central part of the radical program.

Liberalism and the Democratic Caucus

The Democratic Caucus, a coalition of liberals in the Democratic party, achieved majority control of the Berkeley City Council in 1961 after ten years as an opposition movement. Their program was inspired by the 1952 Adlai Stevenson presidential campaign and was a reaction to the conservatism that had dominated the nation during the Eisenhower presidency. Stevenson stressed

(1) civil liberties, in reaction to McCarthy's witch hunts;

(2) racial integration, stirred by the civil rights movement in the South;

(3) a commitment to a system of global collective security, which, in contrast to the isolationism of the 1930s, would intervene against regimes inimical to "democracies"—i.e. communism; and

(4) a relatively more interventionist concept of domestic or local government and administration.

Locally, liberalism in Berkeley meant racial integration in housing, in city appointments, and in schools; it meant a more autonomous and activist city government; and it meant city intervention on physical development issues, particularly around the theme of preserving Berkeley's community character.[1] The city's liberalism was a direct reaction against a history of custodial government and against the view that municipal affairs are or should be adequately regulated by informal consensus, nonpartisan management, and the self-regulating effects of the market. The change in conception did not entail an explicit rejection of the market, but rather the assertion of the city's function as a full-fledged participant in the market, using its own instruments to modify market forces for social ends.

Racial integration was both an ideal and the basis of a coalition of Berkeley liberals. Liberals found the pattern that had developed to be a double burden—a weight of white guilt on the one hand and a social timebomb of black rage on the other—and it was a liberal ideal to use racial integration as a way out of this. Blacks also represented a sizeable block of Democratic voters, at least in the 1950s; as long as the nonpartisan city governments effectively excluded blacks, integration could be a mechanism for rallying the opposition. The liberal Democrats slowly built up their representation as the minority in city government during the 1950s, and as they did so, a degree of black participation developed. Blacks had been on caucus slates starting in 1955, and finally Wilmont Sweeney was the first black elected to the City Council in 1961.

Racial integration was the main liberal struggle of the late 1950s and early 1960s, and when the liberals gained a majority position on the City Council in 1961, the city made a number of very im-

portant moves in the face of stiff opposition. One was the passage of
a fair-housing ordinance in 1963 (later narrowly defeated in a referendum). On the school board, liberals led the way as Berkeley became the only city in the nation to initiate school busing without
outside pressures, in a reorganization plan that distributed the burden of travel on whites as well as blacks. (This prompted a bitterly
fought recall election, as conservatives tried unsuccessfully to oust
the school board that had voted to integrate the schools.) Later, the
liberals' commitment to integration resulted in Berkeley's taxing itself to put the Bay Area Rapid Transit system (BART) underground
to prevent the construction of a physical barrier between black and
white neighborhoods of the city.

The idea that government should be activist, rather than custodial, was manifested in a number of ways: a stronger home-rule
stand in the face of proposals to transfer public health and property
tax assessment functions from the city to the county; a determina-
tion to contain the territorial expansion of the university; upgrading
salaries and the professionalism of municipal workers; and a policy
of generating partisan debate and widespread public involvement in
city boards and commissions.

Planning under the Democratic Caucus

The commitment to intervention in the physical development
of Berkeley—planning—was perhaps the most revealing part of
the liberal program, revealing the strength and the limitations of
liberalism generally. In other places, planning was carried out with
less resolve and clarity of purpose, and with less understanding
of its function on the part of elected representatives, and also
often with less professionalism. Planning was noteworthy in Berkeley for its values and for the constituency it mobilized, for its attitude toward the role of market forces, and for its effort to keep itself focused on the physical environment despite the advent of
new social and economic functions for the city during the 1960s
and 1970s.

The content and early structure of physical planning in Berkeley must be traced to the arrival of T. J. Kent, Jr., in 1948, as chairman of the new University of California graduate planning program. Kent came from a prominent Bay Area family, had studied
architecture at Berkeley in the 1930s, then planning at MIT; during
the 1940s he had been director of planning for San Francisco. Soon

after his appointment to the university, he was made chairman of Berkeley's City Planning Commission. From this position, he was able to test and develop his own ideas about the planning process and to influence Berkeley's development. In 1957, he moved into an elected position on the City Council as part of the Democratic Caucus' push for political control.

Soon after his appointment as chairman of the Planning Commission, Kent was successful in getting the city to hire a professional director and staff and to embark upon a master plan. As planning director, the city hired Corwin Mocine, a colleague of Kent's who had been part of the group of architects and planners (the "Telesis Group") that had thought through and put into practice the graduate program in planning at the university. Working with Kent and the commission, Mocine proceeded to put together a master plan for the city. Kent, who conceived of the plan as a policy document that should be adopted by the City Council, later listed five policies for which the plan stood on completion and to which the city subsequently more or less adhered:

(1) retention of Berkeley's character as a university-residential community in the Bay Area metropolitan core area;

(2) limitations on the physical growth of the univeristy with [the] boundaries of [the] campus now set at 25,000 students—top reached in 1964;

(3) limitation of the population of the city;

(4) metropolitan integration—economic, social, physical, and governmental. The plan ties Berkeley to the metropolitan commuter core, but maintains its specialized role. . . . The key proposals are a regional rapid-transit and a regional plan-making agency;

(5) respect for [Berkeley's] social and architectural heritage. Mixed reasons for accepting a 'cosmopolitan' population . . . Berkeley is a metropolitan reception center.[2]

These general ideas were embodied in the first version of the Master Plan, adopted in 1955 and later updated, amended, and adopted again. They set a frame of reference—for at least some of the people involved, particularly Kent and the planners—for the issues that the liberals defended and for their major achievements in terms of later physical development.

Some of the most important planning issues on this agenda included the establishment of limits on housing densities in the flatlands through down-zoning (finally accomplished in 1963), the successful negotiation and passage of a bond issue to ensure that the BART line would be underground rather than elevated through the city (from the early to the middle sixties), and the exercise of influence on the university to limit its size.[3]

While the effect of the planning effort on the city of Berkeley was physical, it was also institutional and structural. Kent, while he served on the Planning Commission, was developing a set of ideas about the planning process that were unique and distinctive among American writers on planning. His ideas included a strong linkage between planning and city councils and a conception of the limitation of planning to physical development. In arguing for these views—which ultimately appeared in a book, *The Urban General Plan*—Kent was moving against the two strongest institutional changes that were to occur in U.S. planning generally in the following decades: the trend toward locating planning within the staff of a strong mayor or city manager, and the spread of planning across a wide and increasing range of functions.[4]

The Democratic Caucus and Planning after 1969

The Democratic Caucus and its liberal coalition collapsed in Berkeley after about 1967, but a form of liberalism persisted throughout the next decade, and its characteristics are worth noting. The Democrats were no longer the "left" in Berkeley by the late sixties; instead they had become the "moderates," with no significant forces to the right of them. They inherited the largesse of the national "Great Society" programs. Like many other cities, Berkeley began experimenting with the possibilities inherent in these new sources of revenue; the cities developed greatly enhanced municipal roles in a variety of social and business-oriented programs, began paying out much larger municipal payrolls, and developed a kind of project-oriented physical planning that was quite different from the long-range Master Plan of the 1950s.

This was a new kind of "liberalism," an evolution away from the Stevenson-inspired reformers who had moved into city politics in 1952. The earlier liberals had been a minority voice on the City Council until 1961. Many of their proposals involved qualitative changes in the procedures of government, but did not affect its scale, and those that did require more government were often regulatory, such as the fair-housing proposal. These earlier liberals did not develop proposals for increased service delivery involving large amounts of funding. Their planning, finally, was limited to physical development and did not take on the encompassing forms that developed later.

The possibilities of activist government began to develop during the 1960s. On the one hand, many liberals had ambitions to do something about the city's social problems and were willing to create new organizations to help in the attempt. This is evident in the accounts liberal City Council members have given of their goals in participating in local politics, and it is made clear in the commission and staff positions set up during the 1960s and 1970s. Typically, new city functions developed because of the conjunction of federal funding possibilities, the presence of an interested local constituency, and—crucially—the willingness of some local official to move into a new area of responsibility. Berkeley created its Department of Social Planning in the 1960s because of a concern that certain problems were not being dealt with and the idea that the city had a role to play in solving them. The kind of local thinking that led to new initiatives in housing and job development is revealed by Margaret Gordon, a labor economist who served on the City Council from 1965 to 1969. Gordon's research studies had convinced her that unemployment among Berkeley's black youth was a far more serious problem than most had imagined: among blacks between the ages of sixteen and nineteen in 1967 she estimated an unemployment rate of 40 percent.[5] As a consequence of this finding, she worked for the creation of a Berkeley Manpower Commission in 1967. The commission's role would be to get the cooperation of public agencies and local businessmen in programs to educate and employ Berkeley minorities and to seek public and private funds for that end. The work of this commission was frustrated, however, by the desire of the city's antipoverty agency to control all city employment programs. Later, Gordon succeeded in establishing the position of manpower coordinator within the Department of Social Planning. This position was pivotal later in the growth of federal funding for employment programs, enlarged under the Federal Comprehensive Employment Training Act of 1974.

Gordon's interest in housing programs was part of the common liberal Democratic City Council program of the 1960s. During its first four years in power, 1961–1965, the new liberal City Council was absorbed by the issues of down-zoning and the Fair Housing Ordinance, but after the 1965 election, it turned to consideration of ways to subsidize low-income families' housing expenditures. It established a Citizens Advisory Committee on Low-Cost Housing, chaired by John Denton, out of which grew a leased-housing program under Section 23 of the Federal Housing Law. This program was assisting eleven hundred families by 1976 in units spread over a wide range of neighborhoods. Later, Gordon supported the creation of an Urban Redevelopment Authority, which would be able to pursue both housing and job creation programs. Her support of this authority led Gordon and the other council members who supported it into a conflict with local groups. Neighborhood people and radicals attacked the plan because it would demolish existing housing in order to create the West Berkeley Industrial Park. Gordon described being visited by two people who opposed these demolitions:

> They expressed complete shock over the industrial park project and the notion that the council could conceivably contemplate a project that would involve forced removal of any residents whatsoever. Try as I might, I could not convince them that there was a case for a program designed to improve employment opportunities, in the face of severe minority unemployment in Berkeley. . . .
>
> I cannot bring myself to believe, as my . . . visitors apparently did, that there are *never* circumstances that justify forcing some residents to move, in order to carry out a project that promises beneifts for the community as a whole.[6]

After 1971, housing, economic development, and social services programs grew markedly in Berkeley. The political complexion of the City Council had changed drastically: black representation had increased throughout the 1960s to the point where a coalition of blacks and white liberals could dominate the council. Warren Widener was elected the first black mayor in 1971, and in that position, led the government for the next eight years. Meanwhile, the radical coalition (after 1973 somewhat transformed as the Berkeley Citizens Action) acquired council representation for the first time in 1971 and maintained a minority position on the council throughout Widener's term. In this increasingly radical environment, Widener and the liberal coalition adapted their program to new conditions partly by adopting new programs and by taking advantage of increasing flows of federal aid dollars.

Housing programs were one major area of this adaptation. They had started in a relatively small way in the 1960s, but Widener launched a major new initiative in 1974 by establishing a city Department of Housing. He hired a new director, Janet Roche, and a small pilot housing rehabilitation loan program was expanded into the West Berkeley Neighborhood Project, which used community development funds to subsidize housing rehabilitation loans. Meanwhile, the council majority continued to support urban renewal for the West Berkeley Industrial Park and other federally subsidized programs. City expenditures increased from $10.2 million in 1962 to $42.5 million in 1977; of this increase, inter-governmental transfers accounted for an increase of $1.3 million to $18.5 million in the same period.[7] Thus the 1970s were a period of budget growth for the city.

The Left in Municipal Politics, 1966–1981

Even while the Democratic Caucus was winning victories in Berkeley's local government, the Berkeley campus of the University of California was becoming a center of student protest and radical political activism. This began with the Free Speech Movement in 1964, a protest against the university's restriction of student political activities. Soon other radical and antiwar movements became strong at the university, and this university-based political activism supplemented and reinforced the community's. A large group of university-oriented people lived in the city, and Berkeley in 1973—even with university enrollments subtracted—was estimated to have seven thousand more people in the 20–29 age group than would a city with an average age distribution.[8] By the mid-1960s, the antiwar movement had grown very strong both in the University and in other parts of the community, and black activism, led most notably by the Black Panther Party, had greatly increased. The counterculture flourished.

The mobilization of the radical activist constituency as a political force in Berkeley began with the campaign of Robert Scheer for Congress in 1966. Scheer mobilized them as supporters in his primary battle against Jeffrey Cohelan, a liberal who had been reluctant to condemn the U.S. involvement in Vietnam. The Scheer campaign exploited the inability of most liberals to criticize U.S. anticommunist foreign policy and it also connected the development of the war in Asia with political repression and economic and social failures at home. Scheer lost in the primary, but he had built up a local organization, and in 1967 it emerged again for local electoral purposes as the Community for New Politics (CNP). As in many other places, antiwar work became frustrating to many people because the targets of their opposition were remote and abstract; for them, municipal politics came to have more appeal. CNP adopted a platform emphasizing much wider public participation in local government, a variety of municipal enterprises, including the purchase of the city's electricity distribution system (owned by the Pacific Gas and Electric Company), real estate and housing construction ventures, a stronger municipal regulatory stance toward business, and a set of redistributive service and tax initiatives. The CNP slate won no seats, but its platform staked a claim to a share of municipal government for those segments of Berkeley's population that were becoming increasingly radicalized. In the next few years, a number of these radical interests made demands on the municipal government, in many respects as an evolution out of the CNP program. The sequence and order of importance of these demands and the events upon which these forces focused are difficult to discuss objectively, but at least the following points are generally agreed upon:

THE POLICE AS AN ISSUE

Berkeley's police department had long been noted for its professionalism, but as student protests on the university campus were joined to demonstrations in the South Campus area and on Telegraph Avenue, the police use of violence in maintaining order became an important issue. It was not a simple one. On the one hand, even a peaceful mass gathering can be threatening to those who do not share its goals and its methods, and the police facing the surging crowds were in such a position. Claims of deliberate provocation of the police in some demonstrations were also made. Some conservative elements of the community demanded that the police take a hard line against protesters. Eventually, the police did so in enough cases that its own violence became an issue for a great many people.

One police officer gave the following explanation of police action in the *Berkeley Gazette* of October 1970:

> Properly this is the duty of the courts. If they don't do it, then we'll have to . . . because of court decisions and numerous advantages they [the demonstrators] have, we've been reduced to where we'll have to hurt them so bad they won't come back . . . the only effective way to combat these things is to hurt them so bad they won't want to come back.[9]

Instances of the police beating protesters whose only crime was to participate in a demonstration were numerous. The most traumatic event, referred to repeatedly by people in Berkeley at the time, was the violence that took place in Peoples Park on May 15, 1969, when the police, including the State Highway Patrol and county sheriff's department, used shotguns on the crowd, killing one person and wounding over one hundred demonstrators.

This use of police force against protesters, the vast majority of whom felt they were involved in legitimate and nonviolent political expression, profoundly radicalized many people, probably thousands, in Berkeley. Loni Hancock, who later became a radical member of the City Council, described her experience with the police in Berkeley during a Free Speech Movement demonstration in 1964:

> Pushing a baby carriage, I walked down to see the demonstration. The current of anger and hope was strong and exhilarating. It was an example of human beings trying to shape an environment that for too long they had been helplessly shaped by. It felt good to be there. There was no sense of fear because at that time we did not know that police would hurt middleclass people.

Later, she heard a radio account of the police dislodging protesters from Sproul Hall, the university's administration building:

> They're stepping on them and kicking them . . . oh my God, they're kicking them and throwing them down the stairs . . . I don't know what's happening to these kids but it looks, it looks horrible . . . they're throwing them down the stairs, their heads jostling and banging against the bannisters and marble stairs.[10]

Hancock took the lesson to heart. Those who led the university were

> morally bankrupt men who had betrayed their students. . . . Instead of allying themselves with young peoples' desire to be politically active and effective, they allied themselves against it. . . . I was 24 years old. My view of the world had been profoundly altered. . . .

She then quoted Mario Savio's well known statement:

> There comes a time when the operation of the machine becomes so odious, makes you so sick at heart, that you can't take part; you can't even tacitly take part, and you've got to put

your bodies upon the gears and upon the wheels, upon the levers, upon all the apparatus and you've got to make it stop. And you've got to indicate to the people that run it, to the people that own it, that unless you're free, the machines will be prevented from working at all.[11]

Numerous participants have testified that this was in no way a unique experience, but rather these were the common effects (on sympathizers) of actual contacts with the demonstrations and the police violence with which they were sometimes met.

PEOPLES PARK

Peoples Park was a block of land south of the university, cleared by the university, which owned the land and intended to put housing on it, but which, for lack of funds, it was leaving vacant. During April 1969, members of the radical community in the area began to work and to solicit funds to build a park on the vacant land. The concept caught on quickly and got a great deal of support. This was because park land was scarce and needed and because the concept challenged the university, which had torn down much needed housing on the site and then had left it vacant to deteriorate further for several months. For a few weeks, many people worked on the park. According to Joel Rubenzahl,

The days following the founding of the park on April 20, 1969, were filled with joy for those working on the park. Plans developed organically by the users were implemented by the users. The concept of 'user-developed, user-maintained' became basic to the growth and functioning of the park.[12]

The university, after first ignoring the situation, then released statements asserting its property rights over the site. When it became clear that there was wide community support for the park, the university moved in on May 15 to build a chain-link fence around the site, thus precipitating the very large protest demonstrations that resulted in the shootings and arrests described above. These events, after a short time, effectively stopped the park's development. But the idea of challenging property rights, of user control of public facilities, and of high popular participation in the creation of public benefits had caught on very generally in a large segment of the population. Among those so affected were architects and city planners who began to elaborate some of these ideas at length.

BERKELEY TENANTS UNION (BTU)

In the wake of the violence in Peoples Park in 1969, many radicals were concerned to capitalize on the massive outpouring of support for the park and turn it to effecting changes in the basic power relationships of the city. Most of the radicals involved rejected electoral strategies as leading inevitably to compromises with that power system. But political organizing around single issues outside the electoral arena was seen as a way to bring about larger changes. As Rubenzahl put it:

> Radicals understood that efforts in one local problem area would not in themselves solve the much more basic societal problems. . . . It was expected, however, that each separate organizing effort would result in the building of a radical organization that eventually would become part of a broadly based radical movement. Only then could fundamental wealth and power relationships be successfully challenged.[13]

The most important example of single-issue organizing in 1969 and 1970 in Berkeley was tenant organizing, coordinated by the Berkeley Tenants Union. The BTU strategy was to seek recognition as the sole collective-bargaining agent for tenants with landlords. When, as expected, the landlords balked at this, BTU thought that masses of tenants would engage in a coordinated rent strike. With eviction proceedings clogging the courts, the landlords, facing tax and mortgage payments, would be forced to sign favorable long-term rental agreements. In fact, only some five hundred renting units actually withheld rents in a February 1970 rent strike, but in the end several collectives did get favorable rental agreements, and in at least one case, the landlord sold out to the renters. BTU organizers hoped that the rent strike would ultimately enlist the support of constituencies other than renters.

> Homeowners would also reap benefits in the long run. Assessed valuations and taxes are supposed to reflect the market worth of property. Since housing has been in such short supply in Berkeley, speculative investors historically have been willing to invest in rental property with the hope of reaping substantial long-term profits. As valuations rise, taxes rise, forcing up rents. Also with real estate speculation, excessive amounts are paid to purchase property and so mortgage payments rise, in turn raising rents, which in turn raises the amount speculators

are willing to pay for rental property. Homeowners are, however, unable to reap the 'benefits' of this system. Even if they sell for a profit, they are forced to compete with speculators for their new home[s] and thus are forced to pay artificially inflated prices.[14]

The logic of building a broad political coalition around tenant organizing did not result in broad political support; this was made clear from the outcome of the rent strike. But BTU did demonstrate the interconnectedness of housing issues in ways that were to emerge again later.

THE DEVELOPMENT OF RADICAL DOCTRINE

The Peoples Park occupation from April 20 to May 15 and its repression thereafter caused a large number of people in Berkeley to stop believing in the established forms of order and to be receptive to new doctrines. Out of this situation came many different ideas for a new order. The initial situation was not organized, but two main themes did emerge: the devolution of municipal government authority, as symbolized first in a proposal for community control of the police, and second, the challenge to property rights inherent in the occupation of Peoples Park by the street people and other users. The property issue was important because its elaboration as doctrine was capable of undergirding a large number of very popular proposals over the next decade: tenant organizing, municipal ownership of utilities, cooperative housing and businesses, rent control, and the Neighborhood Protection Ordinance.

The elaboration of a political doctrine that catches the imagination of large numbers of people can often be a collective enterprise and its development is not likely to be coordinated or planned. But in Berkeley, Edward Kirshner may be the key figure, the person whose activities before and after Peoples Park revealed the most about the ideas that developed, the person who played the focal role, who allowed a number of people to push their schemes relatively far in the direction of collective control over property, in contrast to the more individualistic doctrines held by most people. Kirshner had been an architecture student at Cornell and then at Berkeley in the early 1960s. At Cornell, he had read a book on town planning, Ebenezer Howard's *Garden Cities of Tomorrow* (1897) and became intrigued with its idea of collectively owned and controlled new towns.[15] He later went to work with the Rouse Company, which was planning the new town of Columbia, Maryland, and was thereby exposed to the economic analyses that went into planning a town of 120,000 in the countryside between Baltimore and Washington. But Rouse was not hospitable to collective ownership, and in 1968 Kirshner went back to Berkeley to enroll in the graduate program in city planning. There he spent three years working on a thesis investigating the economics of new towns in the United States and Europe. His key finding, he said later, was that public investment created land values, and therefore that the public ought to reap the benefits of those values:

> What I did then was spend about three years structuring a model based on Columbia and the other new towns in the U.S. . . . comparing it . . . with that proposed by Ebenezer Howard and the European new towns . . . which were generally locally oriented, with local ownership, cooperative ownership, and see if there was any significant difference in those towns. Nicely . . . it did show a difference . . . that is: land value, all land value, is equal to public investment. . . . Urban value is virtually one dollar to one dollar basis related to public investment. . . . That is all land value, private ownership, is a direct transfer from the public till to the private till . . . someone's private pocket. . . . Now that is not a bad idea *per se* if everyone's pocket is open the same as everybody's pocket is open in paying taxes, but that's not true. Ownership is concentrated. Taxes are broad.[16]

Kirshner had not been a Berkeley activist, and he has described himself as having been rather content to pursue his ideas in a technical, academic way. But after Peoples Park, he did get aroused, like many others. In addition, he was able to relate his studies to the mass sentiment that developed on behalf of collective ownership. After experiencing an example of the collective development of an expropriated piece of property, many people were willing to listen and a few were willing to collaborate on working out collective ownership schemes technically with Kirshner. A series of collaborations began that went on for the next few years.

Kirshner's first actions after Peoples Park focused on the Berkeley Tenants Union, which was coordinating the several groups that had initiated rent strikes in 1970. In 1971 he left Berkeley for a year to work in Cambridge, Massachusetts, at the Center for Community Economic Development. There he met a number of people associated with the idea of local economic development in old

TABLE 4.1. **Required Average Incomes under Profit-Oriented and Community-Owned Development**

Ownership Type	Required Income, Assuming Housing = 20% of Income
A. Profit-oriented	
Investor holds for rent	$18,000
Investor sells to residents	15,000
B. Community-owned real estate and utilities	
Individual mortgages	11,500
Group mortgage	11,000
C. Phased tax shelter sale plus B	
Individual mortgages	10,500
Group mortgage	10,000
D. Partial ownership of enterprises and agricultural sector plus B (rural expanded town)	
Individual mortgages	9,200
Group mortgage	8,800
E. Phased tax shelter plus D (rural expanded town)	
Individual mortgages	8,200
Group mortgage	7,800

cities. At the Center, Kirshner produced what may have been the most central elaboration of his ideas: a monograph that applied his thesis conception more extensively to old cities and revealed the core of his programmatic thinking: "We know from the study results that the larger the proportion of community-owned real estate, utilities, and enterprises in a town, the greater the potential benefits to the residents."[17] His study had analyzed the comparative costs to residents of private and public control of city development. A series of savings were possible to residents, depending on how much was brought under public control: real estate and utilities services, tax savings by providing owners the benefits of tax advantages given to developers, and savings from the share residents might have from collective ownership of enterprises and agriculture. Kirshner demonstrated that, compared to the usual type of development, people would need much less income to get the same standard of living in a new town, depending on the type of collective ownership and operation which was adopted, as shown in table 4.1.[18] But, he wrote, there were other issues that needed to be addressed before community ownership could actually be established in existing cities.

(1)"What social, political, and economic objectives can be achieved through community ownership?" Kirshner drew a contrast between limited and broader objectives that might be achieved. Community ownership would mean not just a shift of political control to a new group of (perhaps more representative) power brokers, but

> the first step toward the establishment of a new social vision: a vision of decentralized economic and political control—with a high degree of citizen participation in government and workers' self-management in industry and commerce—which may eventually be linked to similar arrangements on a regional and even national scale.[19]

More specifically, he listed the following detailed objectives of his program: to use the revenues gathered from collective ownership and enterprise operations to reduce property taxes, upgrade the existing housing stock and reduce housing prices; to provide employment opportunities for local residents; to create decentralized services such as community-run day care or drug rehabilitation centers; and generally to upgrade the local economy by providing for more direct reinvestment of city revenues.

(2) "What forms can community ownership take?" Kirshner in this category considered a continuum ranging from "the community as landlord," involving ownership but little risk, to "the community as entrepreneur," extending toward projects with higher stakes: real estate development, the ownership and operation of utilities, then commercial, and finally industrial, ventures.

(3) "What kinds of existing communities have the most potential for success with community ownership?" The experience of community development corporations in poor areas had convinced Kirshner that sufficient funds would not be forthcoming from governmental or private sources unless the affected populations took

political control or achieved significant political influence. Conditions for this kind of control were most promising, he thought, in cities in the 60,000 to 200,000 population range, those with a large industrial work force. While he cited Berkeley as a possibility for such a takeover, he thought the best chances were in the older industrial cities of the Northeast, Southeast, and Midwest. In those places, he wrote, the leverage of national corporations was an obstacle, but the city populations were politically alert and resourceful. Labor unions had raised wages there high enough so that people could afford to invest in their own housing if it were made cheap enough. Furthermore, these populations might be solidified in their resolve by common ethnic, racial, and class identifications, and thus they might be able to react politically to an economic squeeze caused by an unchecked external corporate extraction of profits from the local economy.

> As happened earlier in the black ghettos of large center cities, these realizations could lead blue-collar people to join together over issues of community control. If current economic conditions continue to worsen, there may be a growing understanding that only by countering outside corporate control of the local economic base will real control of the community by its residents be possible.[20]

(4) "What resources and mechanisms exist for initiating and sustaining community ownership?" An important point in Kirshner's argument was his observation that communities have wealth:

> Even poor and working-class communities are very large economic entities. For example, a typical town of 100,000– 125,000 people who have an average family income of $9000–$10,000 per year has a gross income of $400–$500 million annually—well near the top figures of income on *Fortune*'s list of the nation's 500 largest corporations.[21]

The question was how these communities could recapture this wealth from resident individuals for collective and local purposes. He listed some possibilities: city licensing power for such utilities as electric power, local telephone service, cable TV, gas, and water could be used to acquire ownership. Urban renewal and other land acquisition powers could be used to acquire equity interests in land for development purposes. Various city financial reserves, such as pension funds, and the city's authority to issue tax-free municipal bonds, could be used to acquire land and business enterprises. Cities could also bring various pressures to bear on financial institutions to channel their investment funds locally, and cities could arrange limited partnerships to attract outside investors to joint ventures in enterprises the city would manage.

(5) *"What kinds of political strategy and tactics can be developed by local community groups favoring community owner-ship?"* Kirshner proposed some general principles of political strategy. The most basic one was derived from his continuum of risk, as noted above. The community's ownership of real estate would constitute its most valued political strategy. Real estate was the most important economic commodity for the community to capture, for two reasons: it is the least risky and entrepreneurial of economic ventures and thus requires the least skill for success, and it is the least able to relocate, the least footloose of enterprises, the least likely or able to be stripped of assets while the city is acquiring it. In diminishing degrees, these same characteristics held for utilities, and for commercial and industrial ventures. As a second principle, Kirshner advocated political organizing and education to link the interests of single-issue community groups and labor unions in anti-absentee-ownership themes. Finally, he implied a sequence of political objectives: (1) a mixed local economy with the coexistence of community and privately owned enterprises; (2) community capitalism with community ownership of all local real estate and businesses, but competition among communities on behalf of their own ventures and to attract monopolistic national firms; and (3) a decentralized national economy with monopolistic sectors broken up, and a confederation of communities and regions to provide essential coordination.[22]

Kirshner returned to Berkeley in 1972 and started some political collaborations, which applied these ideas in the specific context of Berkeley, in close association with the radical coalition. Somewhat later, he set up the Cooperative Ownership Organizing Project with a foundation grant. Through that organization, he worked with Eve Bach, Joel Rubenzahl, Tom Brom, Lenny Goldberg, and others to set up a number of separate projects. In 1975, the group pulled many of these together in a book, published by the Conference on Alternative State and Local Policies, called *The Cities' Wealth*. Most or all of its contents could be traced back to Kirshner's earlier work.

In this account, I do not mean to attribute too much responsibility for the development of leftist doctrine to one person, though Kirshner's work is pivotal to the following discussion.[23] Central to planning in Berkeley politics in the 1970s was the challenge to property rights that arose after the Peoples Park events of 1969. To this challenge, Kirshner's analytical work was a natural and constructive counterpoint. Moreover, he and his colleagues had come together out of a common experience in the university's graduate program in planning.

The other important theme in later Berkeley politics was the challenge to government authority structures that grew out of the police initiative and later, in one form or another, worked its way through a decade of debate and change in governmental forums. In relation to this and to other important political themes, such as the women's movement and environmentalism, Kirshner was a minor figure.

The Emergence of a Leftist Electoral Program, 1971–1981

The Community for a New Politics (CNP) campaign failed to get any of its three candidates on the City Council in 1967, but the effort provided electoral experience for a core group of activists, and after the election, the skeleton of an organization remained. Ron Dellums, whom CNP had also supported, won a seat on the council in 1967, and Loni Hancock lost narrowly as the candidate of the CNP group in 1969. But the radical community and students had not voted in great numbers in these elections. This situation changed in 1971 when the southwest Berkeley group of the Black Panthers collected enough signatures to put a charter amendment restructuring the police department on the ballot as a voter initiative.

The police proposal has been described as an Oakland idea, but the time was right for many people in Berkeley.[24] It proposed the creation of three separate police departments for three identifiable Berkeley neighborhoods: West Berkeley, which was largely black; the university and South Campus areas, which was composed mostly of students and the university-oriented radical community; and the hills residential section north of the university, which was a white middle-class area. Each department would have an elected group of commissioners and relatively weak central coordination. The proposal appealed to the radical community and to many others. In the aftermath of the police violence, they could identify with the dramatic protests against the police led by the Panthers. After the Peoples Park experience, they could imagine getting involved in community control schemes. The political initiative, which was provided for by Berkeley's charter and sanctioned by traditional California electoral practices, appealed because it was an option of direct voter influence, bypassing the still unappealing problems of electoral and political organization.

While the police initiative mobilized the radicals, the electorally oriented veterans of the CNP, political elements on the campus, and the city's blacks began to organize for City Council elections. What emerged was the "April Coalition," which, in a series of intense and intricate negotiations, agreed on a slate for the four contested council seats: Loni Hancock, who had run previously with the backing of CNP forces; Rick Brown, a student; and two nominees of the Black Caucus, Ira Simmons and D'Army Bailey. Hancock, Simmons, and Bailey won. Coalition members had also given their informal support to incumbent council member Warren Widener's mayoral candidacy, when he seemed to support the police initiative. Widener came to the coalition victory party and for a time was billed in speaking tours as the "radical mayor of Berkeley." But any hopes for a cohesive radical force on the council were premature. Widener quickly aligned himself with the liberal majority, and Bailey and Simmons refused to work with Hancock; for two years the council was polarized and largely unable to effect a program of any sort. But the coalition now had its first official representatives on the council, and a mode of minority advocacy began to develop over the next eight years. Hancock had access to information about the functioning of the city that she was able to exploit to develop a position on pending issues. Each council member was provided with a packet of items for business prior to weekly council meetings, and she established the practice of holding weekly packet meetings with the coalition supporters who served as a volunteer staff, researching various items. Starting in 1971, she used this staff and its work to question the city's budget, and her staff eventually developed an alternative budget for the city, which, though it had no chance of passing, helped to educate the coalition members and to develop their sense of the needs of a political program.

Hancock quickly discovered that she could get little done through the council directly. Instead, the coalition supporters used the knowledge they were getting on the council to formulate and refine their positions and take them directly to the voters through the initiative process. This was to be the pattern until 1979, as Widener served an eight-year term as mayor and the coalition's council membership varied between one and three seats, in addition to the position of auditor (with additional information-gathering capacities) after 1975. Initiatives that the coalition got passed included rent control (in 1972, overturned by a court decision in 1976), the Neighborhood Preservation Ordinance, and the establishment of a Police Review Commission (in 1973), the setting of limits on local campaign funding (in 1974), and the Fair Representation Ordinance (in 1975). These initiatives were important because they effected significant changes in the way Berkeley was governed. They also influenced City Council elections and council behavior even when coalition members were in the minority. The initiatives brought out the vote for the coalition slate. After 1973, coalition member Ying Lee Kelley was elected to the council, so Hancock was no longer alone at council meetings (this helped, for example, by providing a second for putting matters into discussion). The whole pattern of debate shifted to the left, as the liberal majority was forced to deal with issues raised by and within the structure created by the initiatives and the vote mandate they represented. The council began, after 1973, to pass some ordinances of its own that were influenced by coalition positions, even if they were not identical to them. One example was the establishment of a Charter Review Commission in 1972 in the wake of the police initiative—a more moderate way to consider increases in community control.

The Elaboration of Leftist Planning

Starting with Hancock's packet meetings, the coalition's minority strategy of 1971–1979 provided opportunities for city planners, many of whom had participated in the elaboration of radical doctrine that emerged after Peoples Park, to refine their ideas and tailor them specifically to win voter approval. Kirshner began attending the packet meetings, and it was through them that Eve Bach got involved in the coalition for the first time. What evolved can be summarized as follows: (1) the development of municipal and collective enterprises; (2) the development of a public attitude of intervention and regulation of private activity, rather than acceptance of the wisdom and initiative of entrepreneurs and owners; and (3) the establishment of the principle that the collective wisdom of the community is best derived from the widely based participation of citizens rather than from experts on the municipal payroll. This conception of planning represented a certain expansion of the built-environment focus Kent had favored, but—as events later suggested—it was definitely not an abandonment of the notion of physical planning.

MUNICIPAL AND COLLECTIVE ENTERPRISES

Municipal and collective ownership was perhaps the keystone of Berkeley's radical doctrine as it developed at the end of the 1960s. Collective ownership was important because it would provide direct access to sources of revenue and capital and direct experience and the expertise necessary for popular control of those aspects of the economy that were not owned collectively. It would be of symbolic importance also, a signal that popular forces could manage important sectors of the economy and that collective enterprises, whether or not they were municipally owned, could function as yardsticks according to which privately managed firms could be compared and judged. For these same reasons, perhaps, the establishment of collective ownerships was very difficult to bring about. Kirshner had reasoned that the best targets for municipal ownership were those industries unable to move outside the city and affecting great numbers of people directly: housing, such utilities as gas and electric power, and cable television. In the case of housing, collective or public ownership was to be one element in a more comprehensive strategy that emerged from the 1970 rent strikes, a strategy that included rent control, the neighborhood preservation ordinance, zoning revisions, and housing code enforcement, all regulatory measures. The coalition's chief success in establishing collectively owned housing was the Savo Island cooperative housing project, whose prime mover was Joel Rubenzahl, later a member of the Cooperative Ownership Organizing Project with Kirshner, Bach, and others. Rubenzahl began organizing members of the Savo Island neighborhood in South Berkeley in 1972, and slowly he forged support among its black, elderly, and working-class people for the type of project they wanted. They formed themselves into a Project Area Committee and evolved their own form of ownership and control, a "limited equity" co-op, meaning that the amount of equity any member could accumulate was limited by formula, thus insulating the project from the rising market values in the surrounding community. After much negotiation, the committee convinced the federal Department of Housing and Urban Development that they were a legitimate developer and overcame resistance from within the city administration by persistent lobbying of the City Council. Finally, the city contributed $1 million for land acquisition and other costs. The project finally opened in 1979 with fifty-seven of the seventy-two families paying subsidized down payments and monthly payments.

Berkeley instituted other efforts toward collective ownership. It had a thriving cooperative food sector of the economy, starting with a "traditional" cooperative food store, started prior to World War II and the subject of enthusiastic participation. A series of efforts were also made to acquire the electricity distribution system of the private utility, Pacific Gas and Electric, by referendum, the last of which failed narrowly in 1974.[25]

NEW REGULATORY MECHANISMS

Coalition planners devised new regulatory measures relating to housing and land use in particular. In the wake of the 1970 rent strikes, Kirshner and others had devised a comprehensive and many-faceted strategy for housing, including a substantial move toward collective ownership to be supported by the city. One part of this strategy that gained support after 1971 was the idea of rent control regulated by the city. A Fair Rent Committee was formed in 1971 and a group including Marty Schiffenbauer, Rick Ilgen, and Nick Rabkin went to work writing a rent control law. With support from the April Coalition, the university-based Tenant Action Project, and the Berkeley Tenants Union, the law passed by initiative in June 1972. It was later characterized as a "strong" law. It established base rents, rolled back to their August 1971 levels. It applied to all private rentals for housing. It regulated evictions. Rent increases or decreases as well as evictions had to be approved by an elected five-member rent control board. During the election for the rent control board, a slate of candidates backed by the April Coalition and the Berkeley Tenants Union further explained the rationale behind the law. Regulating rents and evictions, they said, would lower profits on housing, thus discouraging the private speculative development that was causing overcrowding and driving poor people out of the city. But the law would not provide for new housing at low prices. For that, they urged the creation of "a municipal housing materials cooperative that could be financed through city bonds." But they saw rent control and these other programs only as a first step, to regulate the existing property relations between tenants and landlords; a real change in the dependency of tenants on land-lords would require a "political movement that demands basic changes in the property relations of this society."[26]

But while they recognized the limits of a regulatory approach, they did intend to regulate aggressively, as indicated in the following proposals:

> Cost decreases, such as that resulting from reduced property taxes or financing costs, should be routinely passed on to tenants as rent decreases.
>
> In adjusting rents, the Rent Control Board should eliminate speculative profit.
>
> The Rent Control Law ends arbitrary evictions by Berkeley landlords based on lifestyle, politics, or personal dislike.
>
> The Rent Control Board should not allow evictions for demolition until the equivalent housing in the community has been provided for the occupants.[27]

Wherever possible, the coalition slate urged that the Rent Control Board use its powers to regulate discrimination in housing, that it work for a stronger fair housing ordinance, provide counseling services for tenants, and work for the creation of tenant unions to negotiate lease agreements with landlords.

This program and slate proved too radical for many members of the coalition, and it did not prevail in the January 1973 election. Instead, a "moderate" slate won. But many thought the Board still functioned as an effective force. Hancock said,

> They hired Dan Siegal, a radical Berkeley attorney . . . set up working procedures, and began opening lines of communication with the people who had sponsored the rent control measure. The Rent Control Board became a fine example of the possibility of left and middle working together in Berkeley.[28]

Before the rent control law could really be tested in practice, the landlord interests took it to court and won; a series of appeals finally failed in 1976. In the interim, rent control and tenant organizing was in limbo. In 1977, the Berkeley Tenants Union reformed and collected enough petition signatures to put another strong rent control measure on the ballot, but there were divisions within the coalition that would support a moderate but not a strong measure, and it failed. A more moderate rent and eviction control law finally passed in 1980.

A regulatory effort that paralleled the efforts made on behalf of rent control was the Neighborhood Preservation Ordinance, passed by initiative in 1973. This was the first in a series of housing moves supported in the main by moderate-income homeowners in the "flatlands," the two-thirds of the city between the bay and the Berkeley Hills. What these homeowners had in common with the tenants was the perception that speculative apartment building was causing a general deterioration in neighborhood conditions. In this case, the problem was not high rents, but the aesthetic and physical deterioration of the environment. During 1972, John Denton and Martha Nicoloff led a series of community meetings with flatlands neighborhood groups that resulted in a draft of the preservation ordinance. After being turned down by the Planning Commission and put off by the City Council, they collected enough signatures to put it on the ballot in April 1973, at which time it passed.

The Neighborhood Preservation Ordinance effectively removed building permit-granting power from the city staff and gave it to the Board of Adjustment. It prohibited any residential building permit from being granted without the prior grant of a use permit, after a public hearing. Use permits were to be granted only upon a finding that the new construction would not "under the circumstances of the particular case" be detrimental to the neighborhood, that the developer would conform to the city's affirmative action rules, that there would be no significantly harmful environmental impacts from the building, and that for any development of four or more units, at least 25 percent of them would be low-income units. In addition, no demolitions of residential units would be allowed unless it could be shown that they would cause no net loss to the city's housing supply. The ordinance also mandated a review of the city's Master Plan and zoning ordinances with neighborhood participation within two years, after which the Neighborhood Preservation Ordinance would be replaced by a new zoning ordinance. The Master Plan was revised and the zoning law amended eventually along the lines laid down by the Neighborhood Preservation Ordinance.

The Neighborhood Preservation Ordinance set in motion a series of neighborhood-oriented moves by the city, helped along by constant public pressure. Two of particular importance were the Neighborhood Traffic Study and the Neighborhood Parks initiative of 1975. Neighborhood residents in the flatlands had become concerned about the use of their streets for channeling traffic between the freeway along the bay and places of work and residence at the university and hills to the East. They succeeded in getting a study done, and used it as the basis for their demand that certain intersections be blocked off to through-traffic by means of a "diverter" (a barrier that allows turns, but no through-traffic). After resistance from certain city departments, some neighborhoods managed to get the diverters installed. They proved to be both workable and popular, and soon they were in use all over the city. The Neighborhood Parks initiative of 1975 provided a "tax override" that set aside a fund for the establishment of local parks. These were to be planned with neighborhood participation. This procedure was followed with good results in several neighborhoods.

PARTICIPATION VS. STAFF EXPERTS

Among the commitments that infused planning at the beginning of the coalition's participation in the council in 1971 was a commitment to widespread public participation in city politics. Perhaps the major achievement of coalition in Berkeley politics, at least up until 1979, was a series of measures that opened up public participation in government generally. Planning issues played a major, if not leading, role in increasing such participation.

Perhaps this train of events was started by the promotion of the police initiative and by the style of the coalition's participation in the City Council starting in 1971. The police initiative set forth a structural model that both attacked the city manager form of government and appealed to a wide range of voters who felt they were not being well served by that type of government. It would have delivered essential control over an important service into the hands of the neighborhoods, who then would have been free to organize their own representative bodies and to bargain with the city government from a position of some strength. Even though this seemed extreme to a majority of Berkeley voters in 1971, it also dramatized a position from which less strong variants might still be pursued. It launched a debate about a series of public experiments that coalition leaders could put in front of the voters. In a different way, coalition forces assaulted the stylistic traditions of council-manager government. D'Army Bailey and Ira Simmons, the black members of the council elected by the coalition, initiated a confrontational pattern of politics that infuriated and frustrated the other council members; issues were raised in such a way that the kind of collegial atmosphere in which the council had formerly done its business, despite differences, was destroyed. Hancock's lower-keyed but persistent inquiries into the city administration were also damaging to the existing pattern of minimal council involvement. That pattern had established a separation whereby the council tried to set policies based on positions that had been worked up by the city administration. Hancock, who found the city staff to be "a group of polite and supercilious men," reported the following:

> Control of information tends to define what can be done and what sorts of ideas can be discussed productively. With the help of many volunteers, I set out to get as much information as possible about how the city was really run. After great effort, I was able to get an actual line-item budget proposal from the city manager. I was told by an assistant city manager that it was the first time a council member had ever wanted to work from anything other than a summary pamphlet.[29]

Hancock had also been instructed "never to address a question to any staff member except the city manager, because that would 'destroy the chain of command in the city.'" This strict separation of policy making and administration protected a kind of internal unspoken consensus on the rules of operation of the government, a consensus that could not survive the kinds of diversity being produced in Berkeley politics after the 1960s. Bailey's style and Hancock's persistent and well-documented questioning began to break this consensus down, setting in motion a chain of events by which the council and, ultimately, the city administration would come to reflect actual diverse city positions inside their own organizations.

This opening up of debate began to happen in many areas, but land use and housing issues, including the operation of the planning board and planning department, were among the most important battlegrounds. The planning department and the planning commission, after being a focal point for reform during the 1950s and early 1960s, had settled into a relatively minor political role. The planners took no major initiatives and mainly contented themselves with being a locus of zoning administration. Even there, they were sufficiently inactive such that when the neighborhood groups became concerned about apartment building, the initiative process had to be used for passage of the Neighborhood Preservation Ordinance. That measure was passed over the opposition of the planning department and commission. Partly at stake in this opposition was the principle of professional expertise, defined as apolitical, with the policy making function reserved for the council. Later, Dorothy Walker, a member of the planning commission, described the group that put the Neighborhood Preservation Ordinance together as a small segment of the community that simply wanted to stop the construction of housing—a reactionary position in her opinion. In her opinion, they had less legitimacy than did the deliberations of the planning commission and its staff.[30] Similarly, the planning department staff resisted implementing the master plan revision, and only did so after prodding by the coalition and neighborhood forces. But once passed, the ordinance helped to unleash popular forces in the neighborhoods that continued to exert pressure on the planning department and commission, so that, in the context of later measures, public participation continued to open up.

One important contextual factor contributing to this debate was the establishment of the Charter Revision Commission in 1972. This body of fifty-six members, appointed by the City Council, deliberated for three years, initially on the basis of a wide consensus on the failure of the council-manager form of government. The two major reform proposals they presented were for a system of proportional representation (which would guarantee a council seat to any political faction getting one ninth of the overall vote) and for a large council, including six at-large members and twenty-nine members elected from small districts, with a full-time and adequately paid executive committee chosen from among them to replace the city manager. The majority on the Charter Revision Commission ultimately rejected both of these proposals. Apparently when it came down to details, this majority, initially dissatisfied with the manager form, remained unconvinced by the alternative of having elected people involved in the details of formulating policy positions and implementing them. Joel Rubenzahl, a coalition member of the commission, tried to explain the final switch.

> Those opposed argued that the present system was 'democratic enough' and refused . . . to confront the relative merits of the proposed and present systems. I believe that the perhaps unconscious fear of losing influence and power kept the majority from risking short-term losses . . . it had a potential effect on who would be the ruling majority in the future. [But this] was never thoroughly analyzed.[31]

These coalition proposals had roots that linked them to earlier reform Democrat programs of the 1950s and 1960s. The early proposals of T. J. Kent, Jr. for city planning had emphasized the role of the council over that of the city manager, and Kent had seen physical planning as a way of mobilizing opinion and framing issues around land use. He and Rubenzahl authored a minority report to the City Council that argued the advantages of a full-time over a part-time council.

> There is no way that a part-time citizen governing body can effectively control the full-time staff of the city government of a heterogeneous community like Berkeley. In the absence of citizen control, top members of the full-time staff make the difficult decisions that must be made to keep the government operating. Inevitably, many of the important questions . . . involve political judgments. As a consequence, top staff members become political decision makers.[32]

It is possible to formulate a different hypothesis from Rubenzahl's about why the liberal majority of the 1970s was unable to accept the institution of full-time council positions and, therefore, full popular participation in government. The hierarchical structure of council-manager government provides a kind of stability for the relationship between council members and city administrators—not only the city manager, but other department heads. This can act as a shield for the council member. Prevented from knowing too much, the council member has to spend less time on issues, and can deflect constituency demands, while still enjoying participation in *some* policy questions and the fiction of ultimate control in others. Thus, in the past, council members had avoided the details of administration. In the 1970s, this system would also allow them to avoid contact—at times excruciatingly painful—with those people in the city who were radically different from them: blacks, students, and the counterculture, for example.

In the end, little came of the charter revision proposals. The coalition had a chance to think through and air their ideas and to further gauge what they were up against in the Berkeley Democratic Club majority. But little by little, they chipped away at Berkeley's government structure by means of other reforms. They passed initiatives limiting local campaign financing in 1974, and in 1975, they were successful in passing initiatives requiring council confirmation of all department heads, and changing the council voting majority required to remove the city manager from six-three to five-four.

These alterations in the rules by which Berkeley's government operated were capped by the passage by initiative of the Fair Representation Ordinance of 1975, which provided for partisan representation on the city's boards and commissions. The reform Democrats of the early 1960s had tried in relation to City Council appointments to make sure that all political factions were fairly represented, and it was a practice that was followed for about a decade. But political factions were less contentious then, there weren't as many boards and committees, and the committee style was problem-solving in nature, not political. By the 1970s, all this had changed, and when coalition members Hancock and then Kelley found that the council's committee on appointments was excluding coalition members, they sought a change. Not satisfied with the results they were getting within the council, in 1975 they put the Fair Representation Ordinance on the ballot by petition. This measure simply stipulated that all boards and commissions appointed by the City Council would have memberships in multiples of nine, so that each council member would appoint an equal number of committee members. The result was a basic structural change in the handling of issues in Berkeley's government. It provided each council member with his or her own representative person on each board, a person with whom to discuss and analyze the issues. On the boards, on the other hand, interactions continued to be less polarized than in the City Council; more of a problem-solving atmosphere prevailed than was possible in the council. Furthermore, for coalition people at least, these board memberships provided recruitment opportunities and training for council service.

Planning under the Radical Coalition, 1979–1981

The coalition had gone up and down in electoral representation throughout the 1970s. They had Hancock on the City Council in 1971, then Hancock and Kelley after 1973, then in 1975 Hancock, Kelley, and Denton on the council, plus Florence McDonald as auditor. Then in 1977 Kelley lost, but in 1979, McDonald, Fukson, and Denton were elected council members, Gus Newport became mayor, and Anna Rabkin won as auditor. Ironically, it was rent control—the same issue that had dragged the Berkeley Citizen Action (BCA) to defeat in 1977—that contributed to its victories in 1979. What made the difference was the passage of Proposition 13 in 1978, which provided for a cap on property taxes. That measure had been promoted with promises of rent rebates, to be derived when landlords passed on their savings to tenants, but had resulted instead in a wave of rent increases, which had the immediate effect of generating a series of rent control laws that quickly passed in California. As a result of Proposition 13, some local electorates moved to the left, making B C A seem less radical.[33]

Thus by 1979 the coalition had four out of nine council seats (the mayor votes on the nine-member council, the auditor does not). But a fifth member, Carole Davis, joined in alliance with B C A council members on at least some issues, and so there was an expectation that the coalition could effectively govern the city. This expectation resulted in significant changes in the issues the coalition could press, and in its success in doing so. The shift to a nominal leadership position was certainly significant. On the other hand, the instability of actual majority votes in council counted against their success, especially when Davis began increasingly to vote against the coalition. Finally, the worsening fiscal condition of the city as the impact of California's Proposition 13 taxing constraints began to bite crippled many coalition programs.

The 1979 B C A slate was, to begin with, quite different from the one that had operated as a minority position in the previous decade. B C A had broken with Simmons and Bailey and had not elected a black to the council (though it had run some) since 1971. Hancock left the City Council to take a position as director of the regional office of A C T I O N (the federal agency responsible for V I S T A and the Peace Corps) in 1979. In 1973, the coalition had debated its positions vigorously, its two factions being known as the "ideological caucus" and the "pragmatic caucus." By the 1975 campaign, the former group had largely dropped out, and the coalition had reformed itself as B C A.[34] In 1979 many in B C A felt grave misgivings when Gus Newport was put forth as candidate for mayor, because his rhetoric seemed too radical, too ideological. But with Hancock out of the picture, Newport was the main new factor within B C A when it took office in 1979; as it turned out, he was to be an enormous source of strength to them once in office. He was a black and had at least the potential for mobilizing black support that would not be available to any other B C A council member. As it turned out, he got on well personally with the council. He was called the "glue that held B C A together." In practice, although he was a visionary in some of his goals, he turned out to be a pragmatic politician. By 1981, B C A was composed of thirty or more community groups and had 2,300 dues-paying members.[35]

HOUSING AND EMPLOYMENT PROGRAMS

As mayor, Newport took the lead in trying to move two major liberal programs in housing and employment toward B C A objectives.

The major housing program under Widener had been a rehabilitation program, started in 1974 and involving the creation of a new Department of Housing and Development. The program by the end of 1974 had channeled city and federal money into a code enforcement program in several neighborhoods. After that, it used federal community development revenue-sharing funds in the same way. In addition to housing rehabilitation, the city had provided some new housing through the urban renewal program. It resisted building housing in the West Berkeley Industrial Park, but it went ahead with the locally planned and BCA-supported Savo Island project, which opened in 1979 as the new BCA council was taking office. The BCA criticized Widener's housing program because, in focusing on rehabilitation, it was subsidizing lenders and contractors as much as owners and renters, while the proportion of the subsidies passed on to consumers was inadequate. What was needed, they maintained, was direct collective ownership and construction of new housing, along with rent control. The problem with new construction, however, was that financing for housing skyrocketed after 1979 and so the new BCA council was severely limited in what it could do. It got a commitment to convert part of the West Berkeley redevelopment project into housing units, only to be stopped by the costs. It began planning for another limited-equity housing cooperative on University Avenue, a project to be built on the Savo Island model, which was completed by 1982.

Rent control made a comeback under BCA in 1980: A "moderate" rent and eviction control measure was passed by initiative after the council had passed a series of temporary measures amid strong counter-pressures from landlords and realtors and from advocates of much stronger measures. The new law regulated rents and evictions for perhaps 70 percent of the city's residential tenants. It provided for a council-appointed administrative board. It exempted owner-occupied properties of four or fewer units. The operations of the board and staff were to be financed from a $12 per unit registration fee. Operation of the board proved to be both difficult and controversial for BCA. Nearly half of the city's forty-five hundred landlords refused to pay their registration fees, creating the threat that the Rent Stabilization Board could become bankrupt and be unable to enforce the law for lack of funds. All of this meant that a good deal of staff time was spent on court actions to obtain registrations and fees, rather than on the regular operations of the law. A BCA-appointed board member caused embarrassment for the city manager when she was arrested on a minor charge. The appointment of board members became a difficulty later on, when , after BCA lost some council seats in 1981, some new board appointees began to work against the purposes of the rent control proponents—notably by advocating the granting of rent increases based on changes in the market value of property. But no majority was advocating the dismantling of rent control even then, and rent control in principle seemed secure, even if its particulars were at the administrative mercy of the council majority.

Economic development policy was Newport's most important priority when he took office, but, as in the case of housing, it was a policy area fraught with difficulties. Widener's administration, despite the careful thought given to economic programs by such liberals as Margaret Gordon, had been quite traditional on this issue. The West Berkeley Industrial Park had gone nowhere as an attraction for traditional manufacturing industries. CETA and previous employment and job-training programs were being cut. BCA spokespersons had put a good deal of energy into developing alternative economic strategies, but had gotten little official response. *The Cities' Wealth* was one example of such alternative strategies, and Kirshner and Bach, at a BCA press conference before the 1975 election, had described their proposals as an "economic plan," including such components as a large housing-rehabilitation program, the reinstatement of rent control, and a shift of tax burdens from property owners to a progressively structured income tax on corporations, businesses, commuters, and residents.[36]

Hancock had proposed the creation by the City Council of an Economic Development Commission, and this was finally accomplished in 1976. The Economic Development Commission eventually (in 1978) produced a plan, after extensive public meetings and with BCA participation. Widener and the 1978 City Council refused to consider this plan, and the commission was disbanded, so that when BCA moved into leadership in 1979, no real development policy existed. After the election, the new council began serious consideration of the 1978 plan, holding public hearings in May and July.[37] By October, it appeared that BCA wanted a stronger set of economic objectives than had been included in the previous plan: The benefits of economic development should include jobs for young people, for minorities, women, the disabled, and senior citizens; the focus should be on new technologies and services, such as alternative nonpolluting production methods, alternative energy sources, and specialized food products; attempts should be made to reduce alienation and exploitation in the workplace and marketplace; the development effort should include a balanced emphasis on private, public, and cooperative enterprises, rather than exclusive reliance on any-one alone; a greater emphasis should be placed on local control and the avoidance of capital leaks from the community.

Newport supported this shift in the direction of the develop-ment plan, but problems arose, particularly in city staffing, in put-ting together an effective implementation scheme. He contracted with a consultant team for an analysis of the whole economic devel-opment process. Their conclusions, which they presented in a brief report in February 1980, were that Berkeley needed to resolve a cli-mate of conflict between too-simply-conceived pro-business and anti-business factions in the community, to decide exactly what kinds of business ventures and public initiatives could productively interact, and to supply the public staff and funds necessary to start the process. Furthermore, they implied, the leadership of the mayor and a more concrete plan of action were both critical. Sub-stantively, the report warned of serious problems in the way of achieving many of the goals the B C A had for economic development. First, the B C A had made too much of a principle of neighborhood preservation and existing housing interests, to the point where busi-ness interests might hesitate to invest in Berkeley. Second, decision makers in Berkeley were against traditional types of business, to the point where they appeared to be anti-business: "According to the amended economic development plan, 'There is a widely held, and possibly a majority opinion, in this community that businesses whose primary goal is to maximize profits, have not met and cannot meet the community's needs by themselves.'"[38] Instead, the consul-tants found, Berkeley preferred community enterprises, businesses owned or controlled by the neighborhoods, or by worker or consumer cooperatives, or by the community at large. But, they said,

> there is little systematic evidence to suggest that there are stable, long-term employment or business opportunities in the areas chosen as preferred. . . . Simply put, what is known cur-rently about economic development is limited to the more tra-ditional opportunities and strategies.[39]

However sobering this advice may have been for B C A members in relation to their goals, the city nevertheless went ahead with its economic planning. Staff people in both the planning department and the city manager's office proceeded to explore both traditional and nontraditional development possibilities. The planning depart-ment produced a revision of the earlier economic plan, which was adopted late in 1980 by the City Council with its final objectives somewhat moderated. At the same time, the city got a windfall in development funds: a $500,000 grant from the federal government just before the 1980 presidential election, which it used to initiate a revolving loan fund for small businesses. Finally, Newport commissioned a new economic plan to be produced by University of California professors Ann Markusen and Marc Weiss and a team of graduate student researchers. The new analyses, however, were not begun in time to be available before the April 1981 elections, when the BCA group lost control of the council. There did not appear to be any prospect that the new majority on the City Council would use the Markusen-Weiss analyses.

Newport's economic development efforts produced no big successes, although he made some progress by initiating several programs and by mapping out a set of policies that were in place and promised to be continued under the new council. BCA had made a big effort to reach out to alternative energy businesses, but they were difficult to organize into an effective constituency because they were largely apolitical. Another group of businessmen organized themselves under the acronym BUILD to set up a development corporation. This group, characterized by one observer as "hip capitalists," did find it possible to work with BCA and Newport. But one of their key characteristics was an aversion to official government. The appeal of a development corporation was that it was a way to get access to government loan funds and other such support without dealing with City Hall.

THE CITY MANAGER'S OFFICE: ALLEN AND BACH

As it happened, the main energies of the BCA group when it came into office in 1979 were devoted not to housing or economic development, but to the immediate demands of management and budget. The new council was confronted with a city administration that faced severe cutbacks in real financial resources due to inflation and revenue losses. Proposition 13 was beginning to have its effects, and the proportion of the city budget supported by property taxes had dropped from 23.5 percent in fiscal year 1977–1978 to 7.1 percent in 1979–1980.[40] The budget proposed by then-city-manager Michael Lawson had adapted to projected revenue losses by cutting many of the programs that were important to BCA. Upon taking office, the new council took on the budget as its first major task. It appointed a twenty-seven-member Citizens Budget Review Commission, and delayed implementation of the proposed budget while the commission deliberated on ways to change the priorities for cuts and to raise new revenues. Eve Bach, who acted as chairperson for the committee, later described its efforts as "heroic." It made a series of changes that moved the financial burdens in a progressive direction. Where the proposed budget had advocated closing two firehouses and had cut 46.5 fire and police positions at the point of service, the new budget cut nineteen higher-level staff jobs. The commission also changed the fee structures to lift tax burdens for low- and middle-income people: they charged instead higher parking-meter rates, higher building permit fees, new marina use fees. They also proposed a split-roll property tax for library use, with business property taxed at a higher rate, thus taking some pressure off general fund revenues.[41]

For about a year the city staff resisted the new council. Lawson resigned soon after the election, and the BCA forces deliberated on a successor. At the urging of Carole Davis, the non-BCA swing vote on the council, they selected Wise Allen, a black with administrative and faculty experience at a Bay Area college. Allen was on the job by early 1980, and it was not until then that the new council began to get its staffing in order. Eve Bach moved into the city manager's office in mid-1980. But the city administration, between the April 1979 and April 1981 elections, was transitional, because both the leadership and the programs were changed drastically. BCA's style had been to rely on a lot of citizen input from outside of government. When it took control, this pattern continued. The Citizens Budget Commission served as major mechanism for making policy, and each council member had a group of advisors. The mayor had an informal group of advisors. The council staff members became a close-knit group. But it was a year before they were able to start using the formal machinery of government effectively.

THE ROLE OF PLANNING UNDER BCA

When the members of the April Coalition and later the BCA had been in the minority, their planning efforts had been informal, intense, and often dramatic. After 1975, planning by BCA forces moved closer to the government machinery. McDonald spent time in workshops on local economic policy with Bach, Kirshner, and others, and Hancock promoted—with eventual success—the establishment of the Economic Development Commission. The Economic

Development Commission and the Planning Commission became special BCA forums.

When BCA got control of the council in 1979, official governmental planning seemed to go into eclipse, though this may have been a temporary effect associated with personnel shifts. Bach, who had been connected with earlier planning efforts in support of BCA, moved into a more fiscal and management role under Allen. Fukson, who had been on the Planning Commission, was now on the City Council. The chairman of the Planning Commission, Fred Collignon, thought BCA had retreated from its planning interests:

> We got more done substantively on the Planning Commission as a minority. The BCA appointees on the commission could get the assent of the Democratic appointees, so that there was an effective BCA majority on the planning commission, despite their minority status on the City Council. This changed after 1979. The new BCA council majority had all gotten their first experience on the Planning Commission, and now on the council they felt they knew the issues. They asked the planning commission to stop taking initiatives.[42]

Collignon fought for a separate planning function—for the Planning Department to remain performing its clear-cut function of doing comprehensive planning as a basis for land use controls—while Allen considered whether planning ought not to be moved within the city manager's office. In response to these considerations, Collignon addressed Allen in a memorandum:

> That a tension will arise between the planning function—with its comprehensive and longer-range vision of the city's needs and goals—and the short-run budget and political pressures and constraints that invariably fall on any particular city manager or council is inherent in city governance. Such a tension should be expected and encouraged as necessary for the protection of the city's longer-run welfare.[43]

Collignon elaborated on this argument in this way:

> You need a group that *thinks* of itself as independent of council. It can take heat for the council. It can broker negotiations before issues go to council. A member of council acting in public can't as readily compromise as can a member of the commission. Despite being appointees of the council, the commission was able to come to agreement on things the council could not agree on.[44]

Collignon eventually prevailed, at least in principle, and Allen and the council left the Planning Commission intact. At the same time, the main efforts of the BCA planners were concentrated on day-to-day crises. Bach, a key planner in the BCA government, was oriented this way, and she saw little alternative: she wanted to stay where the action was. Collignon thought she was the "soul of BCA," scrupulously honest to the point that, as a result, BCA's fiscal responsibility exceeded that of the previous liberal regime.

BCA's planning stance, however, again raised a problem that had been inherent in the structure of the city's government since Kent had joined the Planning Commission in the 1940s. How could the city do planning and also encourage high public participation? Kent had provided one answer: Keep planning restricted to land use issues, and nail the City Council with the need to face those issues. Later councils had let planning become mainly a bureaucratic affair. The BCA, as a minority, had combined planning functions with popular participation in a vigorous way, and had used them to bludgeon the majority. In office, BCA changed its style somewhat, but its planning efforts continued to come from outside the bureaucracy as well as within it: the rent stabilization ordinance, the University Avenue housing, and some of the economic development initiatives Newport had encouraged all came from groups outside the city government. This was partly due to BCA's ideological commitments and values: having built its strength on participatory innovations, BCA, once it was in City Hall, would find it difficult to turn participation off.

Perhaps the most fundamental function of importance that planning provided to BCA was its provision of a context for many of their actions over a long period of time. Veronika Fukson, the City Council member who guided the 1980 rent control measures through the council, cited the usefulness of her previous participation in several years of planning and programmatic discussions:

> The presence of a plan helped me to do two things. It helped give a context over the years to make you more secure in what you were doing. And because it's a plan to which many people are committed, it maintains a presence in people who want to do it, as well as corrects the tendencies of those who would rather not do it. If we did not have the history of concern for tenants and the 1972 law it would have been harder to stand up to [radicals on the left] and landlords who were calling for our recall—to actually push the 1980 law. And that's a com-

fort from loneliness. It would be lots more difficult to face a hostile audience, and then walk around a community trying to
sell it.[45]

Planners had indeed long been prominent in BCA. Kirshner
and Bach had had their first involvements in professional planning
education in the middle sixties, and later others such as Rubenzahl
and Anna Rabkin got graduate planning degrees at the university.
But the way planning reinforced BCA was general, rather than
specific. It set a context, an agenda, and set forth a repertoire of
problems and approaches to their solutions. It was not a map to be
used in detail, though in some cases the analyses and proposals that
went into planning—only to be changed later—were quite detailed
and specific. The planning function and the programmatic discussions associated with it thus supported later innovations, without
really limiting the spontaneous, problem-solving character of the
administration under a progressive leadership.

Bach, looking back on her and Kirshner's planning efforts
early in the 1970s, was reluctant to give them much practical
weight:

> It is true that [Kirshner] had a coherent plan of many parts
> that I and others helped to elaborate, package, refine, and in a
> few cases to implement. But that is not what held the coalition
> together, or not even what allowed groups of people to bond or
> not to bond.[46]

Bach put more practical weight on day-to-day bargaining:

> More important to the coalition on a practical basis—to any
> political coalition, really—is whether candidates and elected
> officials would (1) give them their traffic light; (2) prevent an
> apartment house from going in next door; and (3) keep their
> rents stable. The more visionary goals of controlling property
> speculation concern very few people.[47]

She even thought that planning—in the sense of an overview or
framework—might be "antithetical" to one of BCA's main achievements, which was untracking the city bureaucracy: "To the extent
that citizen participation means different constituents out there
pushing for their own needs, an overview is antithetical." But even
participation was limited in what it could achieve:

> I believe that citizen participation was an important factor in
> untracking the city bureaucracy . . . but that it has not been

able to retrack it—that is, to integrate redistributive goals. This for a variety of reasons—the interface with other, establishment-controlled institutions (the courts, the county, the Feds, the state); the design of the machinery of local government as the sole provider of service related to protection of physical plant, as provider of infrastructure . . .[48]

BCA planners, in my interviews with them, tended to downplay the existence of coherent planning on their part, even though there was a tangible history of it. They were more interested in project-oriented analyses, in getting things done. But the plans were in their heads, as a collective sense of the future, nevertheless. Neither Bach nor Kirshner could remember the "economic plan for Berkeley," which they had unveiled at a press conference prior to the 1975 municipal elections (mentioned in the previous section of this chapter). When faced with the news clipping, Bach said, "That must have been a press statement we put together from our ideas we had formulated earlier." But they had formulated enough of a program—they had recently finished writing *The Cities' Wealth* —to make the statement. Bach and Kirshner were different from the pragmatists of the left and the right, those who preferred action (or inaction) without the patience to work out the deeper foundation for it or long-term strategy. Kirshner distanced himself from the more impatient organizers and activists who associated themselves with various Berkeley radical causes—"I can't *stand* that stuff," he once said.[49] He preferred careful thought. On the whole, that attitude pervaded BCA planning and was an important influence, through the planners, on BCA generally.

The Liberal Response to BCA Programs

There is a thread of continuity between the early liberal planning movement in Berkeley and the later emergence of the radical coalition in the BCA. Kent's earlier formulation was that physical planning around land use issues should be participatory and taken before the City Council. This was realized by the BCA as it had been, earlier, by the City Council when Kent was on it. Consistent with this, Kent ultimately allied himself with BCA. On the other hand, the differences between BCA and Widener's administration and the council majority of 1971–1979, and between BCA and the council majority elected in 1981, were substantial.

On the one hand, the personal antipathy between the two factions was immense. The main thing I sensed in my 1981 interviews with "liberals" was hurt and anger. My first instinct was to discount these feelings as merely "personal" and to look for structural and economic differences to account for the conflicts among the factions in Berkeley politics. Later, I began to think of the anger itself as a clue, as the key issue itself. I tried to find its roots. One person felt excluded:

> I was initially a supporter of the left in Berkeley but I abandoned them when I saw how authoritarian they really were. That is, the left was only for some people, not others. It was really just a small group of people who had the answers, which they wanted to impose on the rest. The Neighborhood Protection Ordinance was an example. It came from certain people in the neighborhoods who put it together and then, since it was passed by initiative, it couldn't be changed. I think I was naive initially about the level of organization they had.[50]

What none of the liberals had shared was the experience of "radicalization" many BCA people described, particularly around the issues raised by the events of Peoples Park. They had experienced neither the stripping away of confidence in authority that Hancock mentioned, nor the sense of possibility and exhilaration that attended some of the projects adopted after the Peoples Park project, with their suggestion of the peoples' expropriation of property rights. For many liberals, it might simply have been a lack of contact with these experiences that accounted for their lack of impact. As Sennett suggests in *The Uses of Disorder*, a certain type of middle-class liberal could turn his or her back on the real issues of the inner city just by living in the suburbs; and many professionals and bureaucrats did lead similarly insulated lives. Politically, they were not mobilized. This could be even more true, perhaps in a university town.

But perhaps political mobilization was not even the most important question. Many liberals had experienced the main events of this time and been mobilized by them, but they had seen them differently. Andrea Washburn, a newly-elected Democratic council member in 1981, described her first motivation to enter public life in a way that clearly contrasted with Loni Hancock's in substance, but not in relation to the intensity of the experience: She arrived home one day in the early 1970s to find her home broken into. She had little children with her, and the thief was still in the house. It was only because she went in the front door yelling that he went out the back, or the children would have had to confront him. She was outraged at the violation of her home. Soon after, she joined the Berkeley police auxiliary. After training, she rode around in patrol cars. Later, when Berkeley established a Police Review Commission, she had herself appointed to it. Still later, she ran for the City Council and won in 1981.

Washburn was different from the members of the BCA faction, not so much because she had been mobilized, but because she had been mobilized in a different way. Her differences with the BCA, she said, were matters more of style than of actual policy. She thought they had a "lot of crazy ideas," made personal attacks on people in public, and did a lot of grandstanding on issues. Washburn held no major alternative policy conceptions, but she did think that by common sense and a willingness to negotiate she could help the liberal Democrats run the government better than the BCA could.

The members of the new liberal majority that took control of the City Council in 1981 tended to share Washburn's view. In addition, their governing style seemed to have two other differentiating characteristics: a greater tendency than BCA had to entrust government to the staff and city manager, and a greater reliance on the private sector and market. Both of these characteristics cut down enormously on the number of substantive issues facing the majority. BCA, by relying on extensive citizen participation, had faced the issue of exactly how to reform the official city machinery. Perhaps the enormity of this problem was fully demonstrated by the efforts of the Citizens Budget Review Commission. The liberals were much more cautious in using public participation or in criticizing city employees. In these tendencies, they were surely encouraged by many of the professionals working for the city, who preferred more autonomy for their work and less criticism from outside. The result of all these factors was to encourage council members to limit themselves to oversight functions and to allow the details of policy to be formulated by the city manager. The second tendency also simplified matters: by letting the market decide many issues, certain problems could be simply avoided. Liberals, for example, did not face the question of encouraging the cooperative sector in economic policy. They could let the market decide. The great advantage of liberalism was that it cut down the scope and substance of issues.

In reviewing this history, we get a sense that some radicals and some liberals simply caricatured their most basic potentials and beliefs. This happened when radicals truly pushed their points to extremes: for example, in their occasionally over-principled support of neighborhood protection or their hostility to downtown business. The liberal caricature also persisted, as in their tendency to make a fetish of "impartial" professionalism or, sometimes, of the "wisdom of the market." The problem for both factions was how to fine-tune the specifics. For the liberals, this would have required value criteria to determine when to temper their trust in professionalism with vigorous intervention into the workings of the city agencies, and when to admit that the market discriminated against some constituencies. The trouble with the liberals was that these criteria did not automatically arise from their philosophical system, no matter how experienced they were in using it.

For the BCA, on the other hand, the problem was getting the most out of the bureaucracy and the market, while still maintaining control of them. That is, the question was how to bring these potentially useful interests into the service of BCA's constituency, rather than into the service of the most important concentrations of economic power.

CHAPTER 5

Santa Monica and Burlington: Reprise and Refinement, 1981–1984

The defeats of Carbone in Hartford and Kucinich in Cleveland might have suggested an end to progressive local governments in the United States. Reagan's election in 1980 suggested that a general move to the political right, so evident in the policies advocated at the top levels of government and administration and in many prominent interest groups, was also a reflection of changes in grassroots attitudes. There was the Berkeley progressive victory in 1979, but it was not too hard to treat that as an isolated case and to point out the difficulties B C A had had running a government with a plurality instead of a majority.

But progressives came back with stunning victories in 1981 in two small cities: Santa Monica, a satellite city of 88,314 near Los Angeles, and Burlington, at 37,712, the largest city in Vermont. There would also be victories for black and neighborhood coalitions in Chicago and Boston in 1983, a stunning victory for B C A in Berkeley in 1984, and a general revival of certain forms of neighborhood and other mass-based politics and policies occurred, as cities tried to adapt to much reduced levels of federal program funds and to extract resources directly from their own economies.

The initial phases of progressive government in Santa Monica and Burlington are particularly instructive, however, because they show how a set of ideas that had much in common with those developed in the previous decade could be implanted in places with very different economic bases, and at a time when the federal policy context had changed radically.

Santa Monica

Santa Monica had been a quiet, ocean front satellite of Los Angeles throughout the first half of the century, a city of small bungalows and single-family homes.[1] With the development of the Douglas Aircraft factory in the 1930s and the advent of war work in the 1940s, an increasing number of Santa Monica residents became renters, trailers were installed on many back lots, and after 1945, a market for apartment units began to build, a market that included many elderly persons who retired there. By 1960, 69 percent of the housing units in the city were occupied by renters, and a kind of genteel, two-class society had come into existence: property owners and renters. Santa Monica's median family income was somewhat below the $7,646 of the metropolitan area; its median monthly rents and the value of owner-occupied homes were slightly higher than the $72 and $15,900 respectively of the metropolitan area.[2]

The completion of the Santa Monica Freeway to Los Angeles changed all this in 1966. The freeway, in addition to causing a general shift of investment capital into real estate in the 1970s, brought about development pressures: Rental units were converted into larger apartment houses, some single-family units were also converted, small landlords were displaced by larger operators, and housing began to be threatened by office complexes. Most dramatically, land prices and rents rose steeply. This put pressure on the city's middle-income homeowners and renters, and this formed the basis for their support of progressive politics in the 1980s. These changes are demonstrated clearly in the figures shown in table 5.1.

The most striking shifts shown in these statistics are the increases in housing prices in relation to incomes. This suggests speculative housing pressures on homeowners and an incentive for the owners of rental housing to force rents upward or to convert to higher-income-producing forms of ownership. Housing prices exceeded incomes by a factor of somewhat over three to one in 1960 and by over eight to one in 1980 in the city. In comparison, the ratio for the Los Angeles Standard Metropolitan Statistical Area (SMSA) was roughly two to one in 1960, a little over four to one in 1980. For renters, the shifts in values were in the same direction, if less

TABLE 5.1. **Santa Monica Housing Costs, 1960–1980**

	1960	*1970*	*1980*
Median value, owner occ. unit	$ 22,700	$ 36,300	$ 189,800
Median contract rent	83	132	296
Median family income	6,845	10,793	23,263

marked. Meanwhile, the proportion of renters increased in Santa Monica from 69 percent to 78 percent, while it decreased from 56 percent to 49 percent in the Los Angeles SMSA.

The political makeup of the city changed throughout the 1970s. The city had been run by a coalition supported by landlords, small businesses, local banks, and homeowners. Rental housing had been a major industry for a long time—as early as 1940, the proportion of housing units occupied by renters was 69 percent compared to 63 percent for the Los Angeles area.[3] But renters were not strong politically and the city was dominated by its traditional coalition. The city had reformed its governmental structure and had adopted the city manager system after World War II, but the coalition of businessmen and bankers remained in control.[4]

POLITICAL CHANGES

In the early 1970s, all this began to change. First, environmental issues provoked the formation of a new opposition against the city's conservative establishment. The immediate precipitating factor was a proposal, advanced by then city manager Perry Scott, to build a large island on landfill in the bay, which would create a high-rise development, cut off the beach from direct ocean exposure, and demolish the famed Santa Monica Pier. A liberal coalition challenged the city establishment on this issue. It included Republicans Christine Reed and Peter Van den Steenhoven, who won election to the City Council in the 1973 and 1975 elections.

A second factor precipitating change was the political involvements of activists who formerly had been participants in the antiwar and other movements of the previous decade. One result was the formation of the Santa Monica Democratic Club, an affiliate of the liberal statewide California Democratic Council. Another was the community organizing that came to be centered in the Ocean Park neighborhood. Many activists of the 1960s had moved into Ocean Park and had helped to form such new institutions as a community-oriented church, a food cooperative, and an alternative newspaper. These were tied together in the Ocean Park Community Organization (OPCO). The Ocean Park constituency had begun to get involved in local politics around the environmental issues that mobilized liberals in the early 1970s, but their first really organized electoral work began in Tom Hayden's unsuccessful challenge for John Tunney's U.S. Senate seat in the 1976 Democratic primary election. Many activists became involved in electoral work for the first time in this campaign, and after the primary they formed the statewide Campaign for Economic Democracy (CED).

One of Hayden's co-workers in the primary campaign was Derek Shearer, a former antiwar activist and a journalist who had settled in Ocean Park in 1971. Shearer had recently completed his Ph.D. dissertation on public enterprise. Shearer's wife, Ruth Goldway, had her own activist background. While she had been a graduate student in English at UCLA, she had organized a consumer meat boycott that had expanded to encompass the entire state of California. In 1977, Goldway decided to run for a state assembly seat in the June primary, with Shearer as her campaign manager. Thus, for the second year in a row, the local CED base was mobilizing for an election. Like the Hayden campaign, this one was also unsuccessful, but it served to build up the organization further.

In 1978 a different constituency, a renter's group of senior citizens mainly, got into Santa Monica politics. The initial organization came from Sid Rose, a former labor union official from New York, who wanted to organize his neighbors around housing issues. Rose made contact with Robert Myers, then working as a legal-aid lawyer in neighboring Venice, and they began putting together a rent control ordinance that could be put on the June ballot as an initiative. Their work attracted the interest of a larger group, particularly including the organizers in Ocean Park, and they established themselves as the Santa Monica Fair Housing Alliance (SMFHA). Other organizations, which would later make up the rent control constituency, did not get involved at that time, however. CED, for example, did not commit itself to rent control at that time as an organization, although a great many of its members worked for the initiative. Heavily outspent by the landlord interests and outmatched because of the belated participation of other groups, the rent control initiative lost by a 54-46 margin.

After the June initiative, a wider coalition formed around the rent control issue, named Santa Monicans for Renters Rights

(SMRR). It consisted of three components: the Santa Monica Democratic Club, the local CED chapter, and SMFHA. They found themselves with a new issue at this point, for the same election that had defeated rent control locally had passed the statewide Proposition 13, curtailing the amount of revenue cities could collect from the property tax. This measure was to have important ramifications. First, its proponents had argued successfully that limitations on the property tax would result in a comparable limit on rent increases, thus raising tenant expectations. Any subsequent rent increases could then be exploited politically by rent control forces. Second, with property taxes no longer such a significant source of local revenues, one of the main arguments that advocates of intensive real estate development had made—that this kind of development created a tax base to finance needed city services—had to be looked at more critically. SMRR would occupy itself for the next few years with working out the implications of this problem.

SMRR began with a core of forty-five to one hundred activists.[5] Its initial aims were to win on rent control and to get control of the city government by pursuing the rent control issue. In this pursuit of office, the various groups involved were led to make important doctrinal changes away from their previous strategies. Shearer and Goldway, who had positioned themselves in alliance with both the CED and Democratic party groups, adopted a long-standing goal of moving activist organizers into local politics. Tactically, they now diverged from Hayden, who, after his 1976 Senate primary campaign, had continued to operate on the statewide level. CED and the Democratic Club embraced the need for rent control, an issue long politically risky in other cities. It was the housing activists, influenced by the senior citizens, who had seen rent control work in other places such as New York City, who provided the rationale that held the coalition together.

SMRR won a series of victories beginning in April 1979. Their effective organization won the rent control initiative. It ran two candidates for City Council, Bill Jennings and Ruth Goldway, who both won, and it supported Republican Christine Reed, who also won. The successful rent control initiative was hailed as the strongest such ordinance in the nation.[6] It provided for a five-person elected board, so that it had its own electoral base, and the board had strong authority: Rents were rolled back to April 1978 levels in all buildings of four units or more, annual rent adjustments were limited to landlord-documented cost increases, the board could intervene in eviction cases and other landlord-tenant disputes, and all landlords were required to register their units, to report vacancies, and to get the board's consent to remove any rental units from the market.

Once enacted, the rent control law helped to activate its own constituency. The rent control board election was held in June 1979, and SMRR candidates won all five seats. As in the April initiative, SMRR was able to dramatize the personal and pocketbook issues, and the landlords, who ran conservative candidates, played into SMRR's hands. In November, the landlord interests proposed a new initiative that would have gutted the rent control ordinance. Despite their calling it the "Fair Rent Ordinance," the landlord interests lost by a larger margin than they had in April. Meanwhile, one Republican council member had resigned, and SMRR ran Cheryl Rhoden, who won with the aid of the voter turnout caused by the initiative against rent control.

Thus, by November of 1979, SMRR had won three seats on the seven-member City Council and had established a strong rent control law, so it was in an important minority position, able to begin to influence city government from the inside. It began to get small pieces of legislation passed by wielding its minority strength. It joined with Republican John Bambrick after the election to make him mayor and unseat Peter Van den Steenhoven, who had supported the November initiative that would have cut the effectiveness of rent control. It was able to pass legislation establishing a consumer advocate in the city attorney's office. In the summer of 1980, Van den Steenhoven died in the crash of his light plane, reducing the council to six, with SMRR having three members.

THE SMRR PROGRAM

The program that SMRR advocated came from the experience and reflections of a somewhat diverse group of people, and this is worth some elaboration. Basic to the program was what Allan Heskin has called "tenant consciousness," an awareness of the politically and economically vulnerable position that people dependent on others for housing are in, plus a sense of the possibilities of their defense through organization.[7] Barbara Jo Osborne, an Ocean Park activist, became a supporter of rent control after being evicted:

> I had a hard time getting involved in rent control because I saw it as something that helped only everybody, that didn't necessarily help me. I had a wonderful owner and she didn't

want rent control. You know, don't vote for it and I'll keep your rent down. And basically in five years she hadn't increased the rent other than twenty dollars. She was a wonderful person. What happens to these wonderful people though is that other people came and bought her out. And finally I got it. It finally became clear that you do have to take care of the whole community and there was a connection there for me.

I got involved around an issue where I was personally evicted right before rent control. . . . I'm your typical, I thought, white middle-class person who basically gets a free ride. . . . And I just have always believed that it would work out that I would be taken care of. . . . I mean I think I was typical of a lot of people that came to the rent control movement that we were being evicted and that was outrageous. How dare you? How dare you touch where I live? I mean you go get someone else. . . . So I became really involved then because it was touching me personally and there were a lot of people that went through that.[8]

Women were prominent in SMRR. Many thought that the reason for this was that the land use and housing issues that motivated their politics were issues that affected women directly in ways not shared by many men. Cheryl Rhoden said: "The whole concept of rent is focused on the home, which is a woman's domain, versus the poor people's movement . . . "[9]

Heskin had found "tenant consciousness" in Santa Monica. He had found it among the organizers of the rent control movement and he found it to a lesser degree among that much larger public that voted for rent control:

In Santa Monica tenants became a . . . 'class-for-itself,' overcoming both gender and social class divisions. . . . An extraordinary mass of tenants were mobilized, and a sense of collectivity was generated. Tenants who were evicted in encounters with landlords, rather than shying away from future conflicts, became more aggressive; tenants permanently shut off from home ownership, rather than feeling personally defeated, became angered with economic forces contributing to their predicament; and tenants without landlord-tenant problems of their own, upon learning of the problems of others and sensing themselves to be part of a larger group, developed high tenant consciousness.[10]

But Heskin found that many who voted for rent control did so out of monetary self-interest rather than a well-developed political con-

sciousness, and that despite the solidarity that existed, the "net result has been only a distribution of tenant consciousness that approximated that present in the far less organized County of Los
Angeles."[11] In other words, organization was far ahead of a basic
self-awareness in the population. The base for SMRR was broad,
but fragile.

The effect of SMRR, as a coalition, was to broaden political consciousness, to make connections. It tried to get people to tie their
concern with rent control to larger concerns. Overall, that was the
main strategy. Osborne thought SMRR could tie the interests of
home-owners and renters together:

> As the rent control movement started, it was basically getting
> the tenants organized and, as long as we are doing that, let's
> put other more progressive people on the council because the
> people that were on the City Council were really pretty much
> to the right. . . . The city was run by the Chamber of Commerce,
> which is business interests. Now my feeling is . . . the big busi-
> ness interest is not the small business interest . . . the outside
> pressures are not in the same frame of mind. [The outside
> interests] are natural enemies of people who are residents
> whether they are homeowners or whether they are tenants.
> People who live in the city have a vested interest: 'This is our
> town, this is where we live, we care about it and we should
> have priority over you who live in Texas and you just want to
> come in and make money on building this building and then
> you are going to leave and you don't care what happens to the
> building after you are gone." That interest seems to be opposite
> to the people who live there, the actual residents of the city,
> and I think that that is natural and it will always be that way.
> I don't think there is ever any way to change that.[12]

Other SMRR leaders came from different beginnings, but they
came to similar conclusions. Derek Shearer had operated politically
at the national level, but he thought new national and state politics
had to be built on a local base. He had worked in Cambridge on an
alternative newspaper and in Washington at the Institute for Policy
Studies. At IPS, he helped organize a conference on state and local
government alternatives. Then he helped found *Working Papers*, an
important and thoughtful left-leaning periodical, and he was also
involved with Lee Webb in founding the Conference on Alternative
State and Local Policies. In the early 1970s, after moving to Santa
Monica, he divided his time between journalism and public policy

work. In all these efforts, his emphasis was on alternatives. Shearer was reform-minded, that is, he was pragmatic and policy-oriented, in contrast with some people of the left, who at times saw electoral politics as inevitably a sell-out. He said:

> If you are on the extreme left [and have] views that the government is nothing more than . . . the committee of the ruling class, then you take the view that it is better to stay on the outside and build some sort of mass movement. . . . But I think that is wrong on two counts. One: the government is not the committee of the ruling class. Government is an area of contention . . . I mean there are democratic rules. And as long as you have one person-one vote, regardless of how the deck might be stacked against a popular movement, and as long as you have a democratic ethos and you have certain legal structures that recognize that, then you have an opportunity given certain circumstances . . . to build a majoritarian movement. . . . Second, you have to believe that it makes some difference if you win. And everything I know about American history shows that there are a lot of times when it makes a big difference.[13]

Shearer had first entered politics at the state level, when he held a position with the California government for a short time after Jerry Brown's inauguration in 1975. This was what led him into his work with Tom Hayden the next year. But after the Hayden campaign and after Goldway's assembly campaign in 1977, he was more convinced than ever of the need to work at the local level. His contacts in Ocean Park gave him the concrete material to build on. He was an articulator, a person who tried to point out and to convince others of the interrelationships between seemingly separate movements and ideas.

As an undergraduate at Yale, Shearer had been strongly influenced by Christopher Tunnard and had read many books about planning—Lewis Mumford, Percival and Paul Goodman—and such economic historians as Shonfield and Heilbroner, and later he wrote a dissertation on public enterprise. In the late 1970s he was writing a book on economic democracy, and he tried to test his ideas about economic democracy through SMRR and CED. He was teaching at UCLA in the Urban Planning Department, and he led his class of students to produce issue papers on policies for Santa Monica, which he circulated. With such others as Denny Zane, Maurice Zeitlin, and Jim Cohn, he promoted the idea that SMRR should think carefully about its rent control policies and how they were connected to other salient issues.

This radical mix of interests had come into conflict with the liberal Republicans still on the council after 1979, some of whom SMRR had supported. The major issue over which conflict arose was the failure of Van den Steenhoven and Reed to support the rent control law, and this led to a move to unseat Mayor Van den Steenhoven and mayor *pro tem* Reed in 1979. The SMRR faction fought for this change, they argued, for hard-nosed political reasons: They needed all the leverage they could get, and they were very serious about their goals. Van den Steenhoven and Reed, on the other hand, were at best lukewarm toward rent control and were more interested in working on the council in compromise and give-and-take manner. Certainly their goals were much different. They were hurt by the SMRR move, and this put them into strong opposition.

THE 1981 CAMPAIGN

At the end of 1980, SMRR was ready to make a strong bid for control of the City Council. It held an issues conference to plan for the April 1981 council elections. A fourth organization, the Ocean Park Electoral Network, had joined the original three. For the conference, SMRR commissioned a set of working papers and discussed (there is some debate whether they formally adopted) a set of "Principles of Unity" to govern the upcoming campaign.[14] At this point, SMRR clearly was girding itself to move into a majority position, and it was organizing itself in as tight a fashion as it could to wage a cohesive campaign. It was motivated in part by the defection of William Jennings (previously a member of the SMRR slate), who resigned, making a speech denouncing rent control and SMRR's broader aims.

SMRR had matured as an organization, and a set of loosely connected but well-developed positions had been prepared: first, rent control had been conceptualized and elaborated in a robust way. Myers was the principal author of the conception, but the main ideas relating to rent control were developed in a well-established local constituency, which itself was represented in the elected Rent Control Board. This was a powerful organizing device because of the way it touched people: The elected board got people involved in its administration and it was thus possible to avoid the kind of bureaucratization that might have resulted from a board appointed by the City Council.

Second, SMRR had developed its ideas about local politics. Shearer had been active nationally on behalf of this emphasis on local political work, but he was only the most prominent of the Santa Monica faction. Others of its leaders were also very active and formed an important base for electoral work. SMRR issue papers on crime, housing, economic development, government structure, social services, the elderly, women, energy conservation, and other topics reflected the ideas percolating through these organizations, and the "Principles of Unity" declaration forged a consensus for the campaign that followed.

Third, other forces were developing outside of SMRR. Most notable was a group chaired by a UCLA Law School professor, Donald Hagman, and set up as a committee of the Planning Commission to study the "housing element" of the city's Master Plan. They were studying legal devices that could be used to insulate the city from the material costs that new office and commercial construction imposed on it: increased traffic, increased parking demands, and other indirect effects, such as the demolition of existing houses, thus driving up rents for local residents. They focused particularly on a device called "inclusionary zoning," which required developers to provide low-income housing as part of any new development or to contribute to a city fund to build low-income housing and other needed amenities beneficial to the neighborhood.[15]

At the beginning of 1981, SMRR agreed on a slate of candidates for the four council seats that were up for election. They were Denny Zane, a teacher and community organizer who had been prominent in CED, Jim Cohn, a minister and pastor of the Ocean Park Methodist Church, Dolores Press, an active union organizer who had been chair of the rent board, and Ken Edwards, a probation officer who had previously been a City Council candidate and leader of the Santa Monica Democratic Club.

With Shearer managing the campaign, the SMRR slate swept the four open seats. As in the other elections since June of 1978, the landlord, developer, and business interests played the role of foils for SMRR's campaign arguments, which stressed the security of renters and the need for their taking control of their own institutions. Included in the SMRR campaign was a crime control initiative, which supported the police as well as neighborhood involvement in crime prevention. SMRR used direct mail and door-to-door canvassing effectively, against an opposition that relied on money and advertising. SMRR now had a five-two majority on the council and were secure in their majority for the next four years.

TAKING POWER

When the new council majority took office in April 1981, it began to implement its mandate in a dramatic fashion. At a City Council meeting the night after the new members were sworn in, the council passed an ordinance establishing a moratorium on all building construction in the city, at the same time setting up task forces to study, over the next six months, what rules might be imposed governing construction permits more effectively in the interest of city residents.[16]

The moratorium and the task forces were the main story of the first six months of SMRR majority control in Santa Monica. They provided a great deal of access for citizen input into the development process and a vehicle for active involvement by the new mayor, and in doing so they stimulated fundamental thinking by a large group of people on the underlying concepts of land development and the public's role in promoting and regulating it.

The posture of SMRR was initially regulatory — some would say, "consumerist" — rather than committed to operating the local economy. This position was to create administrative and political tension once the new council began to build up its administrative capacity. The task forces were perhaps the first places where this tension appeared and began to be used creatively. They are a key part of the story of SMRR: the story of the transformation of a political process that was mainly regulatory into a somewhat more complex form that could create joint ventures with the private sector.

The most important task force, in terms of the magnitude of land development involved, was the Commercial and Industrial Task Force. A number of large development proposals, which were on the drawing boards with land already acquired by private investors, came before it during the summer of 1981. The moratorium set up a situation in which the developers had to negotiate with the city. The task force, although advisory, clearly had a mandate and the developers knew they had to deal seriously with it. The City Council hoped that out of these negotiations would come both a better arrangement for the city in relation to developments already planned and a sense of the best way to implement and devise new development regulations.

Within a few months, the Commercial and Industrial Task Force had advised the city on three major development agreements.[17] In one case, Welton-Beckett Associates, a national architecture and development firm, had begun planning a large head-quarters office complex, originally planned for 900,000 square feet on fifteen acres. The task force held meetings that included representatives from Welton-Beckett and made a number of proposals: The development might be made with six stories instead of three, and one third of the site would be donated to the city as a park; the developer might pay a "social service and cultural arts fee" to the city equal to 1.5 percent of the project's total cost; it would build a day care center in the park, giving priority to the children of employees and residents; it would provide job training and affirmative action programs; it would build low- and moderate-cost housing. Welton-Beckett had itself suggested other concessions: two $5,000 annual scholarships to the School of Architecture at Santa Monica Community College, support for adult education courses in architecture and urban planning, the provision of a third of the planned 15,000 square feet of retail space in the project to be rented at a favorable rate for purposes deemed necessary by the neighborhood, and the provision of three summer jobs for Santa Monica College students at the company. In the end, the City Council negotiated a compromise agreement that provided for the park, the day care center, and one hundred units of affordable off-site housing.

Other agreements were arrived at in a similar fashion. Kendall Realty had planned a nine-story office building on the beachfront; the council negotiated an agreement that included nine units of low- and moderate-cost housing, and the overall height of the complex was reduced to three stories. Lincoln Properties had planned a seafront condominium project, and the council exacted an agreement from them to build affordable housing on the site and to contribute $7 million to a city fund for additional off-site housing. Greenwood Development Company agreed to build thirty apartment units as part of a $90 million office-condominium project.

The negotiations and discussions involving developers, the council, and the planning task forces that summer were not without rancor. Welton-Becket's representatives, after some hand-wringing at meetings where they expressed a desire to conform to the city's mandate to extract concessions in compensation for the costs of development, finally commented to the press that the city was engaging in "legalized extortion." Describing his reactions to some of the early task force meetings, the president of the architecture development firm seemed both mystified and exasperated that a citizen committee should insert itself into the development process. He said:

The task force process did not accomplish anything it set out to accomplish. Many of the recommendations we frankly don't understand. I think the city has failed to do anything to advance the cause it set out to deal with. It is creating a set of circumstances designed to diminish its chance of getting a good development built.[18]

A minority on the task force echoed the developer's complaints. One member felt the stipulations were too onerous. "If I were Welton-Beckett, I would take a hike . . . I think we're going to hurt the community by putting such onerous development requirements on high quality employers. . . . We're going to scare them out of the community."[19] But the majority held out for an even more stringent set of stipulations than the City Council eventually agreed to, and some were incensed that the council compromised positions they had worked out.

These negotiations illustrated a problem the task forces had (and the council would have) in dealing with private developers: their lack of information about the internal decision making processes the developers were going through. They had a strong political mandate and the capacity to exact stringent requirements from the developers, and they were not about to move from an adversary to a partnership position. Ruth Goldway, who as mayor was serving as liaison to the Commercial and Industrial Task Force, commented to me in 1981 on the development agreement process: "Whenever they agree, I always wonder if we could have gotten more."

In the fall of 1981, the difficulties of the city-developer relationship in Santa Monica were demonstrated when the courts prohibited the city from exacting in-lieu fees from developers. The task force had devised a set of interim guidelines that exacted 1.5 percent of project costs as a fee that could be paid by the developer in lieu of some of the more specific features the city might have wanted. This allowed the developer some flexibility, while providing the city with the means to pay for some of the social costs associated with development: off-site housing or parks, for example. Disallowing the in-lieu fees put the city on more of a collision course with developers.

The Commercial and Industrial Task Force had, by the end of the summer, done most of what it could do. It had given the council some breathing room, it had aired out the issues, and it had gotten a larger number of people involved. But it had not negotiated any agreements; that was left to the council. The council was faced with the need to reconcile the conflicts on these issues, and they faced a dilemma: If they were too harsh, they risked losing the investment and being left with a "hole in the ground," subject to the criticism that they did not care about saving jobs and harvesting whatever benefits development might bring. Denny Zane was the council member who worked hardest on some of the development agreements. He eventually persuaded the rest of the SMRR group to go along with a set of agreements that were less stringent than some had demanded. Later in the fall, John Alschuler arrived as the city manager, and he took a major part in pushing through the agreements.

THE TRANSITION TO MAJORITY RULE

While the task forces occupied much of the public's attention during the first summer of SMRR's control, the new City Council was beginning to face the transition from being an effective opposition to being in majority control. They and others spoke frequently of this transition. They had to master procedures. They had to see all sides of the problems. They had to learn to work with one another and to trust one another at a different level than before, which they did learn through a series of difficult decisions. They had to withstand personal attacks, a problem particularly for Ruth Goldway, whom the new majority had elected mayor.

Though they had a mandate from a majority of the people, they faced institutions that resisted them and gave assistance to their opposition, so that each substantive decision was costly both in terms of time and anguish. The decision to effect the moratorium was a major example. They felt they had to have a moratorium for substantive policy reasons. Two years before, on the eve of the enactment of rent control, there had been a spate of demolitions (popularly referred to as the "demolition derby"). They wanted to foreclose such a possibility by acting quickly after the election. But the result was that they had to hear dozens of cases from developers who had projects going on. They could not get the task forces set up for two months, and in the meantime, they spent hours each week on this problem. Afterwards, some SMRR people thought that the moratorium had been a bad idea. It had been a forum by means of which the victorious coalition had vented some of its anger at the developers, but it had created an atmosphere of confrontation that made it more difficult to work with the developers or with the business community in general.

In general, the council majority faced the question of when to be compromising and when to be ruthless with its authority. With five votes, they had the authority to replace all board members. The memberships of the personnel board and the planning board were particularly crucial, since these boards determined the new council's ability to move ahead on hiring (they wanted to put women in important jobs) and development issues (they wanted the Planning Commission to adopt permanent housing and commercial development rules). Some took the position that they should go ahead and fire the opposition members of these boards, since there would be fights and pain anyhow. They should get their people in, so that they could begin hiring women in responsible positions and get the Planning Commission working in concert wih the council's development goals. Other council members demurred. Ken Edwards wanted to compromise and refused to serve as the required fifth vote for removing people from the commissions. He thought that it would be worth the trouble of having opposition members, not to set the precedent of firing people. Someday, he thought, SMRR might be in a minority position, and it would be well to be able to point to evidence of their compromising when they needed it.

The five majority members had to learn to work with one another. All later said the biggest issue they faced was the selection of the city manager, a problem which came to a head in September of 1981. They had narrowed the choice to Camilla Barnett, who had been assistant city manager in Dallas, and John Alschuler, former assistant city manager in Hartford. Edwards and Press were strongly in favor of Barnett; Goldway and Zane were for Alschuler. This was a difficult issue. Goldway and Shearer knew Alschuler and were convinced of his good qualities, but could not convince the others. They acceded in the end to the choice of Barnett. Fortuitously, Barnett's financial demands were higher than the council majority could meet, and the vote swung back to Alschuler. Edwards later felt this intense negotiation within the majority was a turning point, a crisis that built up trust among them:

> that was very intense among the five of us. . . . We did something very unique almost by accident. We took it to our constituents and had them interview the two which helped SMRR grow because it then brought this debate, this intensity [from us] to SMRR.

> We ultimately didn't work it out. The irony is thank God she didn't take it . . . everything that I thought would be a negative for John has been a positive. . . . I mean it just couldn't have

turned out any better. . . . And I think what that did was it helped me grow. . . . I developed a lot of respect for my colleagues and particularly toward Ruth who I had some problems with over that.[20]

The stress of putting together a majority program generated a good deal of opposition, some of it vituperative. It is hard to exaggerate the undercurrent of resentment that persisted in the community. The newspaper was consistently opposed to the council, and opposition organizations, some of them well financed by outside landlord interests, were formed. In the council, Reed and Jennings remained on the outs with the majority.

ADMINISTRATIVE DEVELOPMENT

One of the Council's first priorities had been to build up an administrative capacity in City Hall. From the start, the new council majority was determined to make an ally of the city administration they had inherited. They replaced three key department heads. The city manager, Kent McClain, resigned soon after the election; they brought in Myers, the lawyer who had fashioned the rent control law, as city attorney; and they shifted the duties of the personnel director. With these exceptions, they worked within the existing structures at City Hall. They were pleasantly surprised, at times, at the support they got in return. Denny Zane said:

> One of the things that you . . . expect . . . when left-leaning people win a majority is that you are going to run into a . . . conservative bureaucracy . . . that they are going to . . . undermine the . . . progressive agenda. But we didn't find that here. We found people who liked the idea of serving the public and liked the idea of getting things done. . . . One of the things about our tenure that marked us as distinct from the prior [council] is that we had things that we wanted to see done.

"Of course," Zane said, there were ". . . lots of gaps in the skills in the bureaucracy . . . because they hadn't been doing the sort of things we wanted to do. . . . They didn't have the training in economic planning or enterprise development."[21]

The important first step had been the appointment of Myers as city attorney immediately after the election. That appointment was crucial, because the SMRR people anticipated immediate attacks on rent control. Myers was available and the council majority agreed to him readily. He turned out to be able to provide them with a good deal more support than they had anticipated. He won over the friendship of the police department, which had been bothered by the slow service they had gotten from the previous city attorney. Myers was running cases through his office quickly, saving the police trouble. He was also a major resource on the development agreements and helped in facing the siege of cases that came before the council immediately after they declared the construction moratorium.

By and large, however, the council felt that it could not make appointments until it had found a city manager. It was November before John Alschuler was in place. But once in City Hall, he began to provide administrative support at a new level. He moved into a key role in the negotiations concerning some of the development agreements. This helped to move some cases to settlement. Early in 1982, Alschuler hired Mark Tigan, who had been an economic development official in Winooski, Vermont, to play the main role in managing local economic development, and slowly they put together policies that made for regularized negotiations between the city and the private sector.

Alschuler, even though he shared many of the goals of SMRR, found himself in somewhat of a middle position. He, in a fashion that has been traditional with city managers, made a number of "good government" improvements. He instituted new budgeting procedures. He saved money on several fronts. He was careful in hiring staff and in many ways took burdens off the City Council, which had immersed itself in many administrative matters. So there were marked changes during the period after he arrived. On the other hand, it fell to Alschuler to integrate the administration with the political process; his unique qualification was his willingness to do this. He wanted to build an organization that could tie together the extremes of efficient administration and responsive, participatory representation. He saw the city government as a

> productive antagonism which develops between the bureaucracy of the city and those people who are involved in the change . . . that grew out of differences that are defined by race and sex and class. People who are brought in here . . . they are all younger. They are 80 to 90 percent women. They are more substantially minority and most important they have more of this generational difference in experience. They are people who experienced the civil rights movements, various antiwar movements.[22]

The organization he inherited, on the other hand, was different. But he valued it also. He viewed the civil service as an enormous resource, "people who have given twenty, twenty-five years of their lives to the public ... with a vision of the public good. Maybe an inadequate or wrong vision of the public good, but it is nonetheless stemming from a vision of the public good." So he wanted the bureaucrats and the activists to work together, for the public sector to build upon itself and not consume itself: "One of the hallmarks of institutions which are successful over time is their ability to grow, building on their past, not building by destroying their past." He thought a good start at this had been made in Santa Monica. He was careful in hiring new people, not bringing in major appointments too fast, but one at a time, so that the existing personnel could respond to the people who had been hired, before the next decision occurred. He said he thought he had a pretty good sense of

> the rate at which they could accept new people. . . . I was very conscious not to bring in more than three or four people every couple of months overall . . . senior major people. . . . I'd bring in three or four people, I'd sit. Let people absorb in before the next wave came in. And I balanced that with things which were attentive to the department heads' needs . . . purchasing systems are inadequate, computer systems are inadequate, personnel systems are inadequate.[23]

Alschuler's other main preoccupation was with development policy and fiscal planning. He needed to get consent from the SMRR base:

> The second thing I've tried to do is positive. . . . There are some enormous political contradictions operating in this city within the progressive movement. That is, I think at this point they have a hard time operationalizing what it means to be a progressive city. There are some major issues for which there is frankly historically not much thought. What is the city's economic development program? How is it going to create jobs? Who is going to get those jobs? . . . . Second there has been and still is no clear notion of how the government can finance its service base. . . . And two things which were, from my experience in Hartford, fundamentals: How do you raise revenue and how do you deal with development policy? Here frankly I think the level of thought has been trivial.[24]

He elaborated on this: The city, he thought, would face a serious fiscal problem in a short time. For a progressive government that had created expectations about housing and social services, this could become a real political problem. The council majority that won election in 1981 had, Alschuler thought (in January 1983), two and a half more years in which to secure their revenue base:

> If they are not successful, then the next three or four years are going to be very very hard . . . that election [in 1985] is going to be very difficult to deal with because it is very hard for them to run as the angels of austerity. They have created very high expectations and they have no strategy on how to raise the revenue.[25]

He found the situation different from Hartford, where Carbone "was a genius at . . . four- and five-year strategies. . . . Nick had enough experience to think three and five years down the road, like any modern corporation would."

In order to shore up the revenue base, Alschuler turned to development policy. With the property tax not being the financial resource it had been before the passage of Proposition 13, he had to create new devices. It was not simply a matter of bringing in commercial and industrial investments, which could then be taxed. Special arrangements had to be devised. The development agreements were the key. But for that purpose, like the revenue question, he was facing a constituency that had not worked out its political priorities. He was trying to bring the council into a more developmental frame of mind, and he had some success. But he knew there were obstacles embedded in the political base of SMRR:

> The basic policy of development has been what we don't want. Their base frankly I think is fundamentally environmentalist. And aesthetic. You talk development policy to members of the progressive community and what you will hear back is neighborhood policy and aesthetic concern. Now both of these are valid . . . [but] that is not a development agenda in general and to the extent that there has been a development agenda it has been a sort of wish list . . . cooperatives . . . fantasies. Fantasies I share but not very realistic: Where is the market? Who gets the jobs? Where does the capital come from? . . . There is an anti-development agenda, but there is no development agenda.[26]

One of his moves during his first year was to bring in David Smith, an economist from Massachusetts who had been involved in some of Hartford's strategy formulation. Alschuler, consulting Smith and his own experience, concluded that, given the California post-Proposition 13 tax structure:

> We need a two-fold strategy. One is on privately held land to push a hotel and visitor-serving strategy. . . . We need hotels because they are the best revenue generators of the city and also they create significant numbers of jobs which are accessible to the . . . unemployed population here.[27]

POLICIES DEVELOP

Between the environmentalist and rent control concerns in the SMRR base and Alschuler's perceptions of finance and economic needs, there was a tension. But it would serve as a creative tension to the extent that the council and SMRR learned ways to turn it to political account. And there were signs, by 1984, that the City Council was taking a more varied and positive position on development questions as part of the more general evolution the council was going through. One dimension of this evolution was simply a shift in priorities; a second was the emergence of a more embracing view of the way government could relate to the private sector. Denny Zane described his shift to a more positive evaluation of the potentials of tourist development:

> I guess I was surprised a little bit by how complicated it all seemed and how much more difficult your decisions were when your decisions meant something. . . . It is not just a question of what the principles are. It has got to work.
>
> And part of it is . . . you got people around you giving you advice . . . and as an activist you don't have quite the same kind of resource to draw from.
>
> My initial inclination about development would have been . . . hostile to enhancing the tourist sector . . . that [it] is a prescription for a non-diversified, parasite economy . . . unhealthy. Much of the Third World is just that. But when you look at the real concrete choices . . . it is not just the generalized question of whether a real industrial base is better than a tourist economy. When your land values are so high and the amount of land is so little, the prospect for doing industrial development is slim. And on the other hand hotels have some real significant virtues. . . . Plus there are people who want to do it.[28]

Alschuler might have taken satisfaction in Zane's discoveries. He had found the anti-tourism attitudes bizarre:

> I have been accused by some people in CED of trying to recreate pre-Castro Cuba, which is bizarre, but it is symbolic of some of the concerns people have about that. . . . And they worry about traffic and are the buildings gonna be too big. If somebody from my background [listens to this] he says, 'this is very bizarre.' You say the city needs money to provide services and there are unemployed people who need jobs and somebody tells you you are going to block my view of the ocean with that building.

> I work for this council, I respect them, and I care a lot about what they say and then still I swallow hard on that stuff. . . . And when you talk to the Pico people [a minority neighborhood organization] I know they swallow hard too on some of that stuff.[29]

Alschuler, like Carbone in Hartford, was part businessman. He had put together a strategy that required the cooperation of private businesses and part of his problem was to find "enlightened" businessmen. After much negotiation, he had gotten the council and the city to agree to set up a tourism committee:

> They agreed to set up the Convention Visitors Bureau, and that has two phases. The first to which there is uniform consensus: let's do a better job of promoting what we have now. But it took me seven months of negotiation to get that thing through. I mean it was not easy. Enormous fear and paranoia on the account of the chamber. And some significant fear and concern on the part of the council. This was not a marriage made in heaven.

But the really subtle problem for Alschuler was to insert the right kind of business representation on the committee:

> My appointment of David O'Malley [of Welton-Beckett] . . . I took a lot of grief for that. I think it was the right choice. . . . One thing Santa Monica doesn't have is a liberal enlightened business group. O'Malley is one of the few people . . . who can provide the core of that. And while they shouldn't control the government and they shouldn't make decisions, there are important contributions they can make. We need them. They need us more than we need them. So I think the bargain we can make with them is more to our benefit than theirs. . . . One

of the perspectives . . . I bring is the sense that we do need to bargain with them.[30]

Zane, who had earlier expressed the anti-development view, had an equally embracing approach to the private sector.

> I think there is an element of the business community who begin to view us as presenting possibilities that didn't exist before, that is, in their interest. Not because we intend to be in their interest, but because [of] our evaluation of what our possibilities are. If, for example, the conclusion we come to after a land use study is that in terms of producing jobs for people who live here and producing revenue for the city with minimum traffic, the hotels are a good idea, okay, well then there are going to be some people in the business community who like us. Namely hotel developers . . . or people who finance hotels. They will like us. But they may have to find that the structure of their relationship to the government is going to be different, that there is going to be equity participation, that there is going to be a way in which some of that flow is returned to the population rather than siphoned off into some other community, that there is going to be a different structure of the relationship, that they nonetheless will probably do very well.[31]

Burlington

Burlington had a substantial working class for a long time, while more affluent classes settled in the suburbs. At 37,712, the largest city in Vermont and the site of the state university, it attracted a sizeable number of the political activists and young professionals who moved to the state in the 1970s. Burlington's politics had been the province of a Democratic party organization for three decades, and Mayor Gordon Paquette was finishing his fifth two-year term. But by 1981, the city's politics were about to change. In part, Paquette's administration had simply lost its vigor and, in retrospect, they were ripe to be beaten. But more basic forces were also at work.[32]

Even so, no one expected Bernard Sanders to be successful in his run for the mayoralty in 1981. Sanders was a professed socialist who had run "educational" campaigns for the governorship and for the U.S. Senate as the candidate of the Liberty Union party in the 1970s. Even though his party's vote had been substantial in Burlington — as much as 28 percent — and there had also been some notable local progressive successes on referenda for utility rate decreases, very few thought he would beat Paquette. Because the Republicans put up no candidate against him and his only other opposition came from two disaffected Democrats, Paquette had been encouraged to run a lethargic campaign. Sanders, in fact, was the leader of what became a substantial coalition. There were several elements in it: the Citizens Party, which had been organized the year before around Barry Commoner's presidential candidacy, ran two candidates for the Board of Aldermen, and two other Aldermanic candidates were also allied with Sanders. During the previous two years 1979 and 1980, a good deal of neighborhood organizing had taken place, and as many as nine neighborhood organizations had been formed, typically around such issues as housing demolitions resulting from downtown development and from highway constructions. These organizations targeted Paquette's actions in his ten years as a Democratic mayor.

With a large working-class vote beginning to mobilize around neighborhood issues, and with Sanders appealing to a diverse activist constituency, and — it was later revealed — with a substantial business and middle-class constituency that had become convinced that Paquette had been in office too long, Sanders won a close election by ten votes.

Paquette's loss put the Democrats on the Board of Aldermen, still in majority control, into a state of shock and confusion. Their behavior in reaction to Sanders, and that of many of City Hall's employees and members of appointed commissions and boards, resulted in a substantial further swing of public opinion toward Sanders' coalition. Sanders' informal alliance, which claimed two votes out of the thirteen on the Board of Aldermen after the 1981 elections, increased its share to five in 1982, re-elected Sanders by an impressive majority in 1983, and added one additional alderman in 1984. The government operated in a substantial stalemate for the first year and was only able to put an administration in place during its second year. By the spring of 1984, Sanders was beginning to put major programs in place, and the outlines of his diverse constituency were beginning to appear.

ECONOMIC AND POLITICAL BACKGROUND

Burlington had been Vermont's major city since early in the nineteenth century, its superior position based on its strategic location on Lake Champlain between the Hudson Valley and Canada.[33] Its first growth came from a wartime positioning of troops occurring between 1812 and 1814. Later a glass production industry developed and, after 1850, lumber transhipment and diversified manufacturing industries were formed. By 1900, the major manufacturing employment in the area was in textiles, and Burlington had become a manufacturing town with a large working class. The textile industry was declining by the time of World War II, but during the war, Bell Aircraft and General Electric established operations in the city, the latter taking over a textile plant in the Lakeside neighborhood of Burlington. By the end of the Korean War, however, both textiles and other manufacturing operations were cutting back on employment. Announcements of layoffs at General Electric and the closing of the American Woolen Company plant in neighboring Winooski followed in quick succession in 1954, and the area's population began to see itself in an economic crisis.

It was at this time that the city's economic leaders took steps to bolster the economy that would, later, feed into the political and economic changes of the 1980s. They established a nonprofit group, the Greater Burlington Industrial Corporation (GBIC) for "aiding the economic development of Greater Burlington." According to the main historical account: "The prime movers included a commercial banker, newspaper publisher, manufacturer, retailer, transportation executive, an architect, two insurance agents, and two attorneys."[34] GBIC was different from most such organizations that had been formed in the past. It was not to be devoted primarily to advertising, and it precluded, in its bylaws, any provision of bonuses to attract industry to the area. Though its initial group of officers and directors was weighted nine to five in favor of Burlington, it saw itself as a regional operation covering all of Chittendon County, and it sought members from all the towns in the county. Its main strategy was to build factories and then to entice stable employers to the area. As its strategy evolved, this ultimately meant an emphasis on developing the outlying areas of the county, because most of the large sites were located there. After a difficult first few years, by 1958 GBIC had succeeded in luring a branch plant of IBM to a plant in Essex Junction, a few miles east of the city. In subsequent years, a good deal of growth in manufacturing employment took place in the county, and the county's population rose from 74,425 in 1960 to 114,018 in 1980.

The city's economic development strategy was not the only result of the layoffs of 1954. Vermont, traditionally a Republican state in its politics, began to elect Democrats after that year, particularly in Burlington and Winooski, and one reason was the perception that the Republicans in the State House had planned no actions in response to the economic problems of those areas.[35] Local Democratic party politics in Burlington can best be understood in the context of the GBIC response to the problems of the local economy. Paquette's economic policy entailed an effort to gather the fruits of suburban growth for the city by modernizing the city's core as a shopping center.

DISSENTING VOICES ON LOCAL DEVELOPMENT

Vermont's political tradition, although it is stereotyped as Yankee republicanism, also shows a history of radical, populist, and labor protest. Some people in Burlington remember militant labor actions in such places as the granite quarries of Barre, and the legacy of the textile-mill operations—extensive in some Vermont cities earlier in this century—was the establishment of a substantial French Canadian working-class population with its own working and political traditions. None of these variants have been dominant historically, but by the 1970s, the state had also attracted a diverse political activist element, and Burlington, the state's largest city and site of the University of Vermont, was the focus of new efforts at political organization that rooted themselves partly in local traditions and in the local working-class population.

Sanders himself was an early example of this joining of political elements in Vermont. He had come from Brooklyn, born in 1941 into a Jewish, middle-class family that had recently emigrated from Poland.[36] In high school he was in track and basketball and later studied at the University of Chicago. He moved to Vermont in 1968, worked as a carpenter, worked for a low-income advocacy group called Bread and Land, and in the mid-1970s began a business that produced educational films. He was known in Burlington as a basketball player, a participant in the antiwar movement, and later as an organizer of the Liberty Union party. On behalf of the Liberty Union party, Sanders ran in two campaigns for governor and two for the U.S. Senate in the 1970s. He never got more than 6 percent of the vote. They were "educational" campaigns. But in these and in his other political activities, Sanders, in a variation of an American political tradition, paid his dues to local institutions and traditions. He met people and his activities paid off for others. He became known, he spread his ideas, and he learned from those he worked

TABLE 5.2. *Age Composition of Burlington and Vermont, 1970–1980*

Age Cohort	State		City	
	1970	*1980*	*1970*	*1980*
20–24	36,009	48,637	5,703	7,469
25–29	28,924	44,845	2,409	3,566
30–34	23,748	42,325	1,734	2,414
35–39	22,713	32,371	1,641	1,575
40–44	23,969	25,023	1,808	1,301
Total, all 20–44 ages:	444,330	511,456	38,633	37,712

with. He did not work only with other persons who had, like him, recently moved into the state; he also worked regularly with old-time Vermonters and absorbed their traditions.

Sanders' history in Vermont and Burlington was far from unique; the integration of outsiders into Vermont life took place all through the 1960s and 1970s. Some indication of the changes can be found in the population statistics for the age 20–44 cohorts as shown in table 5.2.[37] These data attest to a large shift in the city's population composition. Despite a small increase in the median age, the population in the 20–24, 25–29, and 30–34 age cohorts all increased within the city. The most obvious explanation of this would be that it was caused by increased enrollments at the university, which resulted in a relatively larger residue of university-related people living there. This explanation is further suggested by the cohort attrition patterns: The 30–34 cohort for 1980, for example, is less than half the size of the 20–24 cohort for 1970. But the important point is that, despite probably a very large net out-migration as the younger age cohorts get older, the residue of this age group was much larger in 1980 than it had been in 1970.

In Burlington, a number of activists and organizations contributed, throughout the 1970s, to a criticism of local development policies, a criticism which grew in force until Sanders capitalized on it electorally in 1981. Bryan Higgins, in a perceptive paper describing the background of Sanders' election, noted a 1970 Office of Economic Opportunity report that "identified 4,000–6,000 residents of Burlington who did not have the luxury of perceiving as problems the kind of issues the planning department was preoccupied with since they were confronted with basic needs of money, housing, and health." And Higgins added that "in a variety of forums and from a number of perspectives, residents continued to express distress that housing was given low or no priority by the city."[38]

The most important forum of protest Higgins mentions was a neighborhood movement that began developing after about 1977. The neighborhood organizations were not based on large numbers, but effective opposition voices were created through a combination of appealing issues, a citywide support network extending through Burlington's ethnic French community, and timely organizing. Organizer Michael Monte reported that when he arrived in Burlington in 1977 there were two main groups: one, a tenants union organizing effort in the Franklin Square public housing project; the other, a strong indigenous group of neighbors in the King Street area just to the south of the downtown area, which had gotten United Way funding. Monte had been hired as a full-time director by the King Street organization. Initially, the group had mainly been interested in youth and delinquency, a long-standing concern of many city working-class neighborhoods. Monte was able to expand this concern and refocus it on housing issues, and more generally at that time, the King Street and other neighborhood organizations also began to focus on two larger and more dramatic forces. The first was the urban renewal program, which the Democrats had created in the 1960s and which Paquette had enthusiastically developed with downtown business support in the early 1970s. The other was the proposed "Southern Connector"—a four-lane expressway that would link downtown office and retail centers to the suburbs south of the city. Both of these developments threatened neighborhoods in massive and direct ways; both could be linked clearly to the downtown development strategies of the Paquette administration.

After 1977, other neighborhood organizations and related movements began to emerge in the city. People Acting for Change Together (PACT) organized in the Old North End neighborhood and centered its attention on getting rent control and establishing a food cooperative. An informal organization called "Fight Back" began to try to organize people. In 1978–1979 Monte convinced the state office of the federal Law Enforcement Assistance Administration to support organizer salaries in three neighborhoods, and he was also successful in getting two VISTA volunteers for the city. In 1980 the Vermont Alliance, which was a citizens organization operating statewide, decided to focus its efforts in Burlington on neighborhood organizing, and it supported financially two organizers who worked out of the King Street office under Monte. Thus by 1980 there were seven organizers at work in Burlington in addition to Monte. Functioning neighborhood organizations by that time included One Voice in the Old North End, the North Avenue Community Organization, the South End Community Organization, the Lakeside Neighborhood Association, the Franklin Square Action Group, and several others, in addition to the King Street group.

Perhaps the most vocal of these was the Lakeside group. Lakeside was a small neighborhood of less than one hundred families that existed on the lake, just southwest of the General Electric plant and the railroad tracks, and whose only access to the rest of the city was through the Lakeside Avenue railroad underpass. It was a closely knit French-Canadian neighborhood, originally settled as housing for textile workers when the G E plant had been a textile mill. Access to the rest of town had been a problem for the neighborhood for a long time, but what mobilized them to organize were the plans for the Southern Connector. Those plans, drawn up by the State Highway Department with the support of the Planning Commission and the city's downtown business community, called for a four-lane, limited-access road parallel to the railroad tracks. Lakeside people organized, trying to get the plans for the new road changed to allow for pedestrian overpasses or route changes. At first, they got little attention. Joan Beauchemin, who had recently moved to Burlington—she had married a Lakeside resident—became the spokesperson for the community and their main organizer.

Vermont's Act 250, which called for hearings before any major construction projects could go ahead, provided the first major forum for debate on the proposal, and by 1980 the Lakeside Neighborhood Association and other groups were testifying against the road. But they were opposed by the city administration. After rebuffs from Paquette and the Planning Commission, Beauchemin studied the proposed highway in more detail. She became convinced, first, that the engineering studies purporting to show the need for it were wrong—that is, the traffic could as easily be handled by improvements in local streets, at less cost; and second, that the point of view of the business community, which believed that the road was needed to support downtown merchants, was an overly narrow one, and that a more appropriate urban development policy would emphasize housing in the downtown area and the development of food and other stores serving that housing. She came to feel that the strategy favored by the city was one biased toward merchant profits and suburban shoppers, which would place undue burdens on inner-city neighborhoods.

By 1980, Beauchemin had made contact with people interested in broader development options extending beyond the Lakeside neighborhood. She became the coordinator for a group called "Burlington for Better Alternatives." She did research on urban development strategies and found examples of an alternative approach, stressing the introduction of a diverse mixture of social classes into downtown neighborhoods along with a mixture of commercial and other constructions. One example of this approach was in Lancaster, Pennsylvania, which she presented as evidence of the possibilities in a newspaper piece that she wrote:

> As an alternative, let us look at Lancaster, Pa. Faced with a dying downtown and a demoralized business community, Lancaster . . . did what the others tried, a big urban renewal project based on the accepted theory that if you build attractive shopping malls downtown, people will follow. . . . It didn't work. So Lancaster reversed the conventional wisdom and reasoned that if you bring people downtown, stores would follow. It worked. Working with a three-pronged attack, they promoted tourism, renovated housing geared to young couples and retired people, and worked to restore confidence among businessmen — not retailers — that downtown is the best location for offices.

Her solution for Burlington was similar:

> Burlington not only will not die if the connector is not built, it will probably do better. . . . Our intention is not to discourage retail business in Burlington, but to shift the focus to a more balanced approach. . . . Improving our assets, such as the waterfront; neighborhoods such as King Street, Lakeside and South Cove; promoting our rediscovered cultural possibilities; encouraging light clean industry, supplying Vermont-made goods and services — that is what will pump new vigor into Burlington.[39]

In addition to neighborhood organizations, other groups were at work. PACT was organizing on behalf of rent control, a campaign that peaked and ended in 1981. The group had prepared a short analysis of the city's economic structure, which some had called "weak on conclusions." "Fight Back" was organizing, as was the

Redbird Collective, a radical feminist group. These groups varied greatly in the number of people they reached, but all contributed to the climate of ideas in opposition to the administration. Partly, these activities were residues of earlier statewide political campaigns that had created organizations in Burlington that later could be called upon to act in local politics. The antiwar movement was the most important of these movements. Later, the passage of Act 250 marked the advent of an important alliance between established indigenous and new activist elements.

SANDERS' FIRST TERM: STALEMATE

Sanders' close victory in the 1981 mayoral election represented a major defeat for the Democratic party organization. It had been in control of City Hall for three decades and throughout Paquette's ten years in office had dominated the Board of Aldermen. Moreover, during that time, a set of working relationships had developed between the various city boards and commissions, which were relatively independent under the city's charter: their members were appointed by vote of the aldermen to five-year terms and they were not formally responsible to the mayor.

Allied with Sanders in the election in which he defeated Paquette were also a successful aldermanic candidate, Terry Boricius, who had run as a Citizens party candidate, and Sadie White, an independent. However, they faced a hostile majority of eight Democrats, as well as three Republicans who were in no way sympathetic with their aims.

Sanders had campaigned mainly on "equity" themes. He had opposed the Southern Connector and the luxury waterfront condominiums featured in a current development proposal. He advocated tax reform, higher pay for municipal workers, and programs redirecting services to city youth and redirecting housing and medical care to the less affluent. Once in office, his government was dominated by internal administrative conflicts brought on by the intransigence of the Democratic majority on the Board of Aldermen and of some of the commissions, particularly the Planning Commission. A series of dramatic confrontations took place. Shortly after Sanders' inauguration in April 1981, the aldermen voted to fire his secretary, Linda Niedweske; finally, they compromised, after reducing her salary. In June, the aldermen rejected all six of Sanders' nominations for city administrative jobs, prompting Sanders to take them to court. They used parliamentary maneuvers to keep Sanders off the agenda at board meetings. The Planning Commission held meetings with developers without Sanders' knowledge, frustrating his attempts to influence development policies. The obstructionism enacted by the aldermen extended to some City Hall employees, like the city clerk—who locked the door connecting his office to Sanders' and was once caught stealing the mayor's mail—and the director of planning, who was quoted as saying he would not go out of his way to cooperate with the new mayor.

Sanders' responses to this obstructionism, while full of public controversy, were substantially commonsensical and efficient: When the positions of civil defense director and health and safety inspector became vacant in the summer after his election, he was able to appoint two of his supporters, David Clavelle and Steven Goodkind, to these positions. They proceeded to carry out their duties with efficiency and visible results. He appointed a number of volunteer "Mayor's Commissions," which produced highly visible and constructive reports and proposals on youth, the elderly, the arts, women, and city finances and taxes. He paid a "constituency worker" out of his own funds and secured the volunteer labor of a supporter, Jane Driscoll, as director of a youth office.

The net result of Democratic and City Hall obstructionism during Sanders' first year in office was to discredit the Democratic aldermen. A "Citizens for Fair Play" committee was formed, urging a cooperative approach on the part of the aldermen, and the *Burlington Free Press* stated in an editorial that "from the beginning of the Sanders administration, it was clear that the Democrats were more preoccupied with tarnishing his credibility than with the best interests of the people."[40] Sanders and the Citizens party members organized a single slate of aldermanic candidates that ran on the mayor's right to do his job without an obstructionist council. Over one hundred campaign workers volunteered their efforts on behalf of the slate. The six Democrats running for re-election, who used arguments such as a warning "to halt the socialist 'fungus' growing in Burlington"[41] were decimated. The Republicans gained two new seats for a total of five. The new slate won three new seats for a total of five. The Democrats lost five out of six seats, reducing their number to three on the thirteen-member board.

The practical implications of the election were that Sanders now had a sufficient block of support to sustain his veto on any piece of city legislation, and so the Board of Aldermen, even in those cases where Republicans and Democrats formed a majority of eight to five, had to negotiate. The Republicans were able to elect the president of the board, Robert Patterson, and to sustain appointments to such key board committees as finance, ordinance, and salary, while Sanders' supporters were able to get the Community Development Committee expanded. But perhaps the key change was reflected in the board's new willingness to support Sanders' appointments to new administrative posts. In April 1982, he secured the appointment of James Rader as city clerk, Jeanne Keller, former director of the Vermont Public Interest Research Group (VPIRG) as assistant city clerk, and John Franco, a former Liberty Union party organizer and candidate for lieutenant governor, for assistant city attorney, while retaining two officials of the previous administration. Sanders made a number of other appointments in 1982: Jonathan Leopold, a Boston investment counselor and former state official under Massachusetts governor Michael Dukakis, was made city treasurer; Barr Swennerfelt, a former member of a Boston accounting firm, was made assistant city treasurer; and Peter Clavelle, who had been city manager of neighboring Winooski, was made personnel director.

Thus by the summer of 1982, two-thirds of the way through Sanders' first two-year term, he had his administration substantially in place. Through the last part of that year and prior to March of 1983—when Sanders himself, as well as half of the Board of Aldermen, would be up for re-election—a series of events occurred that would consolidate the new slate's position in the government and solidify Sanders' mayorality. What happened was a continuation of the kind of situations that had marked Sanders' first year, but on a new level of intensity. Clear evidence of the administration's competence was demonstrated against the backdrop of Democratic intransigence and incompetence. Elaborate efforts at citizen participation and voter mobilization were made but continued to result in stalemate, particularly on land development issues. All of this ended up being blamed on the previous power clique, instead of on Sanders or his supporters.

ADMINISTRATIVE REFORM

Sanders' new appointments quickly began to make inroads into changing a set of administrative practices that, by any standards, were in need of overhaul. Jakobs says that the city

> undertook an aggressive program of productivity increases and cost containment which, in 1982 alone, saved between $400,000 and $600,000. Departmental purchases were central-

ized, gasoline costs were cut 5% to 10%, low-interest loans
given out to friends of the Cemetery Fund were eliminated.
City insurance contracts were put out for competitive bidding,
rather than leaving them to be handled by a consortium of local insurance firms, as they had been for the last 25 years, resulting in savings of $200,000 or 40%. City pension funds were
invested more profitably. An audit revealed that most retirees
were not receiving their proper benefits due to inattention and
poor management. A new cash management system, investing
the city's short-term cash rather than leaving it in low- or no-
interest bearing accounts was instituted, for a gain of $70,000
a year. A new centralized phone system is expected to save
$100,000 a year. Higher fees for building permits should bring
in $150,000 a year. And then, just before Christmas 1982, the
new city treasurer completed his review of city finances and
found a budget surplus of $1.9 million. The money had been
unaccounted for in the city's annual reports, because they were
so poorly structured that "it was extremely difficult to use them
as a management tool," Leopold explained. Sanders was able to
commit $500,000 to street repairs and propose a small property
tax reduction.[42]

CITIZEN PARTICIPATION

While Sanders was able to show that his government was more
efficient than the previous administration, he also continued his
efforts to reach out to more people and to open the administration up
to wider participation. One dimension of this expansion was largely
internal: an effort to increase communication with the rank-and-file
members of the police and fire departments and with other ordinary
city workers. Sanders had campaigned on a promise to improve city
employees' working conditions and salaries, and now he went directly to groups of workers to hear their own opinions about the
structuring of their jobs and the conditions of their work. These
efforts bypassed department heads and commissions, causing antagonism on their part, but he received at least initial good will from
the city workers involved. Personnel Director Peter Clavelle followed up these discussions with a job reclassification study and the
establishment of a permanent Employee Relations Committee.

The other main move toward a more open government structure involved the creation of Neighborhood Planning Assemblies,
adopted by the Board of Aldermen in September 1982 as a means of

democratizing decisions over the use of the federal Community Development Block Grant (CDBG) funds. Thus, in Sanders' second year, he followed up the main citizen participation initiatives of his first year—a series of task forces—with the establishment of a form of organization that had the potential to shift the locus of decision making in the government. But this alteration would have to wait some time before coming to full realization. It was, for the time being, placed under the Planning Commission, which did not exploit its full possibilities.

STALEMATE ON DEVELOPMENT

Like his first year in office, Sanders' second year was marked by a stalemate on most substantive issues. It was beginning to look as if a "socialist" government in the 1980s might take on some of the same characteristics that had marked the municipal socialists and progressives of the turn of the century: governments that were good on administrative reform, good on expanding public participation in government, but were weak in substantially redistributive programs. Sanders tried a number of changes: he set forth several initiatives that would have reformed taxes, losing a rooms-and-meals tax narrowly to a strong business-financed opposition. He proposed: payments in lieu of taxes from the state university, several state tax reform items, and the expansion of the city's representation on the board of the Vermont Medical Center's hospital. Few of these initiatives succeeded. Probably the central issue of substance, for Sanders, was that of real estate and economic development in the city.

Sanders had campaigned on land development issues; he opposed the Southern Connector project and the Planning Commission's proposal to develop the city waterfront area with luxury condominium housing. He had support in this opposition from the neighborhood interests, who had felt the effects of these urban renewal projects and the threat of further such developments. During and after the campaign, public sentiment had developed for an alternative development policy, one that would emphasize the interests of neighborhood residents and low- and middle-income people. They wanted free access to the waterfront, low- and middle-income housing programs, and downtown and neighborhood commercial development that was appropriate for neighborhood people. Thus, when investors proposed a high-priced department store, the neighborhood interests responded that a low- or medium-priced department store and food store would be more appropriate. When investors wanted to build the four-lane Southern Connector to give the downtown access to the suburban consumers who had settled south of the city around the IBM plant in Essex Junction, the Burlington neighborhood people found themselves strongly in opposition to this plan.

After Mayor Paquette and the majority of the Democratic aldermen were turned out of office, the Planning Commission became the main support for the original development model. Under Commissioner William Aswad and Planning Director Randall Kammerbeek, the Planning Commission had nurtured a well-developed urban renewal program, and they fought Sanders on every detail. Supported by a determined constituency of downtown businessmen and developers, they pursued the building of the Southern Connector, despite Sanders' campaign commitment to stop it. In a 1981 statement, the Planning Commission said:

> The Planning Commission remains convinced that the roads are, in fact, appropriately designed, safe, and badly needed. If we are to return our neighborhood streets to their original purpose and remain a strong retail center, we must construct new access. This foresight by the city is borne out by recent conversations with policy makers for major retailers (who are a key to a successful downtown). They have stated that it would be impossible for them to choose a downtown versus suburban location without this connector system.[43]

But the Southern Connector, while it had been a major campaign issue, was not a main agenda item for Sanders in 1982. The road link remained programmed and was moving toward construction despite many hurdles, including rising costs, while the opposition of the city administration remained largely implicit. The dominant development issue on the agenda was the waterfront, and its continued prominence was at least partly the result of resolute advocacy by Aswad, Kammerbeek, and the Planning Commission, which had put it on the public agenda by means of a plan published in 1971. In 1977 a Canadian developer, the Triad Corporation, had proposed a $22 million project in the waterfront area, to be constructed with the aid of a $3 million Urban Development Action Grant (UDAG) that the Planning Commission had secured from the federal government. Triad later withdrew from the project, selling its option to a local developer, Antonio Pomerleau. Pomerleau later withdrew because of conditions the federal Department of Housing and Urban Development imposed, but by 1980 he had submitted an alternative proposal to be constructed mainly with private financing: a $35 million project including two hundred condominium luxury housing units to sell at $200,000 each, a hotel, commercial space, and a small park. This was the plan that Sanders attacked in his initial election campaign.

When Sanders took office, he first appointed a Waterfront Task Force of architects and developers to produce an alternative plan. Their plan turned out to be similar to Pomerleau's. Sanders, in an interview, later talked about his own goals for the area: He wanted public ownership of substantial parts of the project and the control of development that it would bring:

> It has to be primarily recreational, certainly a park. I'd love to see a public museum, boating, swimming, restaurants that people can afford, perhaps some housing tucked away, but primarily a place where people can enjoy themselves. Public ownership of some key parcels would mean that we will be committed to different priorities. We won't be out to make a profit.[44]

The establishment position, stated most explicitly by the Planning Commission, was that the city should not itself be in the land development business. Kammerbeek was quoted in the *Free Press* to the effect that: "It puts the city in the real estate development business, something we are not really good at."[45]

Sanders and the Planning Commission fought each other to a standstill throughout 1982. Immediately after the election of that year, the Planning Commission took the initiative by proposing to the city a $150,000 feasibility study to be done by the American City Corporation. Sanders and others opposed this proposal on the grounds that the problem did not require more technical information, but rather, a policy decision. In April Sanders proposed the creation of a new board with representation from each of the interested bodies: the Planning Commission's Waterfront Board, the Mayor's Task Force, the Citizens Waterfront Group, and three aldermen. Aswad resisted the idea and Sanders' proposal was voted down by the Board of Aldermen, who compromised by allowing an expansion of the Waterfront Board from seven to ten members. But then it was learned that the aldermen had neglected to reappoint the chairman of the Waterfront Board when his term had expired; he was not reappointed, so Waterfront Board opposition was decreased. In the summer of 1982, Sanders proposed that development affairs be put under his authority and that of the Board of Aldermen, and he proposed the creation of a Community and Economic Development

Office (CEDO). The aldermen refused to adopt the proposal at that time, but, in the fall, Sanders was successful in getting them to create an Economic Development Committee, a community, business, and city government group, on whose agenda would be the consideration of a development function reorganization. Throughout the fall, the stalemate continued. Developer Pomerleau's option on the waterfront project expired in the fall and he withdrew, citing the political climate of the city as one reason. Sanders made a proposal for a two-year development moratorium, while project review would be shifted from the Planning Commission to the Board of Aldermen, a plan rejected 7–6 in January 1983. Then the city held a waterfront symposium in February 1983. Meanwhile, nothing substantial happened.[46]

SANDERS' RE-ELECTION AND A NEW SITUATION

By the beginning of 1983, Sanders and his supporters had fought the opposition to a standstill. Those who favored economic development had no Southern Connector and no waterfront development scheme, despite the best efforts of Aswad and Kammerbeek; Sanders and his supporters had made what they considered to be a beginning, but only that, and they now faced a re-election fight. But they were better organized than before, could put more campaign workers on the street, and could argue that Sanders, having achieved several solid accomplishments and several promising beginnings, despite a series of roadblocks, would now be able to carry forward a program with a new mandate.

The opposition, on the other hand, was in disarray. Speculation throughout 1982 had been that the Democrats and Republicans might run a fusion ticket in order to beat Sanders. Sanders himself doubted they would be that well organized, and, in the end, he was proven correct. The Republicans nominated a conservative, James Gilson, while the Democrats persuaded a liberal, Judith Stephany, to run at the last minute. The downtown business interests, which had sought in various ways to put up real opposition to Sanders, had conducted polls to determine which issues they could use to beat him, but in the end they failed to do so. In the election, Sanders outpolled both of his opposition candidates, gathering 52 percent of the total vote.

Following his re-election, Sanders moved to implement the proposals he had made during the previous year. The main one was the reorganization of the development function within the government: Sanders' proposal was to strip the Planning Commission of its land development functions and create a new Community and Economic Development Office under his authority. He had succeeded in getting this as a recommendation earlier in the year from the Burlington Economic Development Advisory Council, which he had appointed in September of 1982. This was his main order of business after the election. In an April 20 memorandum, he proposed the new office to the Board of Aldermen, citing the need to coordinate "economic" development activities, which had so often impinged on neighborhood interests, with "community" development activities, involving improved housing and neighborhood conditions and also including the citizen participation initiatives that were so important in Sanders' election mandate.

There was some doubt whether, even now, the board would approve the proposal. The recommendation of the Advisory Council would help, but the Democrats and Republicans on the board still held the majority. It was a dramatic moment when several business leaders spoke in favor of the new office at the board meeting, and an affirmative vote resulted. Later, these business leaders gave the reasons for their favoring it. First, they had been convinced by Sanders' strong electoral performance that they could not beat him, and therefore they thought they should try to work with him. Second, they had been convinced that Sanders had put together a competent administrative apparatus and that he had made good appointments. They were willing to prefer a competent administration that opposed them on many points to an incompetent one that supported them on those points. Finally, some at least of these men were convinced that Sanders was operating in their interests. Nick Wylie, manager of the Burlington Mall and a downtown business leader, took this position:

> First, he is competent. He is running the city. Second, he is pro development. He really wants it. He has figured out that it is a cow to be milked. He wants to build his tax base.
>
> Previously there was this lurking presence . . . low-income people who could rise up and stop any project. Paquette was not dealing with them. Sanders has dealt them in.[47]

The creation of the new office made progress possible on two fronts. On one front, Sanders was able to energize the neighborhood assemblies and give them a new importance, which had been unrealized while they were under the control of the Planning Commission. The other front was a series of new development initiatives including, but not limited to, major progress on the waterfront project.

NEIGHBORHOOD ASSEMBLIES

The neighborhood assemblies had been set up by the Board of Aldermen in September of 1982 by authority of the Planning Commission, which had authority over federal Community Development Block Grant funds and was required to implement a "citizen participation plan" as a condition for getting the funds. The Planning Commission set up the associations because it had a former neighborhood organizer, Michael Monte, on its staff who had adopted the idea and who pushed it through, and the commission apparently did not consider the proposal important enough to oppose. Sanders' supporters and Monte had had the idea of setting up a partly autonomous neighborhood participation structure before this, and in instituting the assemblies through the Planning Commission, they were certainly getting less than they wanted. Monte, who was given responsibility for setting up the new organizations, was able to get things started, however. The board resolution called for the Planning Commission to initiate two meetings in each ward, and Monte did that. By the end of 1982, seven assemblies had been set up and had begun to consider issues of interest to them. But it was also clear that they would not get very far under the Planning Commission, which was not going to give them any positive encouragement. Evidence of this attitude can be found, for instance, in the proposal the Planning Commission made in 1983 to adopt uniform association by-laws, to require fifty person quorums, and to restrict the assemblies to quarterly meetings. Monte had resigned his position by the spring of 1983 and had taken a job with the state. Just at that point, the new CEDO was established. This radically changed the prospects for the assemblies, because the Planning Commission had lost control of the CDBG funds and the assemblies.

In June, Sanders asked Monte to return at least on a volunteer, part-time basis to breathe some life into the assemblies. As Monte reports it, "Bernie asked me to come back and provide a little . . . support . . . let's begin to get these things off the ground as regular assemblies, planning assemblies. What are they going to be?"[48]

Monte held a meeting of representatives of each of the ward assemblies, held a discussion about by-laws, got an exchange of information going among the representatives, then held a series of meetings with each separate assembly in which each discussed its by-laws. The new CEDO offered encouragement, most materially by allocating $15,000 of CDBG funds to each of the six assemblies in August, and also by putting Monte back on the city staff payroll where his responsibility would be to nurture the assemblies. Each organization had adopted its own by-laws by October. They proceeded into operation, each with its own different priorities. The aim of their establishment was not to create autonomous neighborhood organizations. Rather, they were to operate as something in-between a simple "decentralization" of the city administration and more autonomous units. Monte saw them as vehicles by which the various city departments could better involve people in their affairs, could get their opinions without relinquishing all control:

> The agenda . . . outside of fifteen thousand dollars [they have for themselves] is to relate to the different departments in terms of information, which is essentially what they were created for. That is a very critical part of the enabling resolution. It talks about [the] many times . . . the different departments have a need to talk to residents of neighborhoods about critically important issues. [This] critical part of the resolution has been my guiding light in terms of what should be happening with the assemblies.[49]

But Monte also welcomed the assemblies' taking control of at least a part of their own agendas and was happy to let them negotiate with him about their substantive concerns:

> At the same time, in an organic way, they have also lent themselves to have critical issues developed by the assemblies themselves. In Ward One, there is a baseball issue that brought out fifty people, in Ward Five, a housing development issue that brought out about fifty or seventy people. In Ward Five, they also by themselves established a South Park Development Committee that worked with the Parks Department on the development of [a] playground. . . . In Ward Six, the development of a residential structure into an office for a lot of lawyers . . . was a critical issue. . . . In Ward Six, because of a previous history in that ward about dealing with the problems of zoning in terms of them wanting to keep a low-density ward, they took on the Master Plan when the Planning Department came to them and said we want input . . . and really worked on it.[50]

Monte operated as an organizer, instead of as a city administrator, for the most part:

> I mean I took a whole lot less control over what should be hap-
> pening. I did not put anything down in terms of "here: use this."
> And so some of them did a little bit of hit and miss. And then a
> lot of times what seems to work in another ward—what I do,
> I will share with another ward. And they may adapt it and
> change it a little bit. So the only way right now for the boards
> to work together, in terms of shared information, is me. I im-
> part information based upon what I think might be useful. . . .
> They have control and . . . there has been a little bit of . . .
> working through some of the stuff in terms of setting the
> agenda and stuff like that. I don't set their agenda. They set
> their agenda. It is a question though of do I want something on
> their agenda and I ask for an hour and a half out of their time
> and they give me forty-five minutes, how do I respond to that?
> And I say I need an hour and a half. Our office doesn't gener-
> ally go in with a sort of saying, here it is, what do you think,
> which is a lot what other departments do as a way of dealing
> with process. We generally come in with a process: write down
> thoughts, think about it, do a whole lot of cute little things that
> get as much information from people as possible.[51]

Monte thought the assemblies were developing as viable organizations under the rather loose rein the city gave them, but he had
no illusions about their being autonomous. He still controlled their
checkbooks, for example; he could negotiate each meeting. He called
them a "hybrid between the centralized planning structure and
a process whereby . . . critical issues in a ward are raised." And,
he said,

> they allow those two things to happen within their own organi-
> zational structure. They elect their own people. I don't like
> some of the people. I really like some of the people. I don't con-
> trol anything in terms of who I am and what happens in city
> government. There is a loose cannon out there going about its
> own way and that is good.[52]

Monte was, however, looking at the neighborhood assemblies
with a critical eye by 1984. In March, he was hoping for some sort of
self-evaluation by the assemblies by the summer, so that the new organizations could determine what purposes they were serving and
see to what extent they really had broadened public participation.

Others in the Sanders administration were wondering about something else. By and large, they noticed, most of the people participating in the assemblies were not part of their coalition. What did that mean? Monte also had this concern, but he expressed it another way:

> Does this enfranchise or disenfranchise? I think it does [en-franchise] . . . a certain group of people. There is a whole num-ber of people who are out there, disenfranchised. A lot of them will tend to be Democrats who were disenfranchised essen-tially from the political process. This is their opportunity to be involved.[53]

ECONOMIC DEVELOPMENT

At the same time that CEDO was setting up the neighborhood assemblies, it was also moving ahead vigorously with its economic development programs. It had been authorized to work on a number of questions by the May 23 resolution: to stimulate investment, to develop projects, to administer a comprehensive housing program, to implement waterfront development, to administer the Commu-nity Development Block Grants program, and to coordinate citizen participation, including the neighborhood planning assemblies. By the spring of 1984, director Peter Clavelle, who had moved from his position as personnel director to head the new office, was able to re-port that a number of these activities were under way.

First, CEDO had taken over the economic development and housing programs that the Planning Department had been oper-ating. It was pursuing Urban Development Action Grants from HUD. In a 1983 report, it described three such projects: the expansion of Burlington Square—a downtown shopping, office, and hotel com-plex—to include a new department store, a parking garage, and ad-ditional hotel space; and two commercial building renovations. These projects were to include investments totaling $25 million, and they would create "nearly one thousand jobs." CEDO was also operating the Housing Improvement Program, a loan program that was helping to finance six hundred housing units.

Second, CEDO was part of an effort to create innovative, new economic development and housing programs. Barr Swennerfelt, in the treasurer's office, had devised the Burlington Revolving Loan Program, for which the Sanders administration had gotten Board of Aldermen approval of a $250,000 allocation aimed at small businesses, with loan ceilings set at $25,000. CEDO was also pursuing a program to stimulate employee-managed businesses by contracting with the International Cooperative Association in Cambridge, Massachusetts, for a feasibility study. And they had also begun a program to aid the formation of a Community Land Trust to build or renovate low-cost housing, with help from the Institute for Community Economics in Greenfield, Massachusetts.

Finally, CEDO was taking the lead in setting up the revitalized waterfront project, which was the most visible economic development project in the city. In 1983, after Pomerleau's withdrawal from the project and while Sanders and the Planning Commission remained deadlocked on the appropriate way to move ahead, a group of local investors had formed the Alden Corporation and had selected a distinguished Boston architect, Ben Thompson, to do the design for the project. They signified their willingness to submit the design to community opinion, and Sanders, having created CEDO, took the opportunity to put a participatory waterfront planning operation into place. Michael Monte, having established the neighborhood planning assemblies on firm ground by the end of 1983, organized a series of meetings on the waterfront project, one in each ward. Over eight hundred people attended these meetings and gave their suggestions about such questions as the degree of setback from the water, the amount of public land and the types of land uses that should be included in the project. The Alden Corporation presented a "concept plan" to the Board of Aldermen early in 1984 and got an acceptance from the board and from Sanders.

THE BALANCE OF INTERESTS IN 1984

By 1984, Sanders had emerged from the deadlocked situation of his previous years in office with a working political coalition and the beginnings of a diverse support base in the city. He was still frustrated by his minority position on the Board of Aldermen, but by making good administrative appointments and improving the management of the city in a striking way, he was able to convince his opponents of his views on many issues, even when he did not have electoral majorities. Basically he had managed to balance the interests of the city's working-class neighborhoods—which needed jobs and improvements in the quality of life associated with their housing and other community services—with the interests of the business community, which needed a stable environment for investment. Sanders succeeded in cutting past the rhetoric of business opposition to find areas of agreement. These included the eventual under-standing that separate projects could be negotiated, with the public interest in each case being represented by the city. He managed to get business leaders to retreat from ritual stands against all pub-lic ownership or in favor of the most damaging versions of the Southern Connector.

CHAPTER 6

Planning

Planning is the application of conscious foresight to making decisions. Public planning is a method of making decisions by communities; it stands as an alternative and supplement to markets, to voting, and to bargaining among major political interests, each of which tend to be reactive. The results that are accomplished by these methods entail little or no conscious foresight applied by the group as a whole.[1] Planning, in contrast, requires the community or its designated officials to look consciously at the causal structures affecting whatever is to be decided.

A city might have to decide between two alternative subdivision layouts proposed by competing developers, for example. Markets, voting, and bargaining—each is a plausible device for arriving at a decision, but only by means of planning is an established way set up for the public or its officials to investigate the cause-and-effect relationships involved in street traffic, work, and residence activities in the subdivision in detail in an unhurried and deliberate fashion and to come up with a plan which meets all the community's objectives.

The preceding chapters are replete with descriptions of major public choices for which these cities used planning. While governments had always used a kind of planning—it was a minor feature of almost all city politics under the governments in power after World War II—for the progressive leaders described in the preceding chapters, planning functioned as a major theme. Carbone's shift to supporting the (expanded) Civic Center came about because, instead of accepting the proposal that was backed by the Chamber of Commerce, he did his own analysis; and his later shift from a physical-construction to a services approach came about because he was convinced by Sid Gardner's analysis of welfare costs. In a less explicit way, Kucinich's policies resulted from Krumholz's earlier analyses, which gave credence to MUNY Light's position and to the anti-tax abatement position; and planning was similarly important in the far-reaching policy positions taken in Berkeley, Santa Monica, and Burlington.

Post–World War II liberal city governments had had an ultimate faith in pluralist bargaining and market processes to settle the most important political issues, and this perspective narrowed the uses made of planning. Progressives, who perceived the increasing economic concentrations that made both pluralism and markets less viable as decision procedures, applied planning to a relatively wider range of topics. In brief summary, this wider scope for planning had the following results:

(1) To a remarkable degree, progressive political leaders used planning and listened to planners, and in some cases, they were themselves central figures in setting forth elaborate planning exercises.

(2) The substance of planning went rather deep, so that the basic elements of a distinctive progressive planning doctrine began to appear in the plan documents.

(3) Progressives adapted previously established official forms and structures to their own ends for doing planning, often finding advantages in using traditional structures and precedents.

(4) Tensions existed between some traditional structures and the participatory style of progressive programs, which often obstructed the whole progressive program.

(5) At least the beginnings of a reinforcement between planning and progressive politics appeared.

Progressive governments, therefore, did not simply use planning to a greater *degree* than their predecessors, but the changes they made, combined with their politics, resulted in differences in *kind*. These differences will be described here, and then I will venture some conclusions as to what planning was all about under these progressive governments.

The Adoption of Planning

For progressive political leaders, the inclination to get involved in planning followed from their disillusion with and rejection of markets and interest-group bargaining as ways of deciding local affairs. For some, this understanding was part of their most basic conceptual apparatus, while for others it came as a slow learning experience. Carbone's development of the downtown Hartford real estate strategy is a good example of the latter. He came from a South Hartford business background. Looking back on his career after he was out of politics, he described himself as having had, early on, more social awareness and public commitment than the city at large had credited him with, but he also claimed to have learned much more, and much more in particular about planning, on the job, once he was on the council. He had initially opposed the Civic Center as not in the interest of his South Hartford neighborhood constituency. Once in office, after hearing arguments from downtown and suburban interests, he worked out a set of conditions under which he would support the idea: the project had to be doubled in size, the major corporations had to make major and visible financial contributions, and he—acting for the city—had to control it. Once he had decided that the city, not private interests, was to be the developer, he was impelled to enter into the planning of it in detail rather than leave it in the hands of the city manager and private developers.

The Civic Center project set a pattern for Carbone. The city manager resigned, leading to a situation in which a succession of city managers and other staff people worked directly with Carbone. Gradually, staffing and control built up in Carbone's City Council office; many other functions began to come under city control instead of being left to the private sector, and they required the city to do planning for them. The Food Plan, the energy program, and numerous other operations begun by Alschuler and other such planning-oriented officials as Coleman and Strecker followed. Still, Carbone's own ability to think in programmatic (as opposed to *ad hoc*) ways was the major force that sustained the others.

In Berkeley, the structure of planning was much looser. The Berkeley Citizens Action people did not have control of the city's administration until 1979, and in their long period as a minority coalition, any planning they did took the form of unofficial drafts and proposals. These studies, however, infiltrated the atmosphere around BCA and helped to shape such specific measures as the original rent control initiatives, the utility takeover effort, and the neighborhood preservation ordinance.

A commitment to planning was characteristic of many of the BCA people who were elected to the Berkeley City Council in the 1970s. They wanted to connect the traditions and concerns of physical planning with broader ends. Loni Hancock seemed to bridge

the poles of traditional planning and new left politics. She had begun political work with the Robert Scheer campaign in 1966 and he
had worked with the Community for a New Politics, working at the
same time on neighborhood planning committees. When she described her motivations for getting involved in local politics,
she wrote:

> The traditional [Democratic] politicians seemed to be talking
> about capital improvements in the city of Berkeley, while the
> new left talked about beginning in Berkeley to address and
> solve the problems of the nation. . . . Only the new left had any-
> thing political to say to me.[2]

A number of BCA candidates infused their local planning interests
into their politics. Veronika Fukson spent time on the planning
board before being elected to the City Council, and Anna Rabkin,
who became the city auditor in 1979, had studied planning at the
university. Prior to 1979, the planning board had been a major focus
of BCA activity because it gave them the chance both to raise specific
issues and to move their less radical board members toward BCA positions. In a way, the BCA planners were following the lead of T. J.
Kent, Jr., the city planner and Berkeley professor who had led
the liberal move to control the City Council in the 1950s and
early 1960s.

It is important to make a distinction between the concrete
ways in which planning came up in terms of specific issues BCA could
address effectively and the much wider set of planning ideas that
influenced the possible moves that political actors could make on
concrete issues. The distinction is between action and context. The
two need to be thought about differently. The fact that the Berkeley
radicals remained on the fringes of power for several years after
1971 meant that they had a relatively small chance to affect official
city actions. But they used this time to create the context for future
actions, that is, to create an agenda of possibilities that the city
could think about until action became possible. *The Cities' Wealth*
investigated this wider set of ideas, and it was itself only one summary of ideas about planning that had been circulating in Berkeley
for some time. The more concrete planning involvement came after
the Fair Representation Ordinance was passed in 1975, when the
BCA people got a foothold in the city boards, including the Planning
Commission, where they were able to be persuasive on numerous issues. Upon taking the leadership of the City Council in 1979, the
BCA people shifted from a planning to a more *ad hoc* administrative

mode of operations, although many of their actions, particularly the work of the Citizens Budget Review Commission, reflected the redistributive thinking that had pervaded their earlier planning work.

Whether planning actually structured the thoughts of the Kucinich administration in Cleveland remains an open question. Ten years of planning analysis had been going on in the City Planning Department under Krumholz, and many of these positions and rationales had been absorbed by Kucinich on such issues as MUNY Light and tax abatements. This pattern was generally consistent with the patterns that held good in Hartford and Berkeley. But Swanstrom describes Kucinich as a political tactician rather than as someone committed to a comprehensive economic program, and his behavior in office—albeit acting under severe external pressures—suggests that there was little or no conscious economic or physical planning in his administration.[3]

Planning—in the more general sense of agenda-setting described here—was also prominent in the thoughts of progressive politicians in Santa Monica and Burlington. Bernard Sanders ran for election specifically using certain planning issues provoked by the development orientation of the Burlington City Planning Commission and the Paquette administration. He put together an alternative strategy for the downtown and the waterfront, which he then elaborated with his close advisors in opposition to the Planning Commission, until he was able to establish the Community and Economic Development Office in 1983. In Santa Monica, Santa Monicans for Renters Rights had tied rent control to wider planning issues by the end of 1980, and its "Principles of Unity" reflected a broad planning strategy. In both Burlington and Santa Monica, this broad sense of strategy, a kind of planning, led to a more detailed form of planning once the city governing institutions came under the progressives' control: in Burlington, planning came under their control with the creation of the Community Economic Development Office; in Santa Monica, with the arrival of Alschuler in the city manager's office and with majority control on the planning commission somewhat later.

Progressive Planning Doctrine

Overall strategic planning by the political leadership was importantly related to the development of more detailed plans by professionals and, occasionally, by citizen boards and committees. This more detailed work comprised a coherent planning doctrine, which I will describe in terms of three themes: public ownership, opposition, and method. All of these themes had been present in traditional planning doctrine, but as minor themes. Progressives incorporated them into a new doctrine. The path-breaking efforts in forging this new doctrine were made in the 1970s, in Hartford, Berkeley, and Cleveland.

First, progressive planners, politicians, and political activists elaborated on the possibilities of *public ownership* of the city's productive resources and investments. The Berkeley group went the furthest with these ideas; Carbone tested them the most; and the Cleveland planners addressed the idea of public ownership specifically in their defense of MUNY Light. Berkeley's conceptualizations of the ·doctrine of collective ownership were most extensively laid out by Kirshner and his colleagues, but they were forged in the political environment surrounding the Peoples Park controversy and later in contacts with collective organizing activists and theorists. The basic set of ideas included, first, the premise that the public had created property values and other forms of social wealth, and therefore that the public should control their use. Second, Kirshner argued for the tactical principle of aiming for control over the most immobile capital first: control of utilities, housing, industry, offices, and stores, in that order. Many specific issues in Berkeley could be connected to these ideas: the Pacific Gas and Electric takeover initiatives, the rent strikes, the fight for rent control and the Neighborhood Preservation Ordinance, all of which asserted the interests of local residents and consumers over those of investors (and speculators).

Hartford's efforts toward establishing public ownership were less all-encompassing in their objectives, but they still amounted to elaborately worked out planning agreements in one area: city co-ownership of real estate. Carbone, Strecker, and their City Council supporters had concluded that the developmental returns of real estate—or at least a share of them—should go to the city's population collectively, rather than to investors. The city's real estate operations came to encompass increasingly more sophisticated deals, but Carbone always justified them in terms of their redistributive effects on the city's predominantly poor population.

In Cleveland, the MUNY Light position first staked out by Krumholz and Bonner and later adopted by Kucinich and by a city referendum simply argued that the existence of a public utility was of concrete benefit to city residents. Cleveland's was the least elaborated position taken in any of these three cities on the issue of collective ownership. But all three cities took mutually consistent positions on the public ownership issue.

A second aspect of progressive planning doctrine as it emerged was the sense of *opposition,* of pitting the interests of city residents against corporate and suburban interests. This adversarial positioning was most dramatically made clear when Cleveland asked HUD to decertify the regional planning agency and Carbone sued the suburbs over their low-income housing plans. This sense of the city's conflictual role was also articulated abstractly as a consciousness that the idea of the "public interest" had been expropriated by business and suburban interests and was being used as a weapon against city people. Therefore, progressives tried either to deny the existence of a public interest or to articulate a new conception of the public interest in which their own residents would be included.

The sense of opposition was not mainly an abstract position, however. There were real conflicts at work, plenty of stimuli to mobilize the energies of planners working in progressive governments. At stake in their conflicts were not just organizational battles (quite common in all kinds of governments), but conflicts in which the planners were in constant contact with real constituencies, at the same time that they were negotiating technical matters with highly organized, and opposing, interests.

These conflictual situations changed the consciousness of the planners. Krumholz reported his initial outrage at encountering racism, when he sat in for Stokes at the Northeast Ohio Area Coordinating Agency, the suburb-dominated regional association of governments. His response stemmed from his own identification with Stokes and his black constituents. Janice Cogger reported similar feelings when she represented the city in the regional transit negotiations.[4] Krumholz generally painted a picture of a staff that met with neighborhood groups at night, then negotiated with corporate interests and suburbs by day. Progressives in Hartford and Berkeley reported similar kinds of dissonance in their political encounters. Carbone's contact with the North Hartford riots was very formative for his sense of politics. Kirshner's contacts with the Berkeley rent strikers and with the Peoples Park demonstrations clearly affected his motivations and his conception of what could be accomplished with planning. Planners were bridges between disparate constituencies, and the conflictual nature of this role changed their consciousness of class and racial relations.

Finally, progressive planners took *methodological* positions that specifically recognized the presence and interests of present residents in the city—in contrast to earlier political methodologies, which focused on such activities as the location of factories, shopping centers, or residential districts, and assumed that the interests of individuals would somehow be derived from these locational economic patterns. One can identify the progressive methodological position in the specific reports and analyses done by the planners. Krumholz and Bonner, who took an individualistic approach, simply asserted the local interest in the need for a redistribution of opportunities. They advocated "maximizing choices for those who have less." The Cleveland Planning Department did a series of studies on several separate issues in which this methodological perspective always came to the fore: the impact of projects on the city's poor was consistently exposed and was weighted heavily against more general and abstract benefits, which often went to people not actually living in the city. The Berkeley group took a more collective tack, but the people they represented were still city residents: the Neighborhood Preservation Ordinance, for example, favored the interests of residents of the local neighborhoods as against those of outside investors.

This methodological perspective was also reflected in the content and the selection of analyses done by the progressive planners. Typically, the initial expression of a progressive consciousness came forth simply as a rejection of the relevance of the traditional city master plan. Master plan documents, common in the background of most city planning agencies, incorporated in their nature the disadvantage of taking a good deal of time to substantiate in terms of data and of being oriented to future populations, almost by definition. Thus the usual method of forming a master plan was to start from certain crucial industrial locations and natural features and then deduce from them the quantities and locations of housing, transportation, commercial, and public investments needed. Alternative methods were conceivable, but this method was the traditional one in American planning and it was supported by local commercial interests. It was natural, then, for progressives first to attack the relevance of master plans. It was more important to them to have *ad hoc* studies done evaluating specific local issues. This was Krumholz's initial planning strategy, as exemplified by the study he made of the MUNY Light sale proposal. It was relatively straightforward politically to take up issues one at a time, to make sure to examine the relatively near-term costs and benefits to present city residents, and to come up with recommendations different from those inherent in master planning studies.

The tendency to retreat from comprehensive plans toward *ad hoc* studies was not, in itself, a people-oriented or progressive methodology. The planning profession was generally moving toward an incrementalist viewpoint, a doctrine associated with Lindblom and others, but much of this type of planning was in fact developed as aid to the kinds of projects the progressives were opposing. Many advocate planners did adopt an incrementalist approach, arguing that ideas about the public interest that had justified the master plans were cover-ups for commercial interests. Some went so far as to deny the possibility of a legitimate public interest.

But the progressives described here took a different tack: accepting the legitimacy of the idea of an overall public interest, they reformulated it in a redistributive way, that is, toward the interests of working, poor, and local people. Thus, Krumholz and Bonner, although not especially articulate about a "public interest," did later evolve a more comprehensive policy statement in the *Cleveland Policy Plan*. In that document, the Planning Commission argued its general position with some rigor and articulated the goal of redistributing opportunities to those who have relatively few opportunities. In itself, it was not a detailed land use or public investments plan, nor was it a proposal to change the basic structure of power or decision making in the city. It was, rather, a presentation of a point of view that might guide decision makers who wanted to make incremental departures from the tradition. In that sense, it was well adapted both to Cleveland's populist tradition of fragmented government and to the Planning Commission's marginal role in that government.

More fundamental proposals for changing the political structure of the city came from planners outside of government in Berkeley and from planners' involvement in government in Hartford. Many of these proposals constituted a move back toward a new sort of comprehensive and physical plan. In Berkeley, the ideas developed in *The Cities' Wealth,* while rather general, were quite sweeping in scope; Kirshner's New Towns ideas were a methodological reversal of master planning procedures. In Hartford, methodological innovations in planning are difficult to discern, because the planning merged closely with Carbone's particular administration and politics. But such reports as can be examined display the structural innovations in city government and economics that occurred there:

the Hartford Food system, the energy proposals, and the various innovations surrounding the real estate development effort.

Urban renewal was the most prominent planning initiative that earlier urban regimes had achieved, and urban renewal, in many respects, involved a delegation of the planning function to private interests or to a special authority. The urban renewal programs in Berkeley, Cleveland, and Hartford (prior to the establishment of the Civic Center) typically depended upon the availability of large private-sector capital. The public role was to certify the public interest supposedly in the project and to put up a subsidy. This made possible the clearance of large parcels of land on terms favorable to the investors. Where the public interest was clear-cut and noncontroversial and where private capital was available, urban renewal was executed rather easily. Problems arose when cities could not reach any consensus on the public interest value of a project. This happened in the case of the West Berkeley urban renewal project: Protests arose over the displacement of residents and stalled the project. Similar protests occurred in relation to the Constitution Plaza project in Hartford, although the city pushed the project through to completion. But in all the urban renewal efforts, a sufficiently elaborate planning apparatus was lacking, one that could take into account all the indirect as well as direct effects of the projects so as to make a convincing case for a public interest. Because local governments failed to take all these effects into account, projects often were attacked and discredited, whether or not they were actually built. By the end of the 1960s, many cities had by-and-large lost interest in urban renewal unless they could define projects as private ones. Instead of trying to improve their planning capacities, their analyses were devoted to enumerating the costs of public actions. The Bay Area Rapid Transit system came under this kind of intense evaluation in the Bay area, and many planners retreated from the very idea of urban renewal.

Government Structure for Planning: Adapting Earlier Forms

Progressives, having adopted planning and used it as a vehicle for somewhat more embracing doctrines than had been used previously by planners, still faced the question of how to institutionalize planning within or around the structures of government. The result of their efforts at institutionalization was a set of structural inventions—and ideas for inventions—that adapted previous forms of planning already in existence to new purposes. Progressive planners and politicians evolved three main ways of operating. They structured a planning function within City Hall, they developed new forms of planning professionalism, and they began to find new forms for an independent planning function. In these ways progressives addressed problems that had been building up for a long time in the profession of planning.

THE PROBLEM

The general problem for planners had been that, although city planning had been somewhat independent structurally and had had many of the privileges associated with professionalism, it had little influence. Jon Coleman testified that, in Hartford, the city planners would learn of development schemes through the newspapers, and then they would be given the job of putting together data to support the projects. The city manager had some power, but the planners did not. A similar lack of influence existed in Cleveland, and Krumholz noted that when Stokes was in office he paid the planners little attention. Berkeley had made land use planning a major part of the liberal push for control of the City Council in the later 1950s, but after they achieved that, the planning office declined in influence.

Thus, a major concern of contemporary planners was to increase their influence and to secure established roles for themselves. In pursuit of this influence, the profession operated under two opposing doctrines in the postwar period. The idea which dominated the period before the 1960s was that planning should be limited to physical land use issues and that the planners should be responsible to the city council or to an independent commission, but not to a mayor or city manager. Berkeley achieved this planning position vis-à-vis the City Council and was in fact the model for its exposition in Kent's writings in the 1950s.[5] Cleveland had successfully established the independent commission form for planning in the 1940s, and John Howard, a contemporary of Kent's, had drawn upon his experience as planning director there to produce a well-known essay advocating the independent commission form.[6]

The independent commission, physical-planning approach found favor in the following way. Many politicians and planners, whose traditions were rooted in reliance on the market and who had learned to trust a pluralism of competing interests analogous to markets, deeply distrusted any planning that would inhibit either markets or pluralism. Limiting planning strictly to land-use issues was a way to keep it within bounds while letting markets and pluralism function in other areas. But if a city was to depart from pluralism, even in this one area, it needed a responsible official body to provide stewardship. This would provide legitimacy for planning. In Berkeley, where the City Council was the responsible body, the legitimacy would come from the representativeness of elected officials. In Cleveland, where the role was played by the planning commission, legitimacy came from the presumed expertise and wisdom of the appointed commissioners.

But planners suffered a loss of independence in the 1960s, when another theory began to dominate planning thinking. Planning, said Robert Walker in an influential book, ought not be limited to land use issues, but should be "as broad as the functions of local government," and placed under the broad authority of the chief executive: the mayor or city manager.[7] Largely as a result of monetary incentives provided by the federal government, this was the form planning began to take after about 1960, and even where formal planning roles continued to specify the more independent arrangements, chief executives and line departments took on planning functions in an informal way. This became true of urban renewal and housing agencies, then of job development and training programs, and then of various social programs, each of which began to have both planning and implementation authority.

But planners were in a dilemma, as Alan Altshuler pointed out in his well-known study: If they stuck to land-use issues, they would have no influence over other areas of policy; but in those other areas, their expertise and consequently their authority would never equal that of the more specialized professionals, such as renewal officials or highway engineers.[8] In Hartford, Berkeley, and Cleveland, planners had long been caught on the horns of this dilemma, and in general they had suffered from both of the problems Altshuler discussed. It was not a dilemma wholly of their own making. Local leaders, under strong pressures including racial violence and economic decline, were adding programs faster than they were building the kinds of synthetic policy-making machinery that could have assimilated the planners' advice. This was certainly true of Stokes's administration in Cleveland, of Widener's administration and earlier administrations in Berkeley, and of the Hartford city councils that immediately preceded Carbone's time in office. The dilemma was not so real in Santa Monica and Burlington, which are smaller cities where government had been more cohesive.

PLANNING IN CITY HALL

For progressives, planning itself began to transcend these problems. As was the case with Carbone, one tendency was for progressive leaders to structure planning within the official leadership in City Hall, or within the office of city manager. This was Walker's solution, and it fit the tendency of progressives to want to use planning across a wide gamut of functions. In Hartford, the executive structure was the main institutional location for planning, and it was a solution adapted to the city's history: There had never been a strong independent planning commission there, and policy direction had always been in the hands of the city manager. When Hartford's city manager resigned, Carbone naturally filled the vacuum. He then added some planning staff, by-and-large in the city manager's office. The advantage was that in that way he could develop one integrated planning unit under his control. He never nourished the Planning Commission. Hartford, however, did have an independent planning operation—Greater Hartford Process, the large and well-funded organization set up by Lumsden and the Chamber of Commerce. Carbone used his City Hall machinery to react to, and often to oppose, proposals coming from Process. There seemed to be a healthy pluralism in this, and the city exploited the Process' planning expertise whenever it could.

In Berkeley, the most radical planning initiatives were begun outside of City Hall. This pattern paralleled the emergence of progressive leadership, which first established itself in the City Council and on appointed boards and committees, and only gradually got established in the city administration. When the B C A gained control of the City Council in 1979, it was soon able to install its own city manager and then to establish some of its supporters in the city manager's office, including Eve Bach. They began to produce planning, but most of their work was managing. Slowly Mayor Gus Newport became involved in the planning process, but he was not as dominant in his administration as Carbone had been in Hartford. He stayed more within the council-manager structure. He played a political role on the council and allowed the city manager a larger place. Eve Bach, in her accounts of her work in the city manager's office, stressed its *ad hoc,* though very constructive, nature. Meanwhile Berkeley's Planning Department remained weak and peripheral. The lead in planning in Berkeley was taken elsewhere, in the city Planning Commission and the City Council.

In both Santa Monica and Burlington, the progressives developed and elaborated their planning staffs under central leadership as soon as they could. Alschuler's thinking about Santa Monica's development strategy with the aid of David Smith was one example of this central management approach; Sanders' periodic statements on waterfront development in Burlington was another; later this pattern was to be much elaborated by CEDO. In both of these cases, there had been independent planning functions outside of the central offices. The Santa Monica Planning Commission served for a short period after the SMRR victory in 1981 as a rostrum for the opposition, and the Burlington Planning Commission served the same purpose there against Sanders.

THE INDEPENDENT COMMISSION

The alternative to a centralized planning function was the independent commission, which had been developed historically in each of the cities considered here. Berkeley had a planning board appointed by the City Council that had a few advisory powers and was separated from the city Planning Department, which was under the city manager; but the planning board had a strong tradition of using its advisory role in a public way. Cleveland's Planning Commission was set up in a more independent way by city charter: commission members and the director were appointed by the mayor, but the director and staff had specified charter powers and advisory functions (no capital budget could be passed by the council without Planning Commission approval, for example.) The director and staff were free from managerial control under Cleveland's weak-mayor system.

In Berkeley, the independence of planning persisted in spite of the city manager. The staff remained marginal to the politics of the council and to the development of the administrative agencies' own plans and programs. But an independent planning function developed in and around the BCA, and this ultimately came to be represented on the Planning Commission and had a political impact through BCA members on the council. In Cleveland, Krumholz was able to build up an independent planning presence, which his predecessors had let deteriorate. He was helped by the existing structure of the Planning Commission as an independent body with certain review powers over the City Council, by mayoral indifference, and by the fragmented nature of Cleveland's large, ward-based council.

The planning commissions in Burlington and Santa Monica served, for a time, as outposts of the opposition to the progressive leadership. These opposing forces were so polarized, however, that no constructive dialogue could occur. In Santa Monica, the seeds of such a dialogue might have existed in the Planning Commission, on the committee that was working on the housing element as SMRR took control in 1981. But the polarized atmosphere that set in following the election was focused on the task forces (another set of committees) and prevented such a dialogue. All this changed later, when Commission terms of office ended and SMRR got a majority on the Planning Commission. Then, influenced by Shearer, the commission used its mandate to promote citizen participation in order to create a constituency around land-use planning questions, and even formed something of a counterweight to the centralizing tendencies that came from Alschuler. The key to this cooperation was the relative consistency of goals that existed between City Hall and the Planning Commission.

In Burlington, the situation was similar to the one that had generated the earlier conflict in Santa Monica. The Planning Commission more and more came to bear the burden of opposing Sanders on development issues, and, in the end, it isolated itself from its support in the business community. This estrangement resulted in the formation of the new Community and Economic Development Office under the mayor in 1983 and the reduction of the Planning Commission and Planning Department to a land-use controls function.

A New Professionalism

Professionalism, nurtured by some form of independence from hierarchical authority, helped planners to operate effectively in the charged environment of progressive politics. Krumholz's professionalism, his sense of calling, which had responded to the prospect of working in Stokes' administration, helped to sustain him throughout most of Kucinich's mayoralty. A similar professionalism sustained Kirshner and Bach in Berkeley. When outsiders called Bach the "conscience" of the BCA in City Hall, they were referring to her integrity in the face of pressures, both from the left in BCA and from the right, as less progressive forces moved back into command after 1981.

Progressive planners were carving out a role for themselves that earlier planners had not needed to play; these contemporary planners were in a new kind of institutional situation. Progressive governments did achieve the beginnings of a new independent planning function and the outlines of a new professionalism, but only the beginnings. If progressive politics had been a fully developed form of government, that is, if there had been a full accommodation between the aims and programs of the progressives and the values and institutions of the wider community and region, then there would have been a lot more support for their programs. As it was, progressives—particularly the planners—were at best in a transitional situation, in which reinforcements did not exist, but in which they were being asked to operate in the face of great obstacles and insecurities. As a result, there were many tensions inherent in planning. These came as much from the weaknesses planning had developed as it tried to adapt itself to earlier political patterns as it did from any defects in the progressive political programs. The more planners had moved, in the 1960s, from their independent roles on planning commissions toward the protective umbrellas of mayors and city managers, the more difficult it became for them to embrace enthusiastically the rather high-profile participatory demands inherent in progressive politics, or to develop their own professionalism.

Krumholz and Bach, perhaps, were exceptional. For others, the planners' professional status sometimes came to be a defense against the demands of elected progressive politicians. Some of Krumholz's staff people took strong exception to being asked by Kucinich's aides to work in election campaigns. Krumholz, himself, had no qualms about giving speeches for his bosses: he had his own well-developed positions, and could support Kucinich (and had on specific issues supported Perk) within his own framework. Staff people in the Berkeley Planning Department, on the other hand, were isolated from the BCA, even after BCA took majority control. BCA was in the habit of attacking the official planners and the city manager under whom they worked (staff planners were under orders not to communicate with the public, except when authorized to by the city manager).

THE INDEPENDENT PLANNING FUNCTION

Apart from the issue of professionalism, the independence of planning lived in a dynamic tension with progressive politics. Progressive chief executives and ruling groups tended to value loyalty in their planners. The BCA, when it was out of power, had infiltrated the Planning Commission in Berkeley and used it as a pulpit and as a training ground for office-holding. When several of these same people were elected to office in 1979, the next group of Planning Commission members felt left out, and one reported that he had been told not to rock the boat for a while by raising new planning issues. The insecurity of power thus became a planning issue; the leadership always wanted to wait until the next election, when their power might be consolidated, before riling the waters. Kucinich certainly had this problem, which led to his practice of installing his political allies as assistants to department heads whose expertise he needed, but whose loyalty to him might be qualified. In Hartford, Planning Commission members outside of Carbone's immediate circle were frustrated by their lack of a policy making role. The planning director worked for Carbone, not for the Planning Commission.[9]

How Planning Reinforced Progressive Politics

Planning relates to politics. Its goals, structures, doctrine, methods, and constituencies reinforce—and are themselves nourished or discouraged by—the structure of city politics. Numerous studies have shown how postwar urban growth politics, a form of interest-group pluralism, encouraged an indicative, business-oriented kind of planning and discouraged a participatory, redistributive kind of planning. Others have argued a complementary point: planning itself has helped to justify and sustain the politics of growth.[10]

Alan Altshuler studied the dilemmas and their possible resolutions facing planners operating in the environment of interest-group pluralism in U.S. cities in the 1950s.[11] He found that planners were boxed in. They could restrict themselves to a land use planning role, a specialty in which they could claim legitimate expertise, but one which the community and its politicians had defined too narrowly, and one which was too much in the hands of the real estate sector for their plans to have the desired impact. Or the planners could try to be generalists, with the result that they would forever be playing second fiddle to other experts with more specialized knowledge, and thus they would inevitably lose authority. Altshuler noted that these problems were specific to U.S. urban politics, and his data were taken from only two cities (Minneapolis and St. Paul). But his argument seemed to apply generally throughout the country.

Taking the nature of urban politics as a given, Altshuler asked city planners to look inside themselves in order to define their roles and their professional knowledge and asked that they elaborate on their basic contributions as generalists. He thought that there were precedents both in planners' experiences and in traditional American institutions for the development of two kinds of generalist roles, not necessarily to be combined in the same person or office: one, "general evaluative rationality," was a function analogous to the judiciary, in which planners, building on their backgrounds as physical planners and on their expertise on the interrelations of different land uses, would comment on the proposals of more specialized planners. He did not see planners as necessarily creating comprehensive plans—their record was not so good at that, and most people saw "master planning" as preposterously overreaching. Rather, he saw planners as creating a body of precedent as they reacted to specialized proposals. Altshuler's second proposal was that planners develop "general inventive rationality": they could use their knowledge of the interrelations of issues and problems to suggest institutions and projects that other specialists could not conceive of.

Prior to these recent examples of progressive city governments, there was not much evidence that U.S. planners often managed to take on these roles. Altshuler's book got a lot of attention when it appeared in 1965 and it is still listed as recommended reading for professional planning examinations, so his ideas are well established in the profession. But more commonly, planners have moved instead in the direction of *ad hoc* project planning or have remained in the physical land use mode. Neither of these roles are incompatible with Altshuler's generalist roles, but they do not themselves achieve what Altshuler was proposing. The most dominant idea in planning after 1965 has been the advocacy of a shift toward incrementalism, which is an emphasis on the short-term, narrow view, and thus antithetical to generalist thinking.

REINFORCING INNOVATION

The progressive planners did very well in implementing both kinds of generalist roles. First, innovation blossomed in these governments, and the doctrinal coherence that was achieved out of early planning efforts reinforced the abilities of all concerned to implement the new ideas that came to them. Carbone found that he was able to be more persuasive in requiring affirmative action hiring and in implementing some of his later changes in service delivery because of earlier analyses of the extent of joblessness and dependency in the Hartford population. Kucinich's successful effort to prevent the sale of MUNY Light to the private utility in Cleveland was based partly on the Cleveland planners' analysis and advocacy of this position several years earlier. Veronika Fukson cited the usefulness of her participation in several years of planning and doctrinal discussions and testified that the existence of a plan was "a comfort from loneliness" when she was guiding the 1980 Berkeley rent control ordinance through the City Council.

The way planning reinforced innovation, however, was general rather than specific. It set forth a context, an agenda, and a repertoire of problems and approaches to their solution. It was not a map to be used in detail, though in some cases the analyses and proposals that went into planning—only to be changed later—were quite detailed and specific. The planning and the doctrinal discussions associated with it thus supported later innovations, without really limiting the spontaneous, problem-solving nature of administration under progressive leadership.

Progressive planners, in their statements in interviews, tended to downplay the importance of coherent planning on their part, even though an observer could spot it. They were more interested in project-oriented analysis, in getting things done. But the plans were in their minds nevertheless. In Berkeley, a news account described an "economic plan for Berkeley," unveiled at a press conference by Eve Bach and Ed Kirshner prior to the 1975 election. In 1981, neither remembered having had any such plan. But they had been able to lay out a comprehensive scheme on short notice because the elements were available to them. The Hartford and Cleveland planners had a similar programmatic capability.

INJECTING MORAL JUDGMENTS

Progressive planners also embodied a kind of "general evaluative rationality." Krumholz may have established the most distinguished record on this account: he had a reputation for fairness and integrity, even among people who thought he had neglected the traditional planning functions and should have been more supportive of business-oriented downtown investments. Many of his studies were evaluations of proposals made by others, and his continual raising of equity issues referred the level of debate to questions of more general principle. Krumholz, more successfully than progressive planners in either Berkeley or Hartford, was also able to build upon and enhance the independence of the planning function. Planners in Berkeley, operating outside of the government hierarchy, at times did play the general evaluative role, while in Hartford very little of this occurred; the possibility of playing the explicit value-raising role seems to be related to the emergence of planning autonomy of some kind.

Progressive planning was, however, distinguished not only by its movement toward these generalist roles, but also by a momentum of the development of plans that linked invention, innovation, evaluation, and coordinated thought. The substance or content of these plans, allowed to be wide-ranging by the wide political perspectives of progressive politicians, ramified and opened up political possibilities, enlivening the broader political debate. Carbone and Strecker, once they had discovered the possibilities of public co-ownership in urban renewal projects, extended this schema to cover city employment policies, contracting policies, policies for the selection of tenants and for public participation in the income-stream and refinancing possibilities of the projects. This explicit making of connections contrasts with the usual practices of urban renewal, which emphasized putting all responsibility for a project's operation in the hands of the private investor, and thus the planners would not face these other questions. Looking toward the interrelatedness of different aspects of projects was especially characteristic of Carbone's administration: the food plan, the energy proposals, the police decentralization schemes, the tying together of all city programs in service of the goal of increasing employment possibilities for city residents which occurred after the middle of the 1970s—all these specific programs were characterized by this kind of thinking, which comes from a focus on planning. The alternative—to leave separate projects in separate hands, hoping for an unconscious coordinating hand to operate them together, at the same time leaving to individual project leaders a maximum autonomy—was more characteristic of earlier governments. This approach inhibited systematic thinking even as it favored the already established interests.

In Berkeley and Cleveland, where most of the planning described here took place outside of the centers of authority, the thoughts of the planners were worked out without the benefits (or costs) of the frequent and immediate implementations that Carbone was able to supply. Yet Krumholz and his staff were able to create a structure of progressive public opinion which extended from the neighborhood groups to the Ohio Public Interest Campaign, and this climate of opinion had at least an initial impact on Kucinich, especially in regard to such issues as tax abatements, MUNY Light and support for public transit. This attitude contrasted with earlier planning positions.

Planning as the Link to the Progressive Movement

Why were progressive planners able to play these roles and to affect the climate of public opinion the way they did? Two main reasons seem evident. First, mass-based politics stimulated them and gave them an opportunity to reinforce the kind of politics they believed in. Second, progressive planners developed both personal and professional strategies that allowed them to overcome the tensions that arose between them and the political and participatory demands of the progressive politicians. Their response to politics and their personal strategies developed as follows:

Leaders of mass movements think hard about how to make a mark on history, and much of the theory of planning focuses upon a similar question: under what conditions will planning make a difference? Progressives involved in planning thought the primary condition was a matter of personal qualities. Krumholz, whose experience is generally thought of as "unique," was bemused by the question of why other cities had not repeated his experience.[12] On the one hand, he thought his own abilities were rather ordinary. But his perception of the planning profession generally was that it was "timid." He urged planners to "take risks." He saw his own accomplishments in rather modest terms. He thought he had had little impact on Cleveland or on other planners in other cities, despite his extensive writings and his many speaking appearances. He tended to evaluate his work in terms of relatively short-term payoffs, although at times he would reflect on his total experience in building the Planning Department over ten years.

The Berkeley planners took a similarly modest, short-term view of their accomplishments. Eve Bach cautioned that the impact of the planners on the BCA, much less on Berkeley itself, had been marginal. Kirshner gave a more expansive description of his goals, but he was similarly restrained in his estimates of the effects of his work. Jon Coleman in Hartford spoke about his role as a staff person for Carbone, and like many of Carbone's staff, he thought in terms of the collective effort, and saw it as not particularly guided by planning. Paul Strecker thought the real estate strategy was "not partic-ularly innovative," although he had never seen it done in the public sector before. Except for Kirshner and Krumholz, none of these planners was interested in writing about or broadcasting his or her achievements. They were too busy doing their jobs, they said, to write about them.

This combination of modesty and pragmatism contrasts sharply with the kind of global assessment of tasks and achieve-ments a historian or social scientist might make. From a historical perspective, two issues come clear. First, political institutions and fundamental economic conditions, as opposed to personalities, ex-plain much of the variation in planners' success or lack of it. The im-portance of the personal qualities of the planners shouldn't be underestimated, but one should recognize as well the intensely emo-tional and conflictual conditions in which they operated and against which they found ways to struggle. Bach, Kirshner, and many of their friends and colleagues were directly or indirectly affected by the events surrounding the violence in Peoples Park in 1969. They participated in the creation of the April Coalition, and through that organization they were able to conceptualize the economic and insti-tutional conditions in which the city was forced to function. There was also an intensely collective atmosphere around Carbone, and in Cleveland, at least during the Stokes's administration, this collec-tive environment also pertained as Krumholz was beginning to put his staff together.

These planners were agents of historic change in their cities. They did not control these historical processes, but they did take conscious charge of the way they perceived them. Perhaps that was the personal part: what they did was to perceive things differently from the way others perceived them, perhaps because they were at least on the fringes of some sort of progressive politics or even radi-cal political consciousness. Looking back on this history later, they may not even have been able to perceive their accomplishments, at least in each detail, in a grand historical light. But for a while at least, they did achieve a certain consciousness, which connected them to larger city changes, and which set them apart. Having people with these qualities in the city government, when many oth-ers around them were stuck in a partial and segmented conscious-ness, made a difference.

An outside observer might see a second issue in the planners' own self-evaluations. Planners tend toward pragmatism; they look at their actions in terms of their immediate impact on politics and administration. But, above all, their work affected the long-term agendas for collective action in their cities. Kirschner, Bach, and the other Berkeley planners associated with the BCA and other groups supplied program ideas, so that when political candidates needed material and arguments and when opportunities existed to use the initiative process, these materials were available and could be used. Krumholz, who could affect the decisions of city government in Cleveland only occasionally, nevertheless kept up a flow of ideas and criticism, which later sometimes had indirect influences. Most notable of these influences were the long-run effects of the Tower City and MUNY Light analyses on the later positions taken by OPIC and Kucinich. Carbone, in full control of his city's administration, also set community agendas by dramatizing such issues as the city-suburb housing and transportation inequities.

The role of agenda-setting in the "mobilization of bias" has long been a basic concept in the study of politics, but it has usually been applied to the actions of those in power rather than to those outside of the centers of control. Bachrach and Baratz introduced the idea in the context of academic debate about community power structure. "Pluralist" thinkers had argued that most decisions in local politics were made in a relatively fragmented way, with different interest groups in control of different types of decision, and with no one elite group dominating the pattern.[13] Bachrach and Baratz countered this argument by contending that the actual making of decisions was only the surface manifestation of a more complex structure. Even if decisions were made within a fragmented structure, they argued, the mobilization of bias concerning the relative importance of these issues was an equally critical dimension of the decision making process, one which might be centrally structured, even if the actual decisions were fragmented.

Wide acceptance of this argument by academics has not often resulted in moving beyond the critical stance or toward analysis of the use of agenda-setting by oppositions. Nevertheless, one can notice such oppositional agenda-setting and mobilization in many real situations. Furthermore, planning has often been a vehicle for these functions.[14] Critics of local power structures have often looked at plans as elite mechanisms for structuring bias. But there have also been cases where oppositions have been able to use planning in this way, even when their direct influence on decision making has been out of the question.

This does not mean that oppositional agenda-setting is a simple matter of writing plans so as to educate people, apart from actual issues. The annals of planning are as full of educational failures as they are full of failures to affect decision making. The experiences reviewed here tell us that the plans of oppositions often interacted with actual interest-group formation, with actual mass mobilizations, and with actual successful pressure being exerted on government decisions. Joan Beauchemin's successful opposition to Burlington's Southern Connector had something of this quality; it connected an alternative development scheme to a general neighborhood movement, a progressive electoral campaign, and detailed negotiations carried out under Sanders later. Similarly, the ideas presented in *The Cities' Wealth* in Berkeley and in many of Krumholz' studies were not *simply* ideas. They were also picked up forcefully by strong political movements.

The ability to respond to and mobilize mass politics was one resource for progressive planners. A second resource was personal and professional strategy. Thus the progressive planning experiences we have reviewed also lead us to modify our conception of the independent planning professional. Earlier formulations had based planners' independence on city charters and on a type of limited physical planning expertise and a particular sense of professionalism. Progressive planners found ways to extend their expertise—along the lines Altshuler had anticipated—and also to modify their professionalism, trading certain formal prerequisites for a more personal sort of autonomy.

Krumholz represented an example of a professionalism that served progressive politics without being consumed by it. There are many other such people who were involved in planning in the cities I have described, but perhaps the particular combination of key positions he held makes a description of the attitudes he took to his work particularly instructive. Krumholz is interesting partly because he was a "transitional" figure, bridging the liberalism of the Stokes administration and the more populist politics of Kucinich and OPIC.

Krumholz was not a mass movement stereotype. He lived comfortably in the Cleveland suburb of Shaker Heights, raised a family, and enjoyed the ordinary life of a white-collar professional. He was remote from the labor movement. His difference from most liberals lay in a combination of his background, his personality, and the opportunities opened up by his job. He had come from somewhat difficult circumstances in Patterson, from a milieu that emphasized the more radical values of the New Deal. Perhaps this is best symbolized by his commitment to the Wallace campaign in 1948. Thus he was at ease with such programs as full-employment through government intervention, and public housing and other collective subsidies. He had a somewhat liberal attitude toward socialist movements in general, in contrast with the red-baiting anticommunism that infected conservatives and liberals alike in that period and the one immediately following.

So, Krumholz never completely joined the "growth coalition." In retrospect, there were several specific times when he resisted it. One such instance occurred in Pittsburgh, where he had been hired by a city planning director engaged in a large modeling effort, only to arrive to see the staff decimated and the agency taken over by the more opportunist John Mauro. Krumholz easily slid into the role of Mauro's assistant, giving up an aspect of professionalism that was to seduce a large number of planners into playing a kind of technician's role, which shielded them from thinking about larger political issues. But being Mauro's trouble-shooter would not, by itself, have turned a planner away from the big-money developer interests of the growth coalition. There also were the meetings in church basements and contacts with the neighborhood residents. Krumholz made these contacts under Mauro and he made them the same way later in Cleveland. He would say what he thought and what the city's position really was, and at times he was screamed at for this frankness.

He was not part of the civil rights movement or any tightly knit support group, but he brought his own personal political convictions to these encounters. His own integrity carried him. At night, he went home to another circle of friends, whose discussions offered him a different perspective on his work. In Cleveland, these friends included such people as Roldo Bartimole, editor of the critical bimonthly *Point of View,* and Harry Fagan of the Commission on Catholic Community Action. The perspective of these people might best be described as skeptical of the existing social order, particularly its distribution of power. They made it their business to stay in contact with people across the range of social classes, and they reacted strongly to what they saw as exploitation. They were not theorists. It was the OPIC group, not Krumholz, who read *Global Reach.*

The people Krumholz hired at the Planning Commission were also not theorists, but they were sensitive to disparities in power, and they were also given to contacts across class barriers, particularly with neighborhood groups and organizers. They themselves, together with Fagan's organizers, formed a support network; but it was a different one from Krumholz's circle. Krumholz, far more than his planning staff, was aware of the uniqueness of his creation, and he authored scores of papers and talks at professional meetings and at professional planning schools, where he was lionized. Thus he played a national, as well as a local, role as a planning professional.

Other progressive planners played a different kind of role. Kirshner and Bach stayed on the edges of many of the radical factions inside and outside of Berkeley politics, but they also had in common their academic work at the University of California, where they went through the professional program in the Department of City and Regional Planning. For them, as for Krumholz, planning professionalism included both an analytical capability and a willingness to commit their support to political figures and organizations. Also like Krumholz, they had a capacity to get angry at imbalances of power, an anger which in their case—more than for Krumholz—led them into the kind of programmatic thinking that was reflected in *The Cities' Wealth*. In positions of responsibility, Bach, like Krumholz, came to be seen as a resource of responsibility and also as a pragmatist, but in terms of action based on thoughtful analysis.

Both Krumholz and Bach—in common with other progressive planners—achieved a kind of professionalism that was less technocratic and more politically thoughtful than that of other professionals. At the risk of trying to clarify what was in fact only muddily distinguished, one can characterize two versions of professionalism current for planners. Progressives, when they were thinking theoretically, focused on the interconnections between institutions and illuminated power disparities between groups and neighborhoods; other kinds of planners would see the same set of relationships more narrowly. Progressives made personal contacts across a wide spectrum of classes; other kinds of planners would seek alliances with other leaders or with other technicians representing interest groups. Progressives could be pragmatic against a background of what was essentially their class consciousness; others assumed that group conflict occurred only within a larger system of rules and markets, and their pragmatism was blind to classes.

CHAPTER 7

Participation:
The Basis of
Progressive Coalitions

For progressive politicians, planning provided a map to guide the political movement. It supplied the cause-and-effect chains that connected their sense of the deterioration of the urban economy to actions that could be taken in support of urban populations. As the economic disparities deepened between the majority of the city's people and the politically dominant business and institutional leadership, the traditional institutions of markets and interest-group bargaining had become abstracted away from this real deterioration, and this absence left an opening.

But planning, though it formed a necessary component of progressive politics, was not sufficient to reach progressive goals. There was another level on which progressive politics operated, that of gaining peoples' motivation and commitment. For these purposes planning could only remain in the background; the main object was mass participation, and the principal and most immediate means toward that end were organizational and procedural. The most important step toward realizing these purposes was to increase public participation so that it rested more on a mass base and less on organized interest groups. In Berkeley, the April Coalition began to open up government by means of attacks on the city manager's control of civic information, then through the ballot initiative that proposed the reorganization of the police department into three autonomous, neighborhood-controlled units. The early Berkeley rent control initiative was in part a procedural reform, which provided for the direct election of the rent control board. The most far-reaching procedural change the Berkeley progressives brought about was the Fair Representation Ordinance, which significantly opened up the processes of government to wide citizen participation. Once Berkeley Citizens Action gained control of the government in 1979, it made certain organizational reforms in the internal processes of government. City employees were to be involved in deliberations on their work conditions and the Citizens Budget Review Commission became a vehicle for wide public participation in what had been a largely closed budget process controlled by the city manager.

In Hartford, the procedural reforms achieved were smaller. Carbone himself took on many of the functions of the city manager, and this represented a movement from a bureaucratic to a representative style of government. For a time, there was wide participation by other members of the City Council. Carbone then initiated the police reorganization as well as certain reforms that aimed to put city services in closer touch with the neighborhoods: the food plan, the energy programs, the placement of paraprofessional workers in the schools are all examples. In the end, Carbone was vulnerable to attack from the neighborhoods for not having created a sufficiently effective structure to handle mass participation. But he had moved some of the distance toward such a structure.

Kucinich, in contrast, operated within a defensive cadre of close advisors and did not open up the government of Cleveland to the people. His support was, nevertheless, to a large extent neighborhood-based. His public acknowledgment of that fact helped to legitimize the neighborhood movement and to encourage it and gave Krumholz at least a symbolic opening—never fully realized—to expand the connections between the neighborhood movement and the Community Development Department, connections he had originally made through the Planning Department under Perk. As was the case with Carbone, the neighborhood movement ultimately turned against City Hall, partly because of its failure to make the procedural reforms demanded. But even in Cleveland the point was made: even the promise of mass public political participation was a powerful organizational instrument. The failure to use the instrument was another issue.

In Burlington and Santa Monica, the procedural opening up of City Hall to large-scale public participation was a large part of the progressive program, and the participatory innovations these cities achieved set them off from Hartford, Cleveland, and in some ways, even from Berkeley. The creation of citizen task forces was one of the main things Sanders could do in Burlington against an intransigent Board of Aldermen during his first year in office; later, his creation of neighborhood planning assemblies was a major factor in shaping important development schemes. Santa Monica opened up the government to its neighborhood and renter constituencies by means of the elected rent control board, by means of a set of commissions, including the development task forces, by transmitting City Council meetings over the radio, and later, by encouraging support for the neighborhood organizations and for some publicly conducted planning commission studies.

Participation as Motivation

The idea that participation in local government can motivate people to make a political commitment and thus can tie an organization together is somewhat unusual, because local government most commonly restricts such participation. Despite the presence of strong participatory values, government is usually left to a party organization and to officials and interest groups. Usually, citizenship means little more than voting for officials whose job it is to watch over a minimal city administration, and the public's participation in this process is mainly oriented toward supporting the economy or else it is siphoned off into largely apolitical voluntary organizations and occasional service on advisory boards.

Within most local governments, as within the private economy, administration is quite authoritarian. Many institutions and practices reinforce a hierarchical, even a patriarchal, mode of operation. The city manager system is among the most hierarchical and patriarchal of these, but some of the traditional local government functions are also strongly both: police, fire, public works, and welfare departments have seldom served as participatory models. Even during reform campaigns, the main political issues have not been the openness of these agencies to the public, but rather their openness to mayors and city councils. The natural tendency of city agencies has been to form their own subcultures, authority systems, and constituencies. The main reform effort has been to coordinate them via the central administration. The increase in federal expenditures during the 1960s and 1970s exacerbated the problem in many cases, directly subsidizing functional empire building rather than mayoral or council control. Mayors, seeking desperately to get control over these fiefdoms, seldom opened them up to the people generally. At times they were preoccupied with coordination, which resulted in authoritarianism at the center.[1]

The different elements that have made up progressive coalitions have reacted against authoritarian government organizations in different ways. Some have found authoritarian patterns inherently unhelpful and unnecessary, while others have found them simply an obstacle to getting access to power and resources. Both of these kinds of groups joined together, however, in seeking participatory reforms. Peoples' experiences with authoritarian power structures led them to organize against them, and then their consciousness of what was possible organizationally was transformed. That is, progressives developed an ability to manage participatory—or incrementally more participatory—forms of organization. In Hartford and Berkeley, police violence was the most important cause of this changed political consciousness. Loni Hancock described her reaction to seeing people such as herself being beaten by police in Berkeley, and said that that generated her motivation to get into local politics. It was police issues as well that got Carbone involved in politics and pushed his evolution forward as an activist City Council leader. Probably Carbone felt less principled objection to hierarchy *per se* than did some of the others, but the effect was similar. Because of the riots, he saw people doing things that were "outside the realm of my experience" and then tried to understand "the denial that was coming from . . . the police and the city manager."

These changes in political perception led progressives to make attempts to change the structure of government, to make large-scale participation easier. Once they had succeeded and participation had been increased, a second kind of shift occurred. People, getting a taste of political participation, desired more. They did not change their attitudes or behavior directly in response to such factors as police violence, but rather they changed in response to the experience of political participation itself. Examples of this second kind of shift were the Berkeley Planning Board members who so appreciated the chance to interact directly with the council members who had appointed them, the Hartford police officers who became converted to the idea of neighborhood policing from the experience of doing door-to-door surveys in the target neighborhoods, and the blacks who helped in the operation of the food system.

At least in the minds of progressive leaders, and possibly more generally, these pressures for participation came to reflect a general value shift in the terms on which they thought about political par-

ticipation. The progressives justified their policies as being representative of the residents of cities, rather than as representative of
property. Property, they said, was an abstraction that, if it had at
one time approximated a local polity, no longer did because so much
control of property now resided outside the city boundaries. It was
not just that control of property skewed power out of the hands of
the masses of people within a city; progressives could also point to
the dimension of external control, thus appealing to sentiments of
localism and local pride.

Developing Participatory Structures

To open up government, progressive politicians and activists
used the existing structures of government and changed the rules
where they could. The methods they used can be categorized provi-
sionally. First, certain initiatives were, in effect, if not in intent,
largely *dramatizations*. The most prominent of these was the Berkeley police reorganization initiative, which would have restructured
the police administration into three autonomous groupings, each
serving a different area and population. As the most extreme of the
proposals—patterned after a Black Panthers' proposal in Oakland, justified by race and cultural arguments and set against the
tumultuous and violent background of Peoples Park cutting to the
essentials of most peoples' sense of security and justice—it opened
up the broad questions of government organization and the role of
the citizenry. The proposal got substantial support in the election,
but it also failed to pass by a large margin. But with the mobilization of that support, a space was cleared for later debates and for legislation of other sorts to open up government and get more participation. These proposals included the city charter revision and other
Berkeley reforms, as described below.

There was drama in other cities too, but it was not so directly
aimed at achieving procedural changes. In Hartford and Cleveland,
city representatives publicized city interests in opposition to those of
the suburbs. Carbone initiated lawsuits over the failure of the suburbs to provide low-income housing, and Krumholz agitated against
the biased regional council of governments. Kucinich's conflict with
the Cleveland banks over MUNY Light and the city's default were
even more bitter dramas. These confrontations, even though they
did not lead directly to participatory reforms, did succeed in raising

the local citizens' interest. They may have increased an awareness of the issues affecting the city at large among the already-mobilized neighborhood constituencies, for example. Later, some neighborhood activists and organizers felt that these conflict tactics had backfired. Yet Carbone had tried to use them in an educational way in Hartford, arranging speaking engagements in the suburbs in order to explain his policies and in the city to rally support for them. The construction moratorium in Santa Monica was another example of a political dramatization that raised political consciousness and prepared the way for structural reforms.

A second participatory strategy involved progressives' *support for neighborhood organizations*. Krumholz's planning department was a model for this in the years prior to the Kucinich administration. Once Kucinich was elected, the issue became the way in which the government would relate to the burgeoning neighborhood movement, and through what agencies, but it was no longer whether the neighborhood organizations constituted an important constituency. In Hartford, Carbone tried to cultivate neighborhood backing, most prominently through his financial support of the Hartford Citizen's Lobby using city funds, but also in other material and symbolic ways. As in Cleveland, a great struggle ensued over the control of these organizations, but no question was raised about their legitimacy or their importance to City Hall. In Berkeley, strong BCA roots developed around land-use planning issues in some neighborhoods. BCA support for the Neighborhood Preservation Ordinance in 1973 and for other neighborhood backed proposals after that served to build up political support for their electoral program, and in a way not matched by the Cleveland and Hartford progressives, BCA incorporated neighborhood constituencies into their movement. In Santa Monica, the city made grants to three such organizations, and Burlington fostered the example of the Neighborhood Planning Assemblies.

Third, progressives pressured local administrations to *depart from the traditional hierarchical models of government*. The Berkeley radicals put pressure on the city manager for information from the earliest days of their participation on the City Council. Similar pressures came both from progressives inside the government on the City Council or in appointed positions and from outside the government through election campaigns and participation on boards and commissions and on city administrative bureaucracies. Eve Bach and Wise Allen, BCA's first city manager, initiated quality-of-work-life programs that did manage to counter the hierarchical traditions developed under previous city managers. Sanders forged similar initiatives in Burlington.

Fourth, sometimes participatory reforms seemed to be *institutionalized,* that is, they seemed to be adopted in a form that most significant parties and interest groups accepted as normal and even claimed as their own—often as a result of the application of the three kinds of pressure just described. One example of this was the Berkeley Fair Representation Ordinance of 1975. In that case, the change made was from board and commission appointments made by the City Council majority to a system in which each council member appointed one or more members of each board. The prior method had left appointments to a more centralized procedure and its supporters felt it was also less "political." But the BCA felt the Fair Representation Ordinance had resulted in a more cohesive and more effective government. Appointees found they had the ear of the council members who had appointed them, while council members had the loyalty and advice of their appointees. This procedure was institutionalized in that it had support from both sides.

In no other city was this level of institutionalization of policy reached. The Hartford neighborhood-policing arrangement, for example, in contrast, was a less complete victory. In that case, the change, imposed by City Hall, won the strong support of the police personnel who were involved in it, but it antagonized some of the police hierarchy that was committed to a more centralized administration. Thus it was vulnerable to revision after Carbone's defeat in 1979. The rent control boards in Santa Monica and Berkeley were other examples of fairly strong institutionalization, but they did not reach as centrally into the general processes of government. Possibly, more will still be achieved in Santa Monica and Burlington, where events had not played out to any conclusion by the end of 1984.

External Pressure from the Neighborhoods

Whatever the levels of commitment to participatory government on the part of the progressive leadership, one would still have to ask whether any participatory innovation could last without strong external support demands from outside the progressive coalition and City Hall. Such demands would reinforce the goals of those inside the government who wished in principle to keep existing participatory channels open and to invent new ones, and would also temper the methods of those who wanted to pursue substantive policy making simply by elaborating administrative functions.

The most obvious example of such support demand was in the neighborhood organizations. They could claim to be the most dramatic political movement of the 1970s. They were particularly strong in Cleveland and Hartford after about 1975, when they started developing very rapidly. They were nurtured by the Catholic Church and got foundation backing: various city administrations tried to support and use them. They tapped a mass need for some effective way to get collective goods in the face of the perception that government was not delivering. They cut across race and class lines. Their economic objectives were similar to those of progressive governments. Yet their relationships to city governments were often complicated. Progressives in Berkeley, Santa Monica, and Burlington found ways, by and large, to use the energy of these organizations. Yet the neighborhoods ended up being very antagonistic to Kucinich in Cleveland and to Carbone in Hartford and were the most cited reason for the defeat of each in 1979. Why was the good relationship possible in the first three cases, and what were the problems in the other two?

The most common explanation for the situations that developed in Hartford and Cleveland is that in both cases the progressive leadership needed to have more control than the neighborhood groups were willing to allow. Carbone and Kucinich, both fully occupied by issues involving the city more generally (default, recall elections, the need to raise federal funds, for example), were unable to create an alternative political system that would have satisfied the neighborhoods.

Second, some progressives blamed the conflicts on the "style" of the neighborhood organizations and their organizers. Many of these organizations built up their own cohesion by attacking City Hall, using tactics that would provoke officials into taking defensive positions and making mistakes, which could then be construed as victories in the neighborhoods. The complaint from progressive city halls was that neighborhood groups tended to miss the fundamental economic issues in their quest for a voice on less important ones. Their problems had an economic basis, and such issues as tax abatements or state aid formulas, which could only be orchestrated through the city administration, were the best ways of getting at underlying causes. The neighborhood movement, on the other hand, based its strategy on questions of empowerment. Such people as Harry Fagan in Cleveland and Jack Mimnaugh in Hartford focused on the system of power as the root cause of local problems. When neighborhood activists saw Kucinich taking issue with the legitimacy of their organizations or when Mimnaugh saw Carbone acting like a machine politician, they saw them as evils to be rooted out. They did not want to be called "Alinsky-style" organizers, and certainly they did have strategies that were far-reaching. But they did not have any alternative economic program to propose.

Even so, relationships between the neighborhood groups and the progressive governments, even in Cleveland and Hartford, were not all bad. Some individual initiatives that came from the Kucinich government got significant neighborhood support, particularly the Cleveland Action to Support Housing (CASH) program that Krumholz had devised, which would have gotten local banks to support the rehabilitation of local residential properties. And Carbone had directly supported many neighborhood organizing efforts. Contacts were extensive between city workers and neighborhood organizers in both places, and the experience generated by these contacts developed over time. The intellectual capital of the neighborhood movements and of the progressive governments overlapped and were therefore mutually reinforcing, to the extent that much of the intellectual structures remained in place despite the loss of jobs and financial resources that occurred after the defeats of Kucinich and Carbone. Foundation resources continued at least partly to support neighborhood groups and other organizations: Hartford's Institute for Criminal and Social Justice and Krumholz's Center for Neighborhood Development were still in operation in 1984, and still had their connections to local universities.

Berkeley, Santa Monica, and Burlington offer an instructive comparison to Hartford and Cleveland. In those cities, the neighborhood organizations were less antagonistic to their governments. Several factors help to explain this. BCA had much more experience in creating a participatory political structure—through ten years in opposition in electoral politics—than either Carbone or Kucinich had, and so the empowerment issue was not a source of conflict with BCA. Instead, BCA had been a vehicle for the establishment of such institutions as the Neighborhood Preservation Ordinance. Second, political participation and city economics did not become separate issues in Berkeley, possibly because the overriding economic issues were land use and rents, for which there were local remedies in which people could readily participate. In the eastern cities, in contrast, the economic problems did not give the appearance of being tractable at the neighborhood or even the city level: Jobs and welfare needs were state and national issues on behalf of which the city had to agitate as a unit.

In Santa Monica and Burlington, the scale of government was smaller, but the neighborhood organizations were just as fundamental to the progressive political movement. In Santa Monica, the progressive coalition was largely based in the Ocean Park neighborhood, which had made itself hospitable to the Campaign for Economic Democracy (CED), the tenants movement, and other organizations. In Burlington there had also been a neighborhood movement, and Sanders brought their support into his campaign. He then continued to work with them through the neighborhood planning assemblies and appointed key organizers to his administration.

But in these cities the neighborhood movement had led less of a separate political life, apart from city politics. Progressive activists and political leaders came partly from the neighborhood movement, to the extent that the worry was voiced that participation in the city administration would vitiate the original organizations. There had not been enough time for such a development in Cleveland and Hartford; Kucinich and Carbone both emerged out of political experiences that pre-dated the neighborhood organizations.

Working with Business

The progressives tried to change the basis on which a government might expect local business support. They challenged the place in liberal values that property rights and market decision making had long held. In Hartford, this challenge resulted in the establishment of the City Council as an equal partner in much of the decision making concerning downtown development; in Cleveland, it meant "standing up to the banks"; in Berkeley, it meant challenging the landlords on rent control and the speculators on land use development issues. The result of this challenge in each case, ultimately, was a business-supported backlash, but the timing of it varied. Carbone was able to work with business, more or less effectively, throughout his ten years in office, though he lost their support at the end. In Berkeley, the BCA was able to work with certain business constituencies in a minor way. It supported small-business development efforts once Newport was mayor, and later got small-business support for commercial rent control. Kucinich, on the other hand, never got anything but opposition from business, which formed a solid front against him. In Burlington and Santa Monica, some substantial and constructive partnerships with business developed, despite some initial conflicts.

The varied experience of progressives in getting business support suggests the variations that persisted within the business community. Business interests were not monolithic, business attitudes change over time, and at least some elements in the business community in these cities could work with progressive politicians. "Big business" interests may have been the strongest in the eastern cities, where they had their headquarters and had made major capital investments in office buildings, but had less concern with new physical plants and real estate. Hartford's insurance elites used the city as a workplace, creating huge concentrations of office employees, who, throughout the 1960s at least, resisted relocation to the suburbs. They needed the continued management of city services and were particularly vulnerable to the upset caused by the racial disturbances of the late 1960s. These needs predisposed them toward extensive corporate philanthropy. They supported Carbone for as long as he seemed capable of keeping his administration together.

Cleveland's business concentration was in basic industries and its leaders were much more conservative than others—even reactionary. Business in Cleveland had a history of leaving the city administration to populist mayors and a fractionalized city council with no particularly high performance requirements. It had, however, created some of the strongest community foundations in the nation. Kucinich got only the enmity of Cleveland's corporate community, orchestrated by Brock Weir at the Cleveland Trust Company, which headed the struggle that led to the city's default. (Krumholz, however, had been able to get at least tacit support from such corporate liberals as existed in Cleveland, and after Kucinich's defeat, the Cleveland Foundation and Gund Foundation supported his operation of the Center for Neighborhood Development at Cleveland State University.)

Corporate liberalism played a less significant role in Berkeley and generally had backed off from any support of BCA. The major business entity in Berkeley was the University of California administration, which was a target for BCA as much as the banks had been for Kucinich and, to a lesser extent, the insurance companies had been for Carbone. An international corporate sector was even less prominent in Santa Monica and Burlington.

Local real estate, developer, and landlord interests formed another segment of the business community in these cities. They thrived on growth and on speculative increases in land prices, and thus the bases of their power were quite local, in contrast to the corporate business segment in Hartford and Cleveland. In Berkeley, these land or property interests formed the spearhead of the opposition to BCA, and they were the dominant segments of the business community in Santa Monica and Burlington. In Hartford and Cleveland, in contrast, they played a subordinate role. Carbone, with corporate allies, was able to single out large-scale developers to work with in downtown real estate projects. In the larger eastern cities, there was less profit to be made in land speculation, so the city may have been in a stronger bargaining position vis-à-vis these interests. Neither in Cleveland nor in Berkeley did progressive governments forge significant alliances with developers; instead they opposed them. Burlington and Santa Monica were different; Sanders and Alschuler found ways to work with at least some developers.

Traditional small businesses were yet another business constituency that progressive governments had to deal with. Carbone came out of a small-business background in Hartford, and he looked on small businesses as his clientele: he installed some small businesses in the Civic Center, for example. Some efforts to support small business were also made in Cleveland. In Berkeley, once the BCA got a working majority on the council in 1979, Mayor Newport made efforts to cultivate a small business constituency. A successful effort was made to get small business support for commercial rent control, a measure that protected them from speculative rent increases, and there was a project to install an organization of small entrepreneurs in an abandoned factory building. In Burlington, city officials enthusiastically administered a small business loan program.

All of these progressive governments were dealing with business interests on two levels. One level involved the general climate of government-business cooperation or antagonism in which symbolic gestures and confrontations were important. Passing rent control ordinances in Berkeley and the building moratorium in Santa Monica were good examples of all these symbolic and confrontational elements combined. On another level, however, in individual cases, progressive government often acted quite pragmatically, particularly in relation to developer and small business interests. Carbone's real estate projects, Alschuler's development agreements, and Sanders' waterfront planning initiatives are good examples of such pragmatic cooperation. These projects depended on the ability of government to deal with business interests on specific issues. This required competent staff work and the capacity to design policies in detail, qualities independent of the question of whether a city government was generally pro- or anti-business.

Most city councils had tended toward the "night watchman" form of government and had minimal policy-making capabilities. Even when they did oversee a city manager structure, they were often weak on policy control of the city bureaucracy and were unable to set new goals and policies appropriate to emerging opportunities and problems. This created a policy vacuum, in effect, which Carbone was able to fill in Hartford and which B C A moved to fill in more modest ways in Berkeley. Kucinich, who had inherited a more populist tradition of city administration that put little emphasis on expertise, and whose situation of confrontation impeded the development of new policy machinery, was not able to make the same kinds of advances. Sanders in Burlington and Alschuler in Santa Monica were, in 1984, moving toward achieving positions similar to the one Carbone had achieved in the previous decade.

At the level of economic structure, two opposite factors seem to have been at work—though one cannot be absolutely sure from only these case histories—one making it easier, the other harder, for progressive governments to establish productive relations with some segments of the business community. On the one hand, there was an ever-increasing tendency toward government involvement in the private sector.[2] New federal finance instruments, such as Community Development Block Grants and Urban Development Action Grants, were part of this story, but these instruments themselves were responses to a more fundamental factor, the inability of the private sector to manage financing alone. Thus in Hartford, it was the weakness of the private investment process that opened the door to Strecker and Carbone when they sought development agreements. On the other hand, corporate capital was disengaging from the central cities. This was apparent in Hartford and seems to have been behind the loosening of corporate liberal support for Carbone. This disengagement was, perhaps, made possible by two factors in Hartford: As the insurance industry diversified, it became less dependent on a central-city location for its workforce, and the workforce itself had gradually been relocating to suburban locations. Corporate disengagement in Cleveland and Berkeley was perhaps more subtle. Corporate remoteness from city concerns had been the norm for some time in both places. Local responses to rather crude intervention policies, to move to sell MUNY Light or to fence in Peoples Park, for example, had caused the corporate sector to seek more subtle forms of insulation and self-protection. The corporate response to Kucinich had been Voinovich; to the BCA, it had been a combination of liberal government, the slow raising of rents and the gentrification of the population.

Most interesting, possibly, in regard to these varied and changing relationships of progressive governments to business constituencies, is the way the progressives learned to be increasingly selective in their strategies. In Hartford, Santa Monica, and Burlington, they were able to work with certain types of developers, even when they were faced with strong antagonism from other business sectors. In retrospect, there is a rationale for this: Developers could make a profit from land development in these areas, even after sharing with the city; they were able to do this because of imaginative and stable goal-setting by city councils and by means of competent administration by mayors and city managers. Faced with a strong government front, it was rational for them to make the deals the cities proposed.

But dealing with business could be inherently antithetical to participatory government. Business interests wanted, above all, a predictability in negotiations and stability in policy making. They got this stability and order from Carbone in Hartford, from Alschuler in Santa Monica, and from Sanders in Burlington. But putting participation into the negotiations was difficult for them. Santa Monica's Commercial and Industrial Task Force was in the end a burden for the renters' coalition in power. But the secrecy that attended private government negotiations in dealing with business offended neighborhood organizations—who had seen too much history to be overly trusting of any government negotiations they did not have a part in. This was a dilemma with which each city's progressive administrations had to deal sooner or later.

Minorities

Minorities were a symbolic part of any progressive government, but various factors—including the assimilationist tendencies existing within minority communities—prevented the development of really effective minority coalitions with the progressives. Blacks had become a potent force in the politics of Berkeley, Hartford, and Cleveland by 1970. In that year, blacks had captured two council seats in Berkeley and the mayor's office in Cleveland and had at least token representation on the Hartford council. The civil rights movement had had a profound effect both inside and outside the black community, changing the attitudes of many liberals. And violent confrontations between ghetto black organizations and the police had forced each city toward a crisis of legitimacy. In each city, a combination of repressive, assimilationist, and more radical responses to this crisis existed. This is too large a story to tell in relation to the case histories I have presented, but here I shall describe the way the progressive political coalitions dealt with blacks and the support the progressives got from blacks. The pattern was different in each city.

In Berkeley, BCA had its strongest roots in the largely white student and antiwar movements. BCA had actively involved a small number of local blacks in its activities, and it had joined for two years in the April Coalition with D'Army Bailey and Ira Simmons on the City Council, two blacks without strong local ties. Indigenous Berkeley blacks had joined more readily with the liberal Democratic faction than with the radicals. Dellums had tied black and radical interests together, but when he left the council to go to Congress in 1969, that cohesion diminished and, except for Bailey and Simmons, most blacks then threw in their lot with the then-dominant Democratic organization. Widener, a black who had won the election for mayor in 1971 with the April Coalition's support, soon moved into the Democratic camp, and the BCA failed to get significant black support until it elected Newport mayor in 1979. Even then, it did not really engage a mass black constituency.

Don Hopkins, in a perceptive analysis, found that the differences between black and radical consciousnesses and backgrounds were simply too great to have been bridged. Also, the immediate rewards of political participation in the Democratic organization were too compelling for most blacks.[3] BCA came to recognize and to respect these differences; it sought black candidates who could work with its political goals, and it sought to convince black voters that its programs were in the interests of blacks. Newport's election may have been the closest thing possible to a fulfillment of that claim, and his subsequent success in working with white BCA people, despite acknowledged differences on both sides, was an affirmation of the possibilities of black-white radical coalitions.

Neither Hartford nor Cleveland achieved the degree of black-white progressive linkages that Berkeley did. In Cleveland, race politics was well entrenched as part of the populist pork barrel, but the city lacked a set of goals that could appeal to white liberals or to blacks on other than the narrowest grounds. Stokes's election in 1967 produced a temporary kind of liberalism: he made a few strong administrative appointments and there resulted a permanent increase in the prominence of blacks in the city administration and city contracts. After 1971, a black city councilman, George Forbes, became the president of the City Council, but the content of black politics remained pragmatic and venal, just like the previous white ethnic pattern since at least the 1930s. Kucinich was, in that context, a threat to the style of Cleveland politics. His urban populist program was clear: economically radical, socially conservative. He tried to appeal to blacks with his economic message and ran headlong into Forbes's opposition. Forbes argued that the interests of blacks lay in cooperation with the business community. Despite several administrative blunders, occasionally racist campaigning, and the solid opposition of the banks and the media, Kucinich did surprisingly well in black neighborhoods. But the predominant black political organizations, and ultimately the neighborhood groups, opposed him.

In Hartford, black politics was less well developed than it was in either Berkeley or Cleveland, until the 1980s. After 1970, Carbone took control of the city government partly by means of alliances with black city councilmen Allyn Martin and Collin Bennett. He provided support for black organizations and expanded social programs affecting black residents, an arrangement that proved viable for him. Only at the end of the 1970s, when opposition to Carbone had developed from various corners, did the lack of a minority political base really hurt Carbone. By then, the indigenous black and Puerto Rican leadership in Hartford was much better developed. In 1981, black leadership took over the City Council and the mayor's office, but this was two years after Carbone himself had left office.

Administration and Participation

Progressives got political commitments by motivating a larger base for mass participation than is usual in local politics. They had plans and programs, but they also attracted participation. They did this through dramatization, through support for grass-roots organizations, by opening up the administration, and sometimes by institutionalizing new participatory rules and structures. They also attracted participation through the administration, using the structures that were there and creating new structures for operating the government openly.

There is a literature that defines political administration as separate from "politics." The argument for this separation is not wholly successful, because in practice, administration interacts with almost everything else. Moreover, the progressives had a tendency to attack administrative values when they were out of office, while, once in power, they tended to politicize administration: to support groups that wanted, at a minimum, to keep the city administration under close legislative and other forms of control and surveillance. Still, certain progressive goals seemed to require the elaboration of a somewhat independent administrative structure and the hiring of top-flight administrators, and administrative success often paid off for them politically because it gave them credibility with the voters, who were skeptical that a participatory government could operate effectively.

A list of the administrative successes of these progressives makes the point. Carbone's real estate strategy produced an alliance with a sector of the business interests in Hartford, and Alschuler's computer operations made the city more effective in dealing with the legislature. Eve Bach's effective role in the Berkeley city manager's office contributed to BCA's credibility, while Kucinich's failure to create a good administration cost him the same. Strong administrative performances in Santa Monica and Burlington gave the progressives credibility with business interests and a wider constituency, and gave a legitimacy to progressive goal-setting.

These apparent achievements raise the question of the real nature of administration under progressive politicians. Did it have a special character, or was it simply that progressive politicians at times supported a standard administrative model? And, if progressive administration was special, how far did it develop?

From the evidence presented so far, the outlines of this relationship can be filled in. We can demonstrate a progression of participatory rules and structures, as indicated above. Based on the frequency of their occurrence, the order of political progression would seem to go from (1) dramatization, through (2) support for grassroots organizations, to (3) the opening up of hierarchical administrative patterns, to (4) the kind of institutionalization established in Berkeley. On this continuum, Cleveland seemed to have achieved the least, Berkeley the most, with the other cities in between: Hartford stuck at step two, Santa Monica and Burlington fixed in 1984 at step three.

A different continuum exists for administration. The impression I have from these case studies is that administration developed the most in Hartford, the least in Cleveland, with Berkeley, Santa Monica, and Burlington in between. The real estate development scheme administered by Carbone and Strecker required a good deal of administrative capacity: legislation to authorize it, a set of rules to govern the city's positions in negotiations, skilled personnel to execute the agreements and so forth. A similar capacity was represented in Alschuler's data-processing operations, used to help the city in its negotiations with state officials. Other administrative initiatives in Hartford were perhaps less striking: The energy operation was quite imaginative in its conception, even if it never got completely carried out; the same could be said for the food plan.

In Berkeley, the BCA's transition from being an opposition voice to full participation in the government administration began in 1979. It was only gradually able to make an administrative mark on the government. Its first city manger, Wise Allen, with Eve Bach, made a few efforts at opening up the fairly closed hierarchy of some city departments. But the BCA continued to have difficulties with some of them—notably the police—even after 1979. With a new city manager in 1982, some progress toward making new rules and carrying out BCA's program commitments did take place. In terms of economic development, Mayor Newport's effort to create a constituency of progressive small-business entrepreneurs resulted in city negotiations to establish a new facility in an abandoned Colgate factory; commercial rent control was established, and the existing moderate rent control operation was strengthened.

Abstracting from these experiences, we can suggest four levels of administrative elaboration in these cases. Cleveland represents the first, a "populist" model. Kucinich's appointment of his close political advisors to administrative posts reflected, many said, the assumption common to earlier city administrations that any citizen could do administrative work. In Berkeley, however, BCA got a significant bridgehead in the city's administration, particularly in the city manager's office, and was able to work with city officials in a regular way after 1979. Carbone in Hartford, to a much greater degree, had essential governmental control over the city administration and was able to effect a much greater degree of administrative development. Finally, hindsight suggests that even in Hartford, where the most administrative development took place, administrative development remained limited and was only partly institutionalized. A fourth level, which we might call "full elaboration" would

FIGURE 7.1. **Participation and Administration Development:
Five Cities, 1969–1984**

Administration

	Dramati-zation	Support for grass-roots	Openings in hierarchy	Fully insti-tutionalized
Fully elaborated				
Elaborated, partly institutionalized		Hartford	Santa Monica Burlington	
Significant bridgeheads				Berkeley
Populist mode	Cleveland			

Participation

occur when administrative procedures have been well established over a period of years, so as not to depend on any one person's administrative leadership. Most of Carbone's achievements were too identified with his personal authority to survive his electoral defeat.

In chapter one, I suggested that participation and administration take somewhat different lines of development and that progressive government involves some particular combinations of the two. Now, after reviewing the evidence, the interaction of these two dimensions of political life is more clear. Figure 7.1 is calibrated in a rough way, using four levels of administrative development and four levels of participatory institutional development. The cities studied lie at different points with respect to these two axes.

This juxtaposition of participatory and administrative elaborations, even though it is an abstraction, nevertheless helps us to see what might have been distinguishing features of these progressive governments. First, these two dimensions do capture essential elements of the tension that persisted within these regimes. Their constituents did make substantial participation demands that were hard to meet. These demands were strongly articulated by the neighborhood movements in Hartford and Cleveland, but they also appeared in the other places. The progressives, once they came into control of government, also needed administrative mechanisms, not only to keep up with the flow of work and to defend themselves against attack, but also to achieve their more substantial goals. They experienced many times—exacerbated perhaps in Hartford, but everywhere generating at least some concern—when these two dimensions of politics were in stark conflict.

This tension in government alone would not be remarkable. What was remarkable was the way in which these progressive governments on many occasions transcended this tension and found ways to develop both dimensions of their political lives. A progressive government's success might be measured by the extent to which it was able to move along both dimensions. The graphic concept is a "frontier," an arc connecting the two axes, and the question for analysts is what factors, apart from administration and participation themselves (shown within the diagram), pushed that frontier outward.

Beyond Participation

As I discussed in chapter six, planning was a feature of political processes emerging both from political administration and from political participation, a feature which, by providing cognitive material for progressive governments, helped them to transcend the tensions between participation and administration. Thus, in the administration or within a neighborhood meeting, when the question of the purposes for which the group was doing something was raised, the existence of the body of concepts and goals contained in planning seemed to be an important resource, helping to create a tolerance between citizens and administrators. But a special kind of planning and planner was emerging: one that had the experience of participation as well as of administration, and that experience helped nurture this kind of tolerance.

Even the most conservative interpretation of the case studies presented in this book would have to emphasize the political mobilization that occurred and note the significant administrative revitalization that took place as newly-elected progressive mayors and city councils tried to consolidate their positions by making administrative and programmatic coups. "Politics" controlled administration. This is certainly part of the story. My own inclination, however, is to go beyond that interpretation to analyze the manner in which the new political mobilizations also created a structure of thought, combining principles of public participation with substantive visions and models of possible reconstructions of the local economy and social structure.

This emphasis entails several other points. First, there is the proposition that a structure of thought, however loose and changing it might be, can and does in reality affect the behavior of voters and officials. This idea can be somewhat counter-intuitive for some people. They decide on concrete issues on a day-to-day basis, and this is as true of progressives as of any others.

The progressives, however, were marked by their constant awareness that, in the background, they needed this structure of thought. They knew they needed it, because they knew the opposition had it, even without ever saying they did. It was impossible to go through the experiences of electoral politics and of organizing on class issues without becoming aware of this prevailing structure of ideas: in the press, in the minds of neighborhood people and labor union members, in the arguments of business leaders and university presidents, progressives came up against a structure of thought that frustrated their efforts and for which they had to come up with an alternative, if they wished to continue the struggle. This necessity of finding alternative ideas sustained their efforts.

Second, this attention to an alternative structure of thought had the tactical advantage that it was an avenue to power and influence. What political scientists had identified as the "mobilization of bias" and agenda-setting, in the sense of mechanisms of elite domination, progressives learned to counter by directly attacking and shaping public biases and agendas. They did this very much by a process of planning, though there were other ways, too. They used planning to shape their own agendas, and later to shape others'.

Much of this process occurred informally and among persons who did not identify themselves as "planners." Nevertheless, it was the formal institutions of planning that at times gave these activities a space in which to operate. The BCA and SMRR people took over their planning commissions; Krumholz was able to operate for a decade in the Cleveland city planning department; even in Burlington and Hartford, where the progressive leadership opposed or ignored the planning machinery, its being there to oppose probably helped these organizations formulate alternative arrangements, if only as reactive moves.

Third, the focus on agendas (and planning) was also a strategic channel, a way of maintaining a conscious link between tactics and an analysis of the fundamental economic forces affecting the city. This analysis, though never completely realized and often in flux, often revitalized and stimulated progressive governments. Alschuler's studies of the Santa Monica economy, *The Cities' Wealth* in Berkeley, Cleveland's *Policy Plan*, and Sid Gardner's work in Hartford were examples, but only the most obvious ones. There were also informal discussions and formal meetings where these issues arose.

A final point on planning: it emerged from the experience of activists as much as from the thoughts of intellectuals. This conclusion opposes a common view that contrasts, too simply, the work of activists and planners. The strongest way to make this point is to refer back to the comments of Nick Carbone and Barbara Jo Osborne, activists who spoke like planners at times, or the statements of Derek Shearer and John Alschuler, intellectuals who nevertheless exposed themselves constantly to activists. They came from different sets of experience, but they got to the same, or almost the same, place.

Carbone and Shearer displayed these contrasting routes to similar conceptions at a panel discussion put on by Planners Network in New York in 1984. They had been billed as speakers for "Socialism in One City" and were to describe their experiences in Santa Monica and Hartford. This they did. Shearer showed the videotape of a segment of "60 Minutes" on the progressives in Santa Monica, which had been shown on network television the previous year. Carbone described his experiences in Hartford in an eloquent and earthy fashion that brought forth a round of spontaneous applause. The first question then came forth from the audience: "All this sounds like a set of good reforms, but by what yardstick is it 'socialism?'" Shearer's response was essentially deductive:

> There is no socialism anywhere. So it's not the right question. You have to ask something more specific. We do find we can get support for more specific positions; rent control, stopping the construction of environmentally disastrous oceanfront buildings, giving people more of a chance to participate in the planning process.[4]

Carbone's answer was more direct:

> If we used the word 'socialism' we would lose the ability to communicate with our people. But by talking about why your taxes are high, it's because a big corporation is building a $10 mil-

lion office building in the downtown and not paying its way
so that you have to pay, and they say 'right.' So you can talk
about specifics. But you can't do socialism because the control
is not at the city level, it's at the state and federal level. . . .
It makes a big difference, for example, who is in the
White House.[5]

Shearer and Carbone were coming from different starting points.
Shearer, certainly, was aware of the larger structural problems
stopping Santa Monicans for Renters Rights from proceeding beyond certain boundaries. His focus on local-level specifics was strategic, but he had thought these specifics through and had connected
them to an analysis of the interrelationships between many larger
different issues and forces. If anything, it was Carbone who was
more explicit about these interconnections as he pointed out the relationship between the city and higher-level constraints. His experience had moved him from the local to the state and national arenas,
where he saw these connections even more clearly. Shearer had
moved in the opposite direction. But they had arrived at similar conclusions.

What we have in these progressive governments—what
doesn't exist in the vast majority of urban governments—is an answer to the problem of the oligarchic rigidity of politics without adequate participation. This is a question of universal importance. Neither liberals nor socialists have come up with a successful answer to
this problem. In the terms of liberal democracy, participation has
mostly been in the economy, through the ownership of property, and
that value system implies that participation in government is to be
the domain of professional politicians or function as a sideline for
rich or retired people, while the most important people are out there
making money with their property. This implication has led liberalism to the rather rigid, bureaucratized position that such contemporary critics as Macpherson or Lowi describe.[6] For the socialists,
there has been a similar problem, though we have no recent experience of socialism in the United States. But the general problem in
the communist countries and the social democratic experience described by Michels is one of delegation of political responsibility
to administrators and party cadres, rather than high degrees of
popular participation. Marxists call this "substitutism": in principle, they begin with "all power to the soviets," but for the soviets
is substituted the party, and for the party, the central committee.[7]

Conclusion

The most general *null* hypothesis in this work was that progressive governments in Hartford, Cleveland, Berkeley, Santa Monica, and Burlington "made no difference." If this expectation of finding no results was not clear to me when I started, it was made clear to me as I listened to the comments of academic observers and of political participants in the cities themselves. My conclusion is that on the contrary, progressive governments did make a difference in these cities. I think a further conclusion can be deduced from this: Progressive government experience in the five cities I studied can be a resource for other cities and for the development of government generally. I base this conclusion on two related factors that figured importantly in the changes that occurred in the cities reported on here. First, there was a shift away from a strict individual and corporate control of property toward government sharing in such control. This shift could be seen in the land development schemes Carbone pioneered in Hartford, which were emulated to some extent in the other localities, and it could be seen in the rent control movement in the California cities. What was innovative about these projects in these progressive cities was not to be found in their legal details, but in the political constructions that Carbone and others gave them. Many other cities were arranging shifts in property relations, as the current focus on "public-private partnerships" makes clear. This shift represents a basic change in the way "capitalism" does business, coming about because of a constriction in private capital availability and flows. Carbone, Kirshner, and others noticed this and found a way to make it a lever for basic public policy changes.

These innovations sprang from the most fundamental sources in the economy. Economic development professionals all over the country were trying to find ways to adapt to this pressure. It was natural that a populist politician like Carbone would find a way to codify this adaptation more generally. If he had not done so, another politician probably would have. But the possibility of these economic changes occurring more generally exists because the economy seems now to demand it. This is a factor that I have not examined closely, but which may be operating in favor of progressive governments.

But the other factor operating to bring about these changes is more traditionally political: What are the chances that politicians will put a progressive construction on current economic adaptations and capture some advantage from them for city residents? What emerges most impressively from these case studies is the way in which such a constructions arose not simply from "the people," and not simply from "professionals," but from the way the two interacted. In Burlington, the original source of alternative economic development policies may have been the neighborhood activist, Joan Beauchemin; in Santa Monica, certain professionals were more in evidence. Carbone was a local who educated himself by standing up to the local professionals and to the business leadership. These sorts of interactions, I think, are replicable, and in this lies the hope for fundamental political innovations in American cities more generally.

Selected Social and Economic Characteristics: Comparison between Cities under Study and Their Standard Metropolitan Statistical Areas (SMSAs)

	1960	
Santa Monica/ Los Angeles:	*City*	*SMSA*
Population	83,249	6,742,696
White	78,122	6,148,220
Black		
Labor force participation[a]		
Median family income	$6,845	$7,646
Housing costs		
Owner units[b]	$22,700	$15,900
Median rent[c]	83	72
Percentage owner units	31	56

	1960	
Berkeley/San Francisco:	*City*	*SMSA*
Population	111,268	2,783,359
White	83,081	2,436,665
Black		
Labor force participation[a]		
Median family income	$6,576	$7,453
Housing costs		
Owner units[b]	$16,600	$16,300
Median rent[c]	70	74
Percentage owner units	44	55

	1960	
Hartford, city of SMSA:	*City*	*SMSA*
Population	162,178	525,207
White	137,027	495,879
Black		
Labor force participation[a]		
Median family income	$7,211	$7,187
Housing costs		
Owner units[b]	$16,400	$17,000
Median rent[c]	67	67
Percentage owner units	25	59

	1970			1980	
	City	SMSA		City	SMSA
	88,289	7,032,075		88,314	7,477,503
	81,935	6,006,499		75,696	5,135,540
	4,218	762,844		3,594	943,124
	75.2	79.6		65.8	64.9
	$10,793	$10,972		$22,263	$21,125
	$36,300	$24,300		$189,800	$87,400
	132	110		296	244
	23	49		22	49

	1970			1980	
	City	SMSA		City	SMSA
	116,716	3,109,519		103,328	3,250,630
	79,041	2,574,802		69,159	2,362,964
	27,421	330,107		20,671	391,235
	66.1	77.6		61.2	65.8
	$19,987	$11,802		$20,360	$24,648
	$26,600	$26,900		$96,400	$99,000
	128	130		223	267
	35	52		38	53

	1970			1980	
	City	SMSA		City	SMSA
	158,017	663,891		136,392	726,089
	111,862	610,041		71,169	638,448
	44,091	50,518		46,131	61,826
	75.3	81.3		60.4	67.1
	$9,108	$12,282		$14,032	$23,853
	$21,000	$25,100		$45,700	$63,400
	109	118		174	210
	21	59		23	62

	1960	
Cleveland: City/ SMSA:	City	SMSA
Population	876,050	1,796,595
White	622,942	1,535,829
Black		
Labor force participation[a]		
Median family income	$5,935	$7,036
Housing costs		
Owner units[b]	$13,900	$17,700
Median rent[c]	67	71
Percentage owner units	45	62

	1960	
Burlington/ Chittendon Co.:	City	SMSA
Population	35,531	74,425
White	35,399	74,141
Black		
Labor force participation[a]		
Median family income	$5,487	$5,407
Housing costs		
Owner units[b]	$13,900	$12,300
Median rent[c]	56	54
Percentage owner units	48	—

SOURCE: These figures are from the U.S. Bureau of the Census and include: 1980 Census of Population, *General Social and Economic Characteristics,* PC80–1–66, Sect. 1, Tables 54, 56, 57, 58, 120; 1980 Census of Housing, vol. 1, *Characteristics of Housing Units,* Chap. A, General Housing Characteristics, Tables 1, 18.; 1970 Census of Population, vol. 1, chap. B, *General Population Characteristics,* Tables 23, 27, 34, 85, 89, 104, 107, 121, 124; 1970 Census of Housing, vol. 1, *Housing Charac-*

1970		1980	
City	SMSA	City	SMSA
750,903	2,064,194	573,822	1,898,825
458,084	1,721,612	309,299	1,525,865
287,841	332,614	251,084	345,536
75.1	80.2	55.3	62.3
$9,107	$10,407	$15,991	$22,721
$16,700	$22,800	$30,400	$53,900
792	93	127	182
46	62	48	65

1970		1980	
City	SMSA	City	SMSA
38,633	99,131	37,712	114,018
38,353	98,461	37,228	112,427
148	310	149	390
—	—	59.3	65.3
$9,908	$10,757	$18,560	$20,209
$21,500	$20,900	$53,300	$52,900
102	107	210	213
48	—	43	64

teristics for State, Cities and Counties, Tables 1, 8, 18, 29; 1960 Census of Population, vol. 1, *Characteristics of the Population,* Tables 20, 27, 73, 76, 83, 86; U.S. Census of Housing: 1960, *State and Small Areas,* Tables 1, 12, 17, 18, 21, 28, 30.

[a]Labor force participation: percentage of population, 16 years old or older, who are in the labor force.

[b]Median value, owner-occupied units.

[c]Median contract rent.

Notes

Preface

1. Interview, Derek Shearer, July 26, 1981.

2. A critique of this practice can be found in William Foote Whyte's presidential address to the American Sociological Association. See William F. Whyte, "Social Inventions for Solving Human Problems," *American Sociological Review* 47 (February 1982): 1–13.

Chapter 1

1. On the coalitions that put postwar mayors in office, see Stephen Elkin, "Cities without Power: The Transformation of American Urban Regimes," in Douglas Ashford, ed., *National Resources and Urban Policy* (New York: Methuen, 1980); John Mollenkopf, "The Postwar Politics of Urban Development," in William K. Tabb and Larry Sawers, eds., *Marxism and the Metropolis* (New York: Oxford University Press, 1978); and also John Mollenkopf, *The Contested City* (Princeton: Princeton University Press, 1983).

2. Recent analyses have documented this point. See, for example, Barry Bluestone and Bennett Harrison, *The Deindustrialization of America* (New York: Basic Books, 1982).

3. See, for example, William W. Goldsmith and Michael J. Derian, "Is There an Urban Policy?" *Journal of Regional Science* 19 (1979): 93–108.

4. Elkin thought these changes described a transition from infrastructure and development orientations to coalitions organized around the delivery of social services—a formation increasingly characteristic of the 1970s. The most trenchant formulation of the dependence of urban governments on such services is to be found in James O'Connor, *The Fiscal Crisis of the State* (New York: St. Martin's Press, 1973).

5. On trends in housing costs, see Michael Stone, "Housing and the American Economy: A Marxist Analysis," in Pierre Clavel, John Forester, and William W. Goldsmith, eds., *Urban and Regional Planning in an Age of Austerity* (Elmsford, New York: Pergamon Press, 1980), pp. 81–115.

6. The most extensive treatment of the neighborhood movement is perhaps that of Harry Boyte, *The Backyard Revolution* (Philadelphia: Temple University Press, 1980). Harvey Molotch describes the beginnings of the opposition to growth politics in environmental, neighborhood, and other organizations in "The City as a Growth Machine," *American Journal of Sociology* 82 (September 1976): 309–332. See also John Mollenkopf, *The Contested City*, chapter 7.

7. The idea of an "underclass" was forcefully argued by Edward C. Banfield, *The Unheavenly City* (Boston: Little Brown, 1970) without explicit race connotations. The argument that minority hiring had undermined minority grass-roots leadership was current in Cleveland at the end of the Stokes administration. See the exchange between Don Freeman and Roldo Bartimole in the periodical *Point of View* 4 (April 1972): 4–8.

8. This argument is made in William K. Tabb, *The Long Default: New York City and the Urban Fiscal Crisis* (New York: Monthly Review Press, 1982).

9. Quoted in Sidney Schanberg, "Will the Best Man Win?" *New York Times*, July 10, 1982.

10. Theodore Lowi, *The End of Liberalism* (New York: W.W. Norton, 1969). The concern for substantive or substantial (as opposed to functional) rationality, which appears in Lowi's argument, was prominent in the work of Karl Mannheim. See Karl Mannheim, *Man and Society in an Age of Reconstruction* (London: Routledge and Kegan Paul, 1940), pp. 52–60.

11. Mollenkopf, in *The Contested City*, chapter 7, suggested that the neighborhood movement was only an incomplete alternative to the growth coalition; Molotch, in "City as Growth Machine," suggested the existence of an anti-growth coalition without describing its basis in any detail.

12. This estimate is corroborated by Mel Scott, *American City Planning since 1890* (Berkeley: University of California Press, 1969), p. 614.

13. The ways in which national programs began to require local planning are suggested in Peter Marris and Martin Rein, *Dilemmas of Social Reform* (New York: Atherton Press, 1967).

14. See Britton Harris' particularly influential article, "Plan or Projection: An Examination of the Use of Models in Planning," *Journal of the American Institute of Planners* 26 (November 1960): 265–272. For a review of alternative planning approaches in the 1960s, see Richard Bolan, "Emerging Views of Planning," *Journal of American Institute of Planners* 33 (July 1967): 233–245.

15. For example, a group called Planners for Equal Opportunity had a membership of perhaps five hundred to a thousand by the end of the sixties compared to the membership of the American Institute of Planners, which peaked at about fifteen thousand. I have not been able to get a better esti-

mate for the first figure, but on AIP membership, Scott suggests the figure of "over 3,800" in 1965, and Kaufman lists 10,000 in 1974. The 15,000 figure is my estimate for membership at the time when the AIP merged with the American Society of Planning Officials to form the American Planning Association at the end of the 1970s. See Scott and Jerome Kaufman, "Contemporary Planning Practice: State of the Art," in David Godschalk, ed., *Planning in America: Learning from Turbulence* (Washington, D.C.: America Institute of Planners, 1974).

16. On official and unofficial advocacy, see Martin Needleman and Carolyn Emerson Needleman, *Guerillas in the Bureaucracy: The Community Planning Experiment in the United States* (New York: Wiley, 1974).

17. On Cockrel, see Jim Jacobs, "DARE to Struggle: Organizing in Urban America," *Socialist Review* 12 (May-August 1982): 85–104.

18. Madison, Wisconsin, was (along with Berkeley and Hartford) an early example of such a new departure, and I regret having omitted it from this account. On Madison and other progressive city government experiences of the 1970s, the best single source is the reports of the Conference on Alternative State and Local Policies, accessible through the newsletter, *Ways and Means* (Washington, D.C.: 1975).

19. Earlier treatments of these ideas and experiences include Eve Bach, Nicholas R. Carbone, and Pierre Clavel, "Running the City for the People," *Social Policy* 12 (Winter 1982): 15–23; and Pierre Clavel, "Planning under Progressive Majorities," Cornell University, Department of City and Regional Planning, Working Papers in Planning, no. 59, (Ithaca, N.Y: February 1982).

20. For a work comparing modern with earlier municipal experiments, see Richard J. Margolis, "Reaganomics Redux: A Municipal Report," *Working Papers*, 10 (May/June 1983): 41–47. On municipal progressives, see Blaine A. Brownell and Warren E. Stickle, eds., *Bosses and Reformers: Urban Politics in America, 1880–1920* (Boston: Houghton Mifflin, 1973); Melvin Holli, *Reform in Detroit: Hazen S. Pingree and Urban Politics* (New York: Oxford University Press, 1969); and Tom L. Johnson, *My Story* (New York: 1911). On early socialist city governments, see Bruce Stave, ed., *Socialism and the Cities* (Port Washington, New York: Kennikat Press, 1975).

21. Stave, *Socialism and the Cities*, chapter 1.

22. These aspects of liberal democracy are analyzed critically in C.B. Macpherson, *The Life and Times of Liberal Democracy* (New York: Oxford University Press, 1977).

23. Robert Michels, *Political Parties* (Glencoe, Ill.: The Free Press, 1949). This work was first published in Germany in 1911.

24. In fact, in the rationale of growth politics that developed after 1945, planning did tend to function in this way, and local planning practices were constrained by their dependence on administrative project successes. Planning without implementation came to constitute an exercise in futility for many within the profession.

Chapter 2

1. These and subsequent summaries of Hartford's political and economic organization are drawn from published sources, from interviews, and from the news files of the Hartford *Courant.* I made eight trips to Hartford between January 1981 and May 1982, conducted thirty-five interviews there, and also had two people from Hartford, Nicholas Carbone and Robert Wiles, visit Ithaca to give seminars, at which times I conversed with them extensively. I am indebted to the Hartford *Courant* and its librarian, Kathy McKula, for letting me use the news files. I also relied on published articles and reports, though there has been little written on Hartford politics. Interested persons might consult Harry Boyte, *The Backyard Revolution*, (Philadelphia: Temple University Press, 1980), chapter 6. I also made use of a mimeographed report, Community Renewal Team of Greater Hartford, *Draft of Action Program*, mimeographed, February 17, 1964.

2. Interview with Jack Dollard, November 13, 1981.

3. Interview with Arthur Lumsden May 7, 1982.

4. Community Renewal Team, *Draft*, pp. 28–31.

5. Paraphrased from the *New York Times Index.* (New York: New York Times Co.) July, August, September 1967; April, July 1968; June, September 1969; April, June, August 1970. The heading was "Negroes—Urban Hartford, Conn."

6. Interview with John Wilson, November 24, 1981.

7. Interview with Jon Coleman, November 24, 1981.

8. Interview with Nicholas R. Carbone, November 23, 1981.

9. Ibid.

10. Ibid.

11. Ibid.

12. An account of this transaction is to be found in Anthony Sampson, *The Sovereign State of ITT* (New York: Stein and Day, 1973), pp. 150–156.

13. Interview, Nicholas R. Carbone, November 23, 1981.

14. Nicholas R. Carbone, Seminar Presentation, Cornell University, Ithaca, N.Y. May 6, 1981.

15. Interview with Sanford Pariski, November 23, 1981.

16. Interview with Nicholas Carbone, November 23, 1981.

17. Ibid.

18. Carbone seminar, Cornell University, May 6, 1981.

19. According to William Cochran, Executive Director of the Hartford Development Commission, three statutes got the most use: (1) Section 12–65B of the Connecticut Statutes, enacted in the early 1970s, authorizing seven-year tax-fixing agreements for projects worth $10 million or more in cities of over 100,000 population; (2) the City and Town Development Act of 1975, authorizing twenty-year tax contracts on developments where the city owned the land and also authorizing revenue bonds for such projects; and (3) Section 8–215 of the Redevelopment Statutes, enacted much

earlier, allowing forty-year tax agreements for low- and moderate-income housing.

20. The following exposition is drawn from an interview with Paul Strecker, March 31, 1982.

21. Carbone Seminar, Cornell University, May 6, 1981.

22. Ibid.

23. This description of Hartford's police reorganization is drawn from interviews with Robert Wiles, Neil Sullivan, Leroy Bangham and Dan Ward. See also such documents as Brian Hollander, *et al.*, *Reducing Residential Crime and Fear* (Washington, D.C.: U.S. Government Printing Office, 1980).

24. "Save the Cities: A Report on Welfare and Taxes in Hartford," prepared at the request of the Court of Common Council of the City of Hartford by the Greater Hartford Process, Inc., (Hartford, Connecticut: April 1975).

25. The original data for these figures appears on page A–4, "Letter of Transmittal" from John A. Sulik, city manager, attached to *Fiscal Year 1979–80 Recommended Budget*, City of Hartford, (Hartford, Connecticut: 1979).

26. These and the paragraphs immediately following have been adapted from Eve Bach, Nicholas R. Carbone and Pierre Clavel, "Running the City for the People," *Social Policy*, (Winter 1982): 15–23. This article drew upon a number of speeches and other materials made available to the author by Carbone.

27. See Catherine Lerza, *A Strategy to Reduce the Cost of Food for Hartford Residents* (Washington, D.C.: Public Resource Center, 1978).

28. On Hartford energy policy, see Chris Merrow, *The Role of Local Governments in Delivering Energy Assistance Programs*, U.S. Department of Health and Human Services, no. 100–80–0107 (Washington, D.C.: May 1981).

29. The following description of John Alschuler's work is drawn from an interview with him on November 4, 1981.

30. Ibid.

31. Ibid.

32. Ibid.

33. Ibid.

34. Interview, Jon Coleman, January 23, 1981.

35. Interview, John Wilson, November 24, 1981.

36. Interview, Jack Mimnaugh, May 6, 1982.

37. Interview, Robert Wiles, November 23, 1981.

38. Hartford *Courant*, September 2, 1979.

39. Hartford *Courant*, November 9, 1977.

40. Hartford *Courant*, October 29, 1978.

41. Interview, Jack Mimnaugh, May 6, 1982.

42. Ibid.

43. For example, this was Boyte's main conclusion in his study, *Backyard Revolution*.

44. *Washington Post*, September 9, 1979.

45. Interview, Mildred Torres-Soto, November 13, 1981.

46. Interview, John Alschuler, November 4, 1981.

47. Interview, Nicholas R. Carbone, November 23, 1981.

48. Interview, Paul Strecker, March 31, 1982.

49. Interview, Richard Suisman, April 15, 1982.

50. Interview, Arthur Lumsden, May 7, 1982.

Chapter 3

1. The original source for these data is the U.S. Census, from various years. I also consulted a number of economic and demographic analyses dealing specifically with Cleveland. See Joseph T. Bombelles *et al.*, *Regional Economic and Demographic Analysis for Cleveland, Ohio*, John Carroll University, Urban Observatory Program, Research Project no. 10, (Cleveland, Ohio, n.d.); Timothy K. Kinsella, *Overall Economic Development Program for Cleveland, Ohio*, Cleveland Division of Economic Development, (Cleveland, Ohio: 1977); Edrich A. Weld, Jr., *The Population of Young Adults in Cuyahoga County, 1960–1990, Expected Changes and Implications*, Cleveland State University, College of Urban Affairs, (Cleveland, Ohio: 1978). For a further explanation of the implications of these figures, see William W. Goldsmith, "Poverty and Profit in Urban Growth and Decline," in Clement Cottingham, ed., *The Urban Underclass* (Lexington, Massachusetts: D.C. Heath, 1982).

2. On the structure of power in Cleveland, I benefited from reading a number of books and papers. Particularly useful was Roldo Bartimole's *Point of View*, a bi-weekly newsletter that provides both current news and historical perspectives, and has been published since 1968 (P.O. Box 99530, Cleveland, Ohio, 44199). Todd Swanstrom's *The Crisis of Growth Politics: Cleveland, Kucinich and the Limits of Electoral Reform* (Philadelphia: Temple University Press, 1985) is the single best source on Cleveland politics. Other useful works include Robert S. Allen, *Our Fair City* (New York: Vanguard Press, 1947); Charles H. Levine, *Racial Conflict and the American Mayor* (Lexington, Massachusetts: Lexington Books, 1974); Philip W. Porter, *Cleveland: Confused City on a Seesaw* (Columbus: Ohio State University Press, 1976); Carl B. Stokes, *Promises of Power: A Political Autobiography* (New York: Simon and Schuster, 1973); and Estelle Zannes, *Checkmate in Cleveland: The Rhetoric of Confrontation during the Stokes Years* (Cleveland: The Press of Case Western Reserve University, 1972).

3. Stokes, *Promises*, p. 49.

4. Swanstrom, *Crisis*, p. 95.

5. Stokes, *Promises*, p. 12.

6. Swanstrom, *Crisis*, p. 104.

7. Stokes, *Promises*, p. 122.

8. Timothy Ambruster, "'Cleveland Now': One City's Program for Change," *Current History* 54 (December 1968): 357–364.

9. Stokes, *Promises*, p. 130.

10. Donald Sabath and Roldo S. Bartimole, "Planning Board in Power Vacuum," *Cleveland Plain Dealer*, February 27, 1966.

11. John Howard, "In Defense of Planning Commissions," *Journal of the American Institute of Planners* 17 (Spring 1951): 89–95.

12. Donald Sabath and Roldo S. Bartimole, "City Planners Must Take Stand," *Cleveland Plain Dealer*, March 1, 1966.

13. Donald Sabath and Roldo S. Bartimole, "Planners Last to Hear of Plans," *Cleveland Plain Dealer*, February 28, 1966.

14. What follows is drawn from a series of interviews and conversations that took place between myself and Norman Krumholz during 1981 and 1982. Krumholz's own account of his public activities can be found in his article, "A Retrospective View of Equity Planning: Cleveland 1969–1979," *Journal of the American Planning Association* 48 (Spring 1982): 163–183.

15. Communication to the author from Norman Krumholz, February 1981.

16. Ibid.

17. Ibid.

18. Ibid.

19. This quotation has been attributed to Daniel Burnham, the architect and planner who designed the layout for the Chicago World's Fair in 1893.

20. Norman Krumholz and Ernest R. Bonner, "Toward A Work Program for an Advocate Planning Agency: And Some Examples of Work Accomplished," (Paper prepared for a session on Advocacy Planning for Social Change, American Institute of Planners, Fifty-fourth Annual Conference, San Francisco, October 1971.

21. Ibid., p. 1.

22. Ibid., p. 2.

23. Norman Krumholz, Janice Cogger, and John Linner, "The Cleveland Policy Planning Report," *Journal of the American Institute of Planners* 41 (September 1975): 298–304.

24. Ibid.

25. Norman Krumholz, "A Retrospective View of Equity Planning," pp. 163–183.

26. Harry Fagan, *Empowerment: Skills for Parish Social Action* (New York: Paulist Press, 1979), p. 5.

27. Interview with Harry Fagan, December 14, 1981.

28. Fagan, *Empowerment*, p. 6.

29. Fagan interview, December 14, 1981.

30. Interview with Ed Kelly, December 16, 1981. The citation refers to Richard Barnet and Ronald Muller, *Global Reach: The Power of the Multi-National Corporations* (New York: Simon and Schuster, 1974).

31. Ed Kelly, *Industrial Exodus*. Washington, D.C. Conference on Alternative State and Local Policies, 1977.

32. Don Freeman, *Point of View*, 4, (April 1972): pp. 4–8.

33. Ibid. See also Bartimole's comments on Freeman's argument in the same issue.

34. The text of this speech is reprinted in the *Cleveland Press*, October 3, 1978, p. A–9.

35. See Dan Maraschall, ed., *The Battle of Cleveland: Public Interest Battles Corporate Power*. Washington, D.C. Conference on Alternative State and Local Policies, 1979, and Swanstrom, *Crisis of Growth*, chapter 8, "The Politics of Default."

36. Swanstrom emphasizes that the default was political, an attempt to get Kucinich defeated.

37. Swanstrom, *Crisis of Growth*, p. 287.

38. Norman Krumholz, "A Strategy and Program for the Revitalization of Cleveland's Neighborhoods and for the Neighborhood Use of Community Development Block Grant Funds." HUD Conference on Housing 2—Neighborhood Revitalization, xeroxed document, February 9, 1978, p. 3.

39. Ibid.

40. Ibid., pp. 5–6.

41. Swanstrom, *Crisis of Growth*, p. 301.

42. Norman Krumholz, "A Retrospective View of Equity Planning," pp. 171–172; and Interview, December 10, 1981.

43. Interview with Mindy Turbov, December 10, 1981.

44. Norman Krumholz, "A Retrospective View of Equity Planning," p. 19.

45. Interview with Norman Krumholz, December 10, 1981.

Chapter 4

1. For this account, I have relied heavily on T. J. Kent, Jr., "Berkeley's First Liberal Democratic Regime, 1961–1970: The Postwar Awakening of Berkeley's Liberal Conscience," in Harriet Nathan and Stanley Scott, eds., *Experiment and Change in Berkeley: Essays on City Politics, 1950–1975* (Berkeley: Institute of Governmental Studies, 1978). I have also relied on other essays in that volume and on interviews with twenty-five people in Berkeley. In the narrative following, these sources are not cited directly, except when specific quotations are germane or when identification of the particular source is part of the meaning of the information I wish to convey.

2. T. J. Kent, Jr., "A Case Study of Orthodox City Planning," Department of City and Regional Planning, University of California, mimeographed, (Berkeley, 1968), p. 7.

3. Ibid., pp. 3–4.

4. T. J. Kent, Jr., *The Urban General Plan* (San Francisco: Chandler, 1961).

5. Margaret Gordon, "From Liberal Control to Radical Challenge," in Nathan and Scott, *Experiment and Change*, pp. 269–316. The data cited are on p. 288.

6. Ibid., pp. 299–300.

7. U.S. Bureau of the Census, 1962 *Census of Governments*, vol. 7; 1977 *Census of Governments*, vol. 4, no. 4, Table 22, p. 172 (Washington, D.C.: 1962, 1977).

8. These figures are cited by Wallace J. S. Johnson, "Berkeley: Twelve Years as the Nation in Microcosm, 1962–1974," in Nathan and Scott, *Experiment and Change*, pp. 179–230. The figures appear on p. 182.

9. Joel Rubenzahl, "Berkeley Politics, 1968–1974: A Left Perspective," in Nathan and Scott, *Experiment and Change*, pp. 317–361. The quotation is on pp. 337–338.

10. Ilona Hancock, "New Politics in Berkeley: A Personal View," in Nathan and Scott, *Experiment and Change*, pp. 363–408; quotation on p. 366.

11. Ibid., p. 367.

12. Rubenzahl, "Berkeley Politics," p. 325.

13. Ibid., p. 333.

14. Ibid., p. 335.

15. Ebenezer Howard, *Garden Cities of Tomorrow*. (London: Farber and Farber, 1945).

16. Transcript of a lecture by Edward Kirshner, Cornell University, (Ithaca, New York: 1981).

17. Edward M. Kirshner and James L. Morey, *Community Ownership in New Towns and Old Cities* (Cambridge, Massachusetts: Center for Community Economic Development, 1975), p. 24. The actual writing dates from 1972. The source for much of the work was Edward M. Kirshner, "New Town Development Costs," and Peter L. Bass, "New Town Development: Financial Aspects" (Joint masters thesis, Department of City and Regional Planning, University of California, Berkeley, June 1971).

18. Kirshner and Morey, *Community Ownership*, p. 21.

19. Ibid., p. 25

20. Ibid., p. 29.

21. Ibid., p. 28.

22. In these tentative suggestions, Kirshner drew upon ideas that had been advanced by Gar Alperovitz, *Notes toward a Pluralist Commonwealth* (Cambridge, Mass.: Cambridge Institute, 1971) and James O'Connor, "Inflation, Fiscal Crises and the American Working Class," *Socialist Revolution*, 2 (March–April 1972): 9–46.

23. Some members of Berkeley Citizen Action, reviewing an earlier draft of this chapter, thought I had attributed too central a position to Kirshner and the planners. I think not, although the subject could stand more research than I have given it.

24. Rubenzahl, "Berkeley Politics," pp. 338–342.

25. For a description of all of these efforts, see Eve Bach, Thomas

Brom, Julia Estrella, Lenny Goldberg, and Edward Kirshner, *The Cities' Wealth: Programs for Community Economic Control in Berkeley, California.* Conference on Alternative State and Local Policies, (Washington, D.C.: 1976).

26. *Platform of the Community Rent Control Coalition*, pamphlet, Berkeley, California, no date.

27. Ibid.

28. Hancock, "New Politics," p. 389.

29. Ibid., p. 383.

30. Interview with Dorothy Walker, July 1981.

31. Rubenzahl, "Berkeley Politics," p. 358.

32. Ibid., p. 359.

33. John Westcott, "The 'Respectable Radicals' and the Politics of Berkeley," *California Journal*, 12 (April 1981): 143–144.

34. Rubenzahl, "Berkeley Politics," p. 346; Hancock, "New Politics," p. 401.

35. Westcott, *"Respectable Radicals,"* p. 143.

36. *Grassroots*, weekly newsletter, April 9–23, 1975, p. 8.

37. The relevant documents are: City of Berkeley, Economic Development Commission, *Economic Development Plan, Proposed October 1978, Adopted November 1980, and Environmental Impact Report*, photocopied (no date); City of Berkeley, Comprehensive Planning Department, *Summary of Berkeley's Economy and Proposals for Economic Planning*, photocopied, October 1976; "Comments of David Romain on the Economic Development Plan," transmitted by memorandum to the Berkeley Planning Commission by acting director Mary Reynolds, October 8, 1980; and U.S. Conference of Mayors, *An Analysis of the Economic Development Process in Berkeley, California*, photocopied, February 26, 1980.

38. U.S. Conference of Mayors, *Analysis of Economic Development*, p. 7.

39. Ibid., pp. 8–9. Later, the Markusen-Weiss report found the cooperative sector to be strong and worthy of added policy attention. See Marc Allan Weiss and Ann Roell Markusen, *Economic Development: An Implementation Strategy for the City of Berkeley*, Institute of Urban and Regional Development, Working Paper No. 354 (Berkeley: June 1981).

40. U.S. Conference of Mayors, *Analysis of Economic Development*, p. 4.

41. See Bach, *et al.*, *Cities' Wealth*, "Running the City for the People," pp. 20–23.

42. Interview with Fred Collignon, July 14, 1981.

43. "Recommendations on Budget and Future of the Planning Department," Memorandum from Fred Collignon, Berkeley, California: February 4, 1981.

44. Ibid.

45. Interview with Veronika Fukson, July 16, 1981.

46. Communication to the author by Eve Bach, 1982.

47. Ibid.

48. Ibid.

49. Interview with Edward Kirshner, January 1983.

50. Interview with Dorothy Walker, July 16, 1981.

Chapter 5

1. On the history of Santa Monica, I am indebted to Aubrey Austin, Jr. See also Les Storrs, *Santa Monica:Portrait of a City, Yesterday and Today* (Santa Monica: Santa Monica Bank, 1974).

2. These figures are drawn from the U.S. Census on Population and Census of Housing, cited fully in chapter 1, n. 3.

3. U.S. Bureau of the Census, Sixteenth Census of the United States: 1940, *Housing*, vol. 1, "Data for Small Areas," pt. 1., Tables 4 and 5.

4. Derek Shearer, "How the Progressives Won in Santa Monica." *Social Policy* 12 (Winter 1982): 7–14. See also Derek Shearer, "Planning and the New Urban Populism: The Case of Santa Monica, California." *Journal of Planning Education and Research*, 2, (Summer 1982): 20–26.

5. Shearer, "How the Progressives Won in Santa Monica," p. 9.

6. See the following sources for information on rent control and related developments: "City of Santa Monica. City Charter, Article XVII: Rent Control," in John Gilderbloom *et. al.* eds., *Rent Control: A Sourcebook* (Santa Barbara: Foundation for National Progress, 1981); Mike Jacob, "How Rent Control Passed In Santa Monica," in Gilderbloom, *Rent Control*, pp. 178–182; David Lindorff, "Left Face in Santa Monica." *Village Voice* (December 2–8, 1981); Eric Shuman, "Sleepy Santa Monica: A Berkeley for the 1980s," *Los Angeles* 25 (November 1980) pp. 202–207, 309–315; Maurice Zeitlin, "Tenant Power to Political Power," *The Nation* (July 4, 1982).

7. Alan Heskin, *Tenants and the American Dream* (New York: Praeger, 1983), pp. 66–90.

8. Interview with Barbara Jo Osborne, January 13, 1983.

9. Interview with Cheryl Rhoden, January 13, 1983.

10. Heskin, *Tenants*, p. 250.

11. Ibid., p. 251.

12. Interview with Barbara Jo Osborne, January 13, 1983.

13. Interview with Derek Shearer, January 12, 1983.

14. Photocopies of this document exist: "Principles of Unity between Members of the Santa Monicans for Renters' Rights Coalition—Adopted January 1981—Working Papers" (Santa Monica: January 1981). Brief statements covered: Airport, Commercial Development, Housing, Self-Government, Crime and Public Safety, Social Service Programs, City Administration, Energy, Environmental Health, and Human Rights.

15. Hagman's contribution may be inferred from some of the documents that bear his name, e.g. "Taking Care of One's Own through Inclu-

sionary Zoning: Bootstrapping Low and Moderate Income Housing by Local Government," Draft, no date; "Landowner-Developer Provision of Communal Goods through Benefit-Based and Harm-Avoidance 'Payments' (BHAPS)," in *Zoning and Planning Law Report*, 5 (March 1982): 16–32.

16. The procedures adopted are described in: City of Santa Monica, Community and Economic Development Department, *Interim Guide to Property Development*, February 1983. The development agreements are described in Shearer, "Planning and the New Urban Populism," p. 22.

17. Shearer, "Planning and the New Urban Populism," p. 22.

18. "Stringent Terms Sought on Project," in *Santa Monica Evening Outlook*, August 5, 1981.

19. Ibid.

20. Interview with Ken Edwards, January 11, 1983.

21. Interview with Denny Zane, January 12, 1983.

22. Interview with John Alschuler, January 4, 1983.

23. Ibid.

24. Ibid.

25. Ibid.

26. Ibid.

27. Ibid.

28. Interview with Denny Zane, January 12, 1983.

29. Interview with John Alschuler, January 4, 1983.

30. Ibid.

31. Interview with Denny Zane, January 12, 1983.

32. For this and much of the background material for the following story, my basic source is Renée Jakobs, "Planning and Politics: A Case Study of Progressive City Administration in Burlington, Vermont, 1981–1983," (Master of Regional Planning thesis, Department of City and Regional Planning, Cornell University, 1983).

33. Donald R. Gilmore, "The Economic Redevelopment of the Burlington, Vermont, Area, in W. Paul Brann, *et. al.*, *Community Economic Development Efforts: Five Case Studies* (New York: Committee for Economic Development, 1964), pp. 37–104.

34. Gilmore "Economic Redevelopment", p. 49.

35. Frank M. Bryan, *Yankee Politics in Rural Vermont* (Hanover, N.H.: The University Press of New England, 1974).

36. Available biographical information on Sanders is limited. Typical of what exists is Debbie Salomon, "Bernie Sanders: The State of the City," *Burlington Citizen*, 10 (February 1984), pp. 1–2, 10, 11.

37. U.S. Bureau of the Census, 1980 Census of Population, PC 80–1, B–47, *General Population Characteristics*, Table 20, "Age by Race and Sex, 1910 to 1980"; and Table 26, "Persons by Age for Areas and Places, 1980 and 1970," (Washington, D.C.: 1980).

38. Bryan Higgins, "Burlington, Vermont: Private Interests Masquerading as Public Policy?" (Paper presented at the 24th Annual Meeting of

the Association of Collegiate Schools of Planning, Chicago, October 23, 1982).

39. Joan Beauchemin, "Connector-Type Highways have Failed to Meet Goal: Drawing People into Cities," *Burlington Free Press*, November 17, 1981.

40. Jakobs, "Planning and Politics," p. 40.

41. Ibid.

42. Ibid., pp. 64–65.

43. Burlington Planning Commission, *An Overview*, photocopied document, (Burlington, Vt.: 1981), p. 12.

44. David Moberg, "Burlington Loves Bernie," *In These Times* 7 (March 23–29, 1983), p. 13.

45. *Burlington Free Press*, April 12, 1982.

46. My source for this story is Jakobs, "Planning and Politics," pp. 114–150.

47. Interview with Nick Wylie, March 27, 1984.

48. Interview with Michael Monte, March 28, 1984.

49. Ibid.

50. Ibid.

51. Ibid.

52. Ibid.

53. Ibid.

Chapter 6

1. The idea that planning is an alternative to markets was forcefully put forward by Friederich Hayek, *The Road to Serfdom* (Chicago: University of Chicago Press, 1944); later, a more expanded argument for this interpretation was made by Robert Dahl and Charles Lindblom, *Politics, Economics and Welfare* (New York: Harper and Row, 1953). They described markets, bargaining, polyarchy, and hierarchy as the main alternative public choice mechanisms, thus subsuming planning *per se* under hierarchy, but maintaining the principle of the need for alternative ways for communities to make collective choices. My position is that the activity of planning as a hierarchical ordering of alternative social choices is a conceptual and practical alternative to markets, bargaining, and polyarchy, whether or not the community adopts hierarchy as a method of making political decisions.

2. Ilona Hancock, "New Politics in Berkeley: A Personal View," in Harriet Nathan and Stanley Scott, eds., *Experiment and Change in Berkeley: Essays on City Politics, 1950–1975* (Berkeley: Institute of Governmental Studies, 1978), p. 371.

3. Todd Swanstrom, *The Crisis of Growth Politics: Cleveland, Kucinich and the Limits of Electoral Reform* (Philadelphia: Temple University Press, 1985).

4. Janice Cogger, "The Regional Transit Negotiations," mimeographed ms. Cleveland Planning Department, (Cleveland, Ohio: 1977).

5. T. J. Kent, Jr., *The Urban General Plan* (San Francisco: Chandler, 1961.

6. John Howard, "In Defense of Planning Commissions," *Journal of the American Institute of Planners* 17 (Spring 1951): 89–94.

7. Robert Walker, *The Planning Function in Urban Government* (Chicago: University of Chicago Press, 1941).

8. Alan Altshuler, *The City Planning Process* (Ithaca, N.Y.: Cornell University Press, 1965).

9. Andrew Gold, who was Planning Commission chairman for part of the period of Carbone's tenure, felt that Carbone, by not using the Planning Commission, had lost a potentially valuable independent critic and source of ideas. Gold, who had earlier worked with Krumholz in Cleveland, tried to have Krumholz hired as planning director when the position became vacant, and he felt that Carbone was resistant to the idea out of a desire to keep political control in fewer hands. He told me this in an interview, September 21, 1981.

10. John Mollenkopf, *The Contested City* (Princeton: Princeton University Press, 1983).

11. See Altshuler, *The City Planning Process*, chapter 6.

12. Norman Krumholz, "A Retrospective View of Equity Planning: Cleveland 1969–1979," *Journal of the American Planning Association* 48 (Spring 1982): 163–183.

13. Peter Bachrach and Morton S. Baratz, "The Two Faces of Power," *American Political Science Review* 70 (December 1962): 947–952.

14. This point is argued at length in Pierre Clavel, *Opposition Planning In Wales and Appalachia* (Philadelphia: Temple University Press, 1982).

Chapter 7

1. This point is made best by Roland Warren, in Joseph D. Sneed and Steven A. Waldhorn, eds., *Restructuring the Federal System: Approaches to Accountability in Post–Categorical Programs.* (New York: Crane, Russak, 1975), pp 35–60.

2. Interpretations and documentations of the increasing presence of government in the economy have come from the left, right and center of the academic and ideological spectrum. For two well-known presentations, see Andrew Shonfield, *Modern Capitalism* (New York: Oxford University Press, 1965) and James O'Connor, *The Fiscal Crisis of the State* (New York: St. Martins Press, 1973).

3. Don Hopkins, "Development of Black Political Organization in Berkeley Since 1960," in Harriet Nathan and Stanley Scott, eds., *Experi-*

ment and Change in Berkeley: Essays on City Politics, 1950–1975 (Berkeley, Ca.: Institute of Governmental Studies, 1978), pp. 105–177.

4. These remarks were made at a panel discussion held at CUNY Graduate Center, May 11, 1984.

5. Ibid.

6. C. B. Macpherson, *The Life and Times of Liberal Democracy* (New York: Oxford University Press, 1977); Theodore Lowi, *The End of Liberalism* (New York: Norton, 1969).

7. The literature on this subject is extensive. I have relied particularly on Ralph Miliband, *Marxism and Politics* (New York: Oxford University Press, 1978).

Index